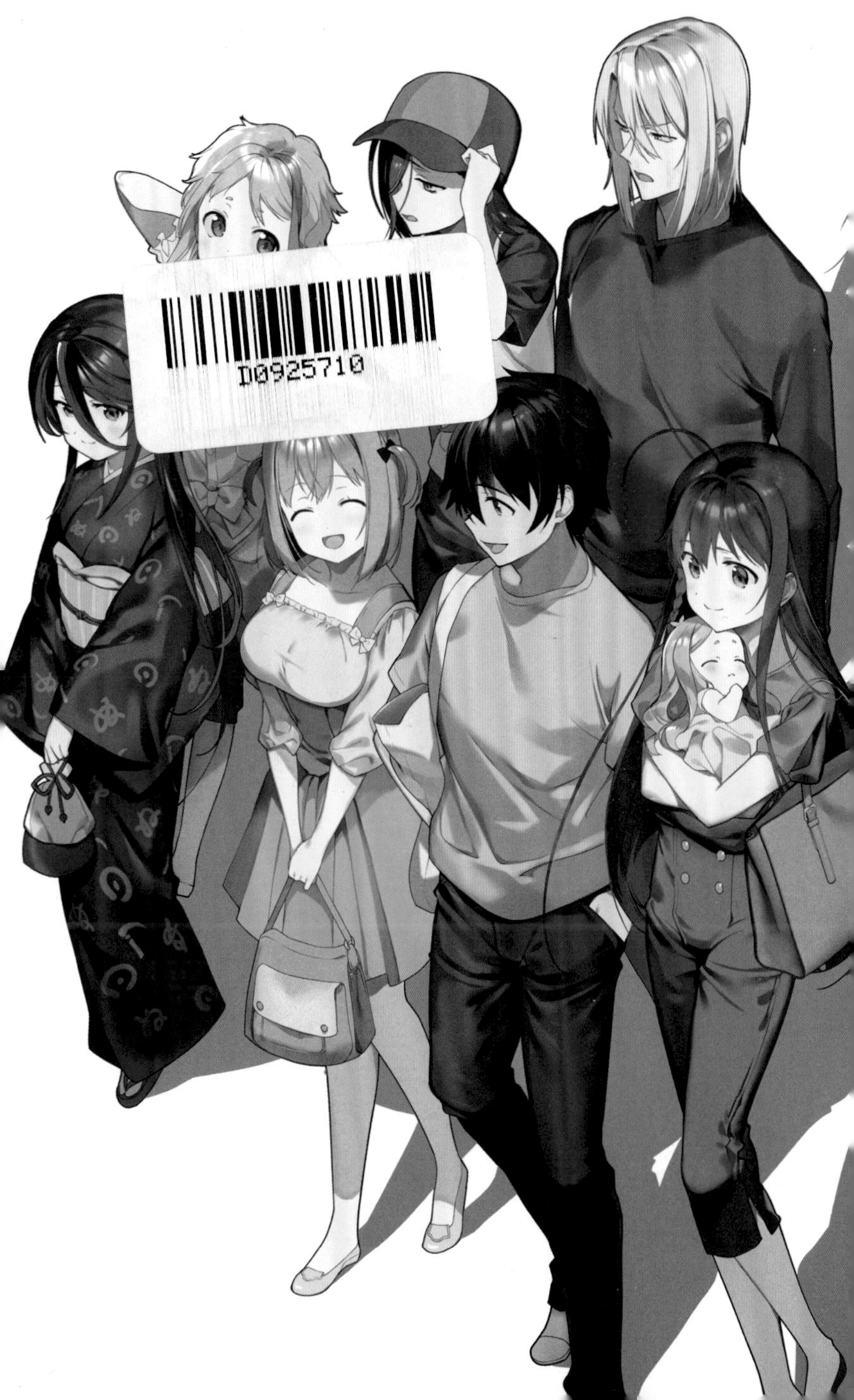

JUN / 0 2022

THE DEVIL IS A PART-TIMER! ⑱

Chapter 90: The Cleric Shows How She Earned That Title ・・・・・・ p3

Chapter 91: The Hero Is Cheered by a Cryptic Missive ・・・・・ p35

Chapter 92: The Devil Is Rocketed Into the Air ・・・・・・・・・・ p69

Chapter 93: The Hero Kicks Off the Final Battle ・・・・・・・・・ p93

Chapter 94: The Hero Quells her Anxieties for the Future ・・・ p121

Afterword ・・・・・・・・・・・・・・・・・・・・ p160

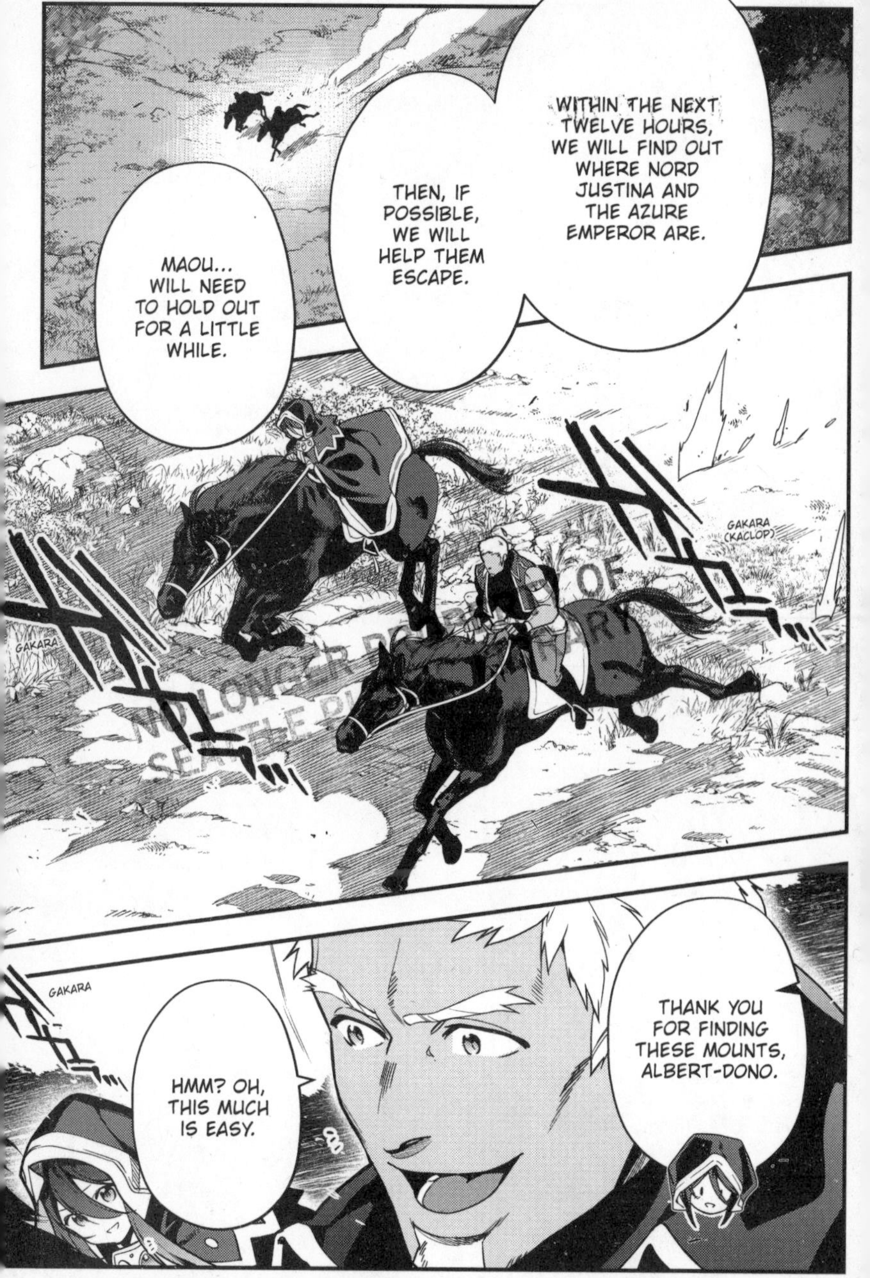
WITHIN THE NEXT TWELVE HOURS, WE WILL FIND OUT WHERE NORD JUSTINA AND THE AZURE EMPEROR ARE.
THEN, IF POSSIBLE, WE WILL HELP THEM ESCAPE.
MAOU... WILL NEED TO HOLD OUT FOR A LITTLE WHILE.
GAKARA (KACLOP)
GAKARA
THANK YOU FOR FINDING THESE MOUNTS, ALBERT-DONO.
GAKARA
HMM? OH, THIS MUCH IS EASY.

CHAPTER 90: THE CLERIC SHOWS HOW SHE EARNED THAT TITLE

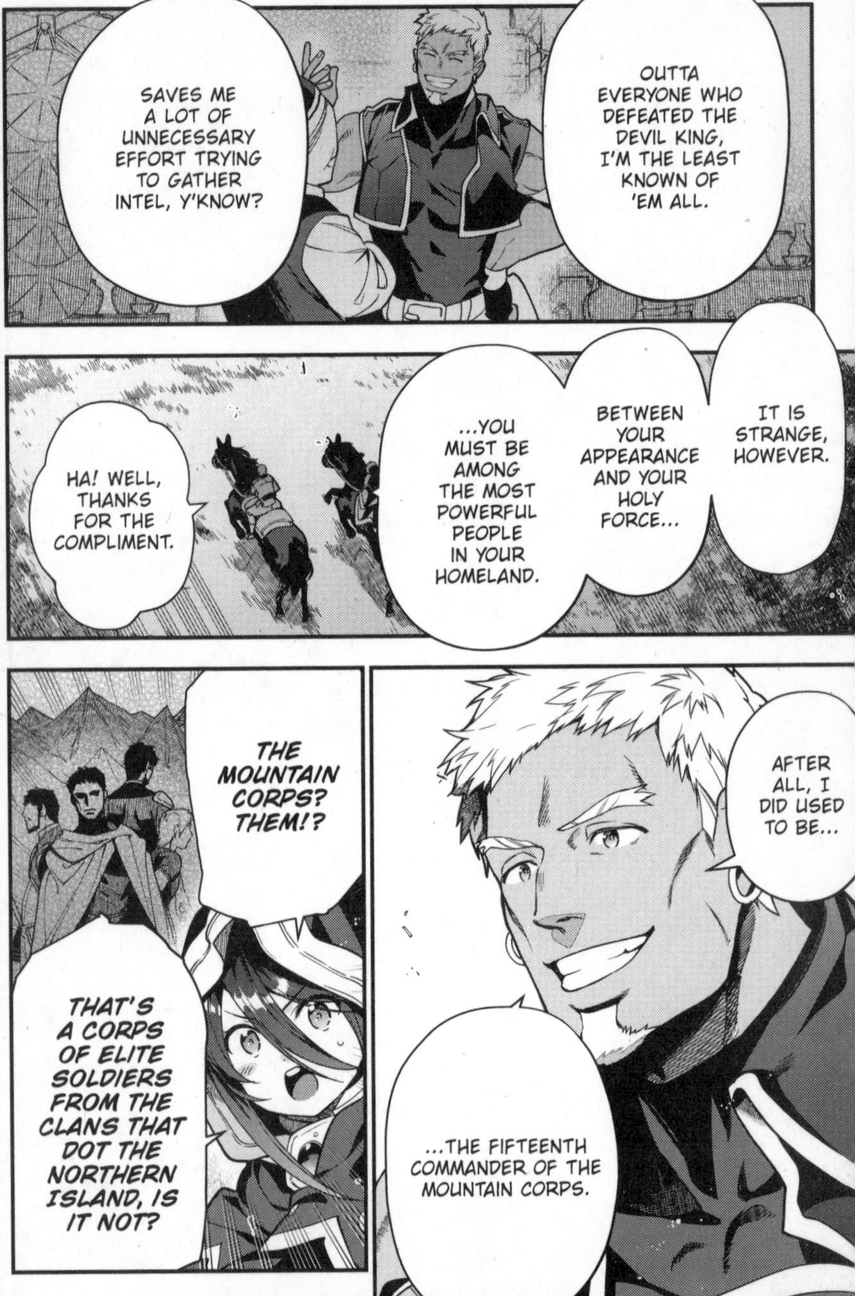
OUTTA EVERYONE WHO DEFEATED THE DEVIL KING, I'M THE LEAST KNOWN OF 'EM ALL.
SAVES ME A LOT OF UNNECESSARY EFFORT TRYING TO GATHER INTEL, Y'KNOW?
IT IS STRANGE, HOWEVER.
BETWEEN YOUR APPEARANCE AND YOUR HOLY FORCE...
...YOU MUST BE AMONG THE MOST POWERFUL PEOPLE IN YOUR HOMELAND.
HA! WELL, THANKS FOR THE COMPLIMENT.
AFTER ALL, I DID USED TO BE...
...THE FIFTEENTH COMMANDER OF THE MOUNTAIN CORPS.
THE MOUNTAIN CORPS? THEM!?
THAT'S A CORPS OF ELITE SOLDIERS FROM THE CLANS THAT DOT THE NORTHERN ISLAND, IS IT NOT?

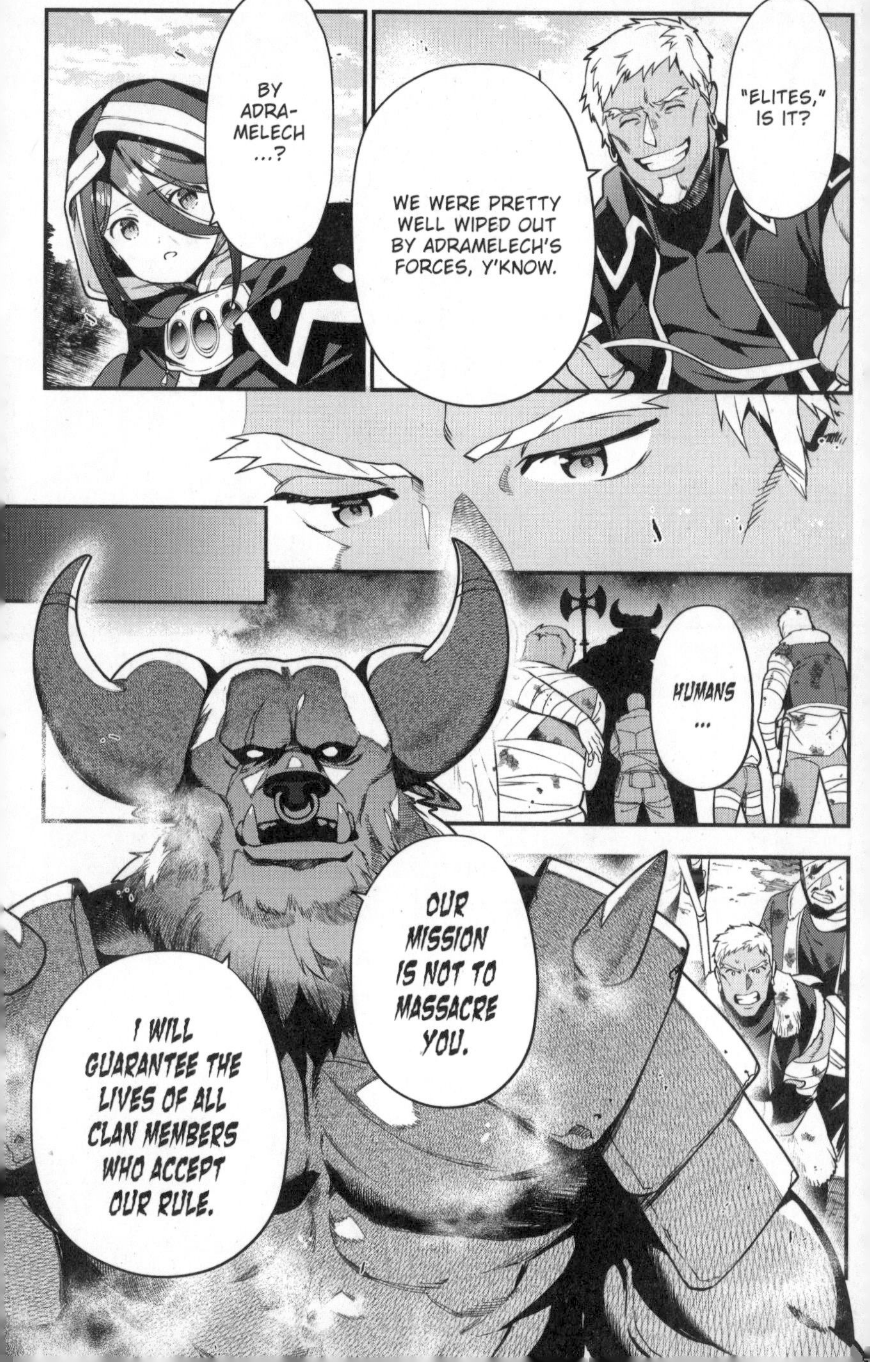
"ELITES," IS IT?
WE WERE PRETTY WELL WIPED OUT BY ADRAMELECH'S FORCES, Y'KNOW.
BY ADRA-MELECH ...?
HUMANS ...
OUR MISSION IS NOT TO MASSACRE YOU.
I WILL GUARANTEE THE LIVES OF ALL CLAN MEMBERS WHO ACCEPT OUR RULE.

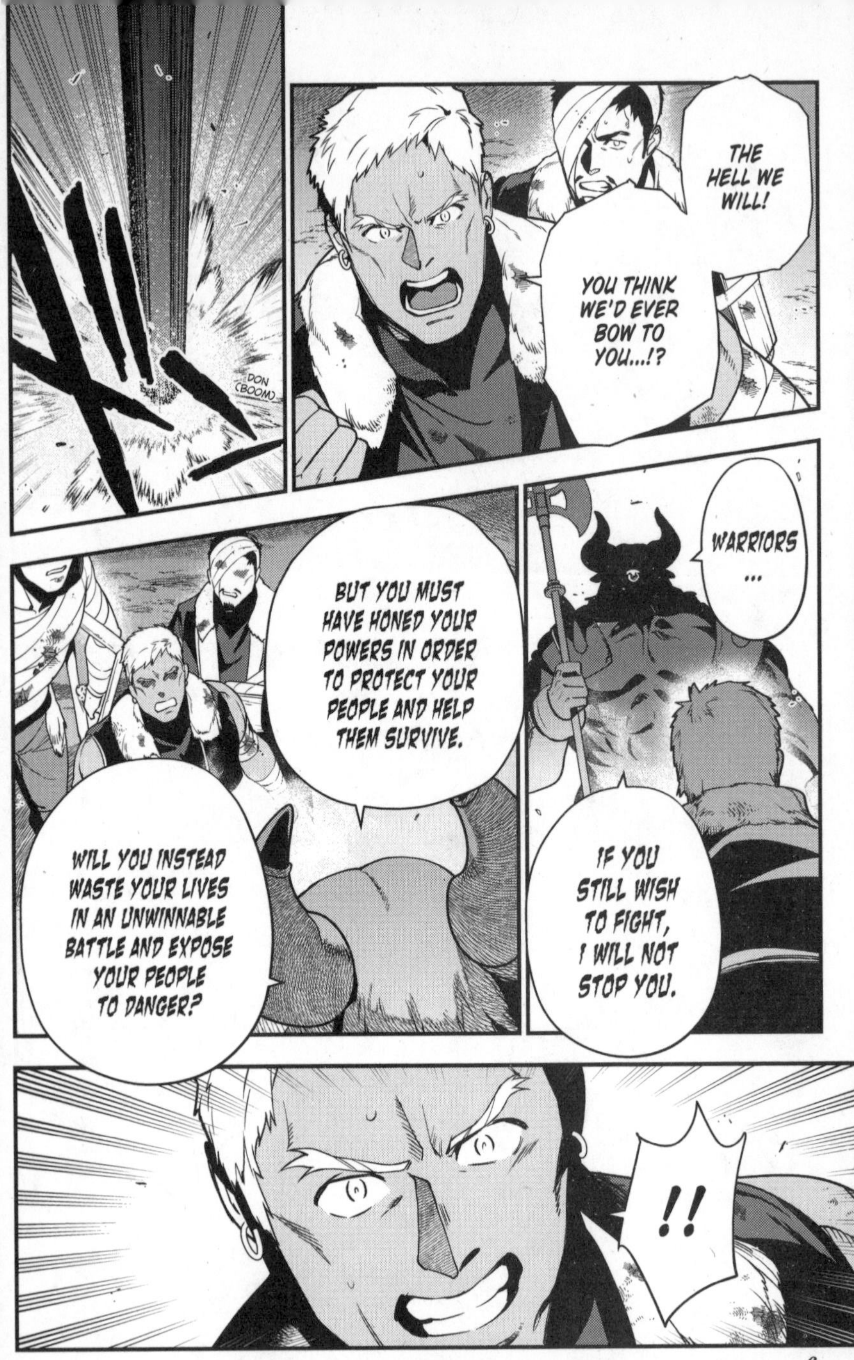
THE HELL WE WILL!
YOU THINK WE'D EVER BOW TO YOU...!?
DON (BOOM)
WARRIORS...
IF YOU STILL WISH TO FIGHT, I WILL NOT STOP YOU.
BUT YOU MUST HAVE HONED YOUR POWERS IN ORDER TO PROTECT YOUR PEOPLE AND HELP THEM SURVIVE.
WILL YOU INSTEAD WASTE YOUR LIVES IN AN UNWINNABLE BATTLE AND EXPOSE YOUR PEOPLE TO DANGER?
!!

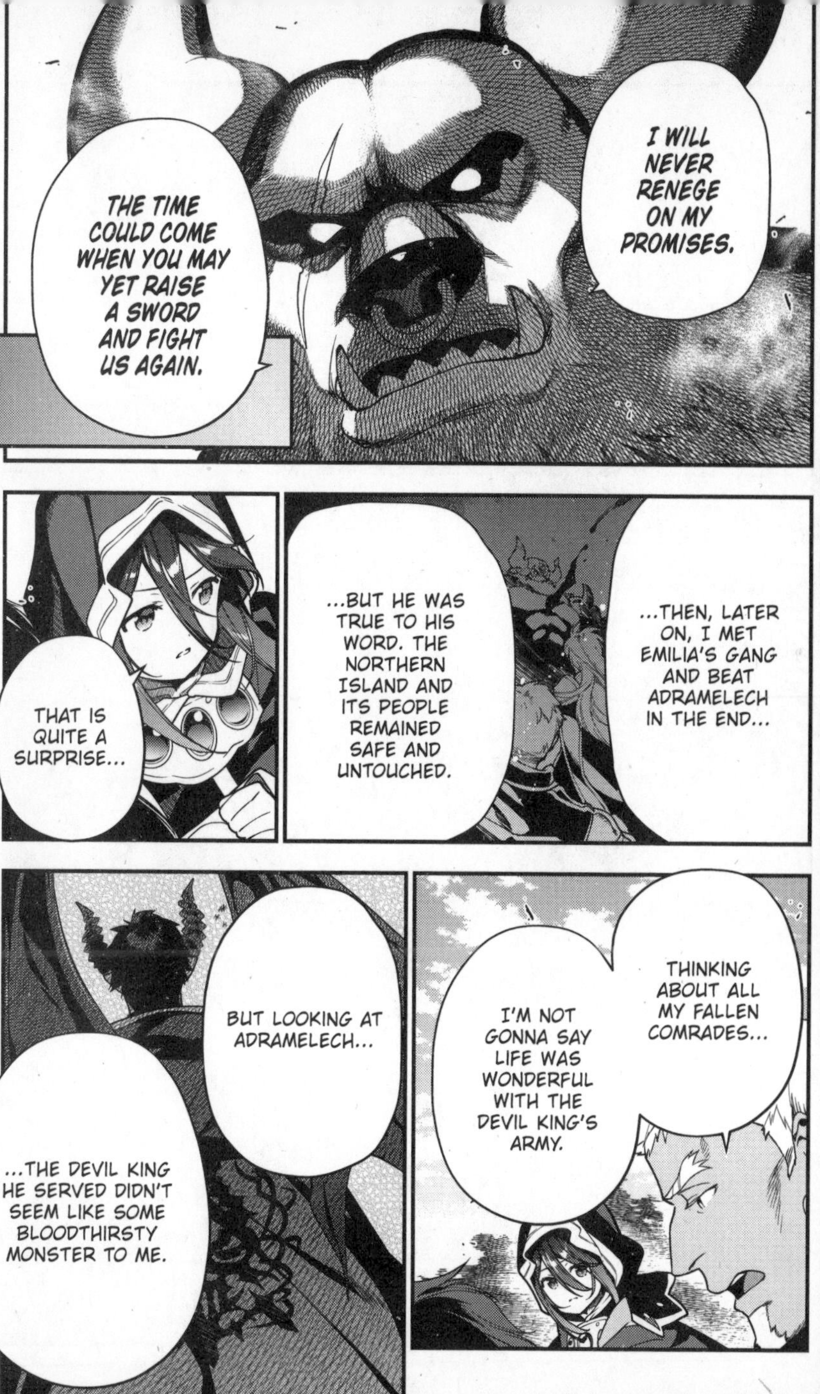
I WILL NEVER RENEGE ON MY PROMISES.
THE TIME COULD COME WHEN YOU MAY YET RAISE A SWORD AND FIGHT US AGAIN.
...THEN, LATER ON, I MET EMILIA'S GANG AND BEAT ADRAMELECH IN THE END...
...BUT HE WAS TRUE TO HIS WORD. THE NORTHERN ISLAND AND ITS PEOPLE REMAINED SAFE AND UNTOUCHED.
THAT IS QUITE A SURPRISE...
THINKING ABOUT ALL MY FALLEN COMRADES...
I'M NOT GONNA SAY LIFE WAS WONDERFUL WITH THE DEVIL KING'S ARMY.
BUT LOOKING AT ADRAMELECH...
...THE DEVIL KING HE SERVED DIDN'T SEEM LIKE SOME BLOODTHIRSTY MONSTER TO ME.

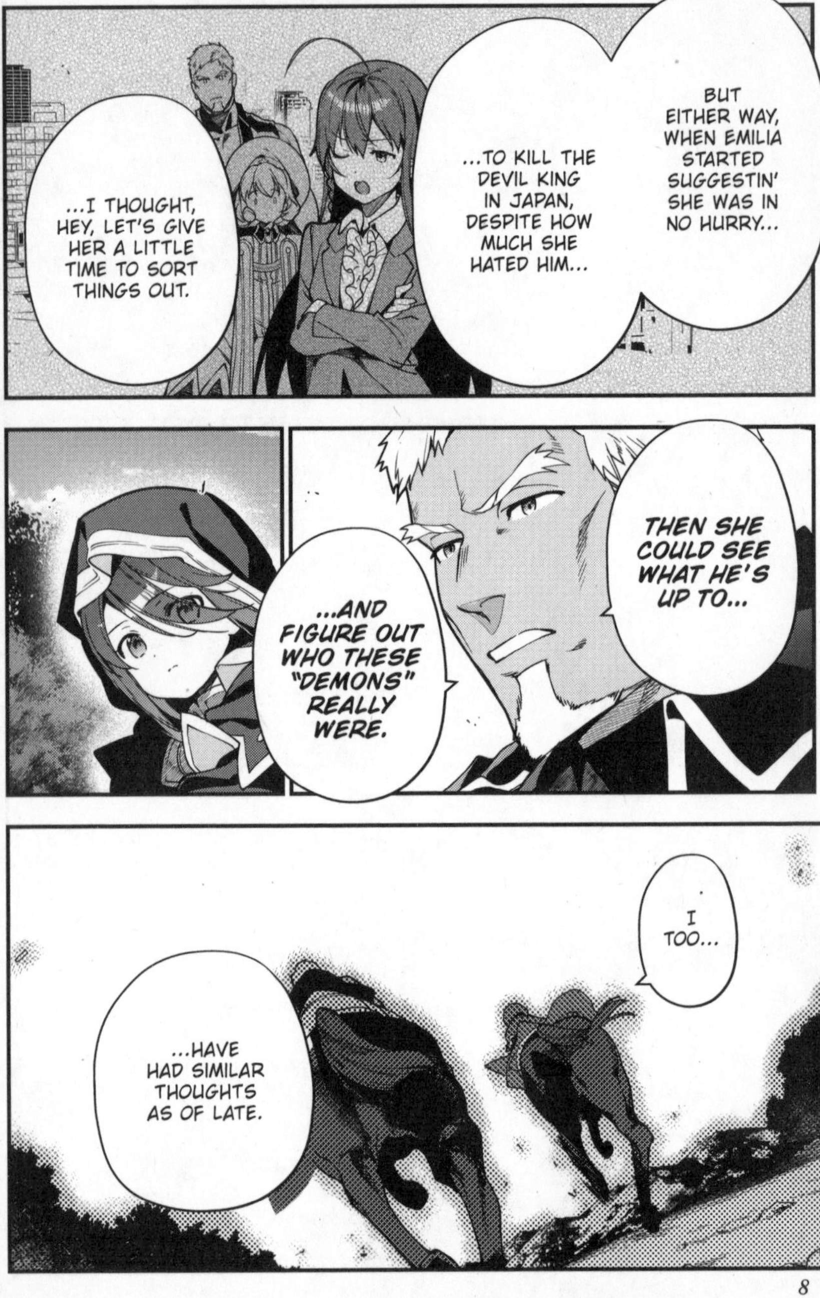
BUT EITHER WAY, WHEN EMILIA STARTED SUGGESTIN' SHE WAS IN NO HURRY...
...TO KILL THE DEVIL KING IN JAPAN, DESPITE HOW MUCH SHE HATED HIM...
...I THOUGHT, HEY, LET'S GIVE HER A LITTLE TIME TO SORT THINGS OUT.
THEN SHE COULD SEE WHAT HE'S UP TO...
...AND FIGURE OUT WHO THESE "DEMONS" REALLY WERE.
I TOO...
...HAVE HAD SIMILAR THOUGHTS AS OF LATE.

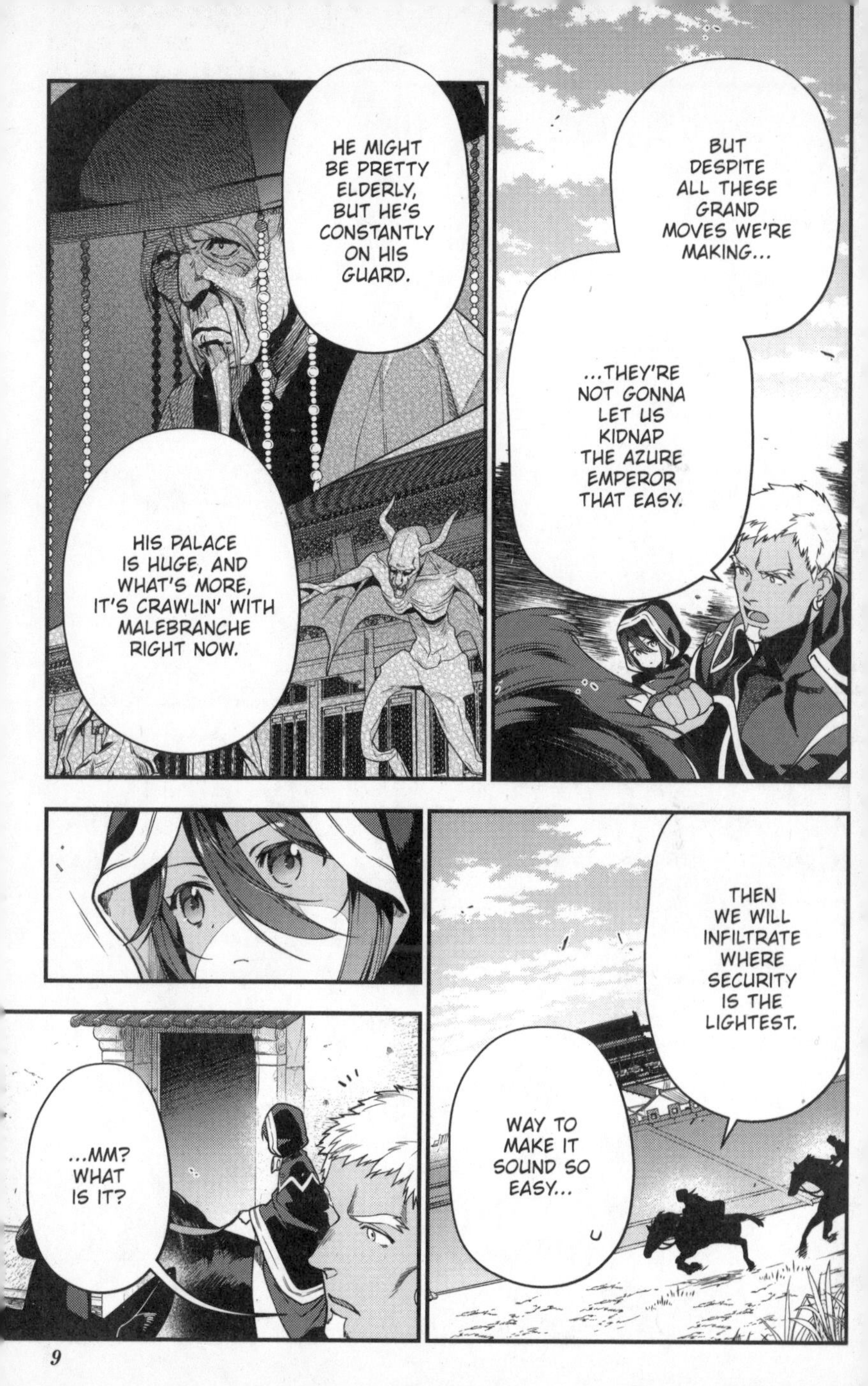
BUT DESPITE ALL THESE GRAND MOVES WE'RE MAKING...
...THEY'RE NOT GONNA LET US KIDNAP THE AZURE EMPEROR THAT EASY.
HE MIGHT BE PRETTY ELDERLY, BUT HE'S CONSTANTLY ON HIS GUARD.
HIS PALACE IS HUGE, AND WHAT'S MORE, IT'S CRAWLIN' WITH MALEBRANCHE RIGHT NOW.
THEN WE WILL INFILTRATE WHERE SECURITY IS THE LIGHTEST.
WAY TO MAKE IT SOUND SO EASY...
...MM? WHAT IS IT?

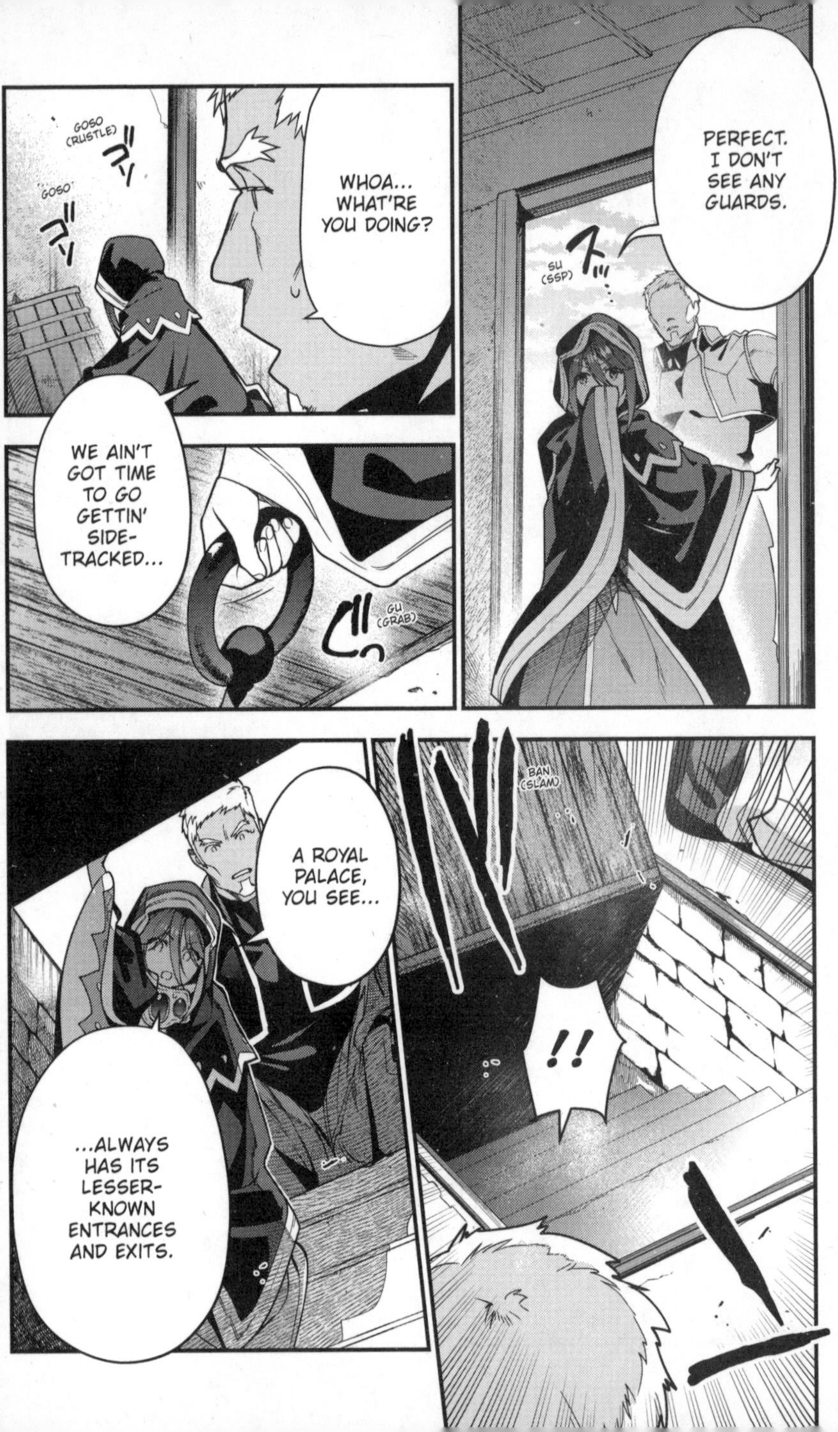
PERFECT. I DON'T SEE ANY GUARDS.
SU (SSP)
WHOA... WHAT'RE YOU DOING?
GOSO (RUSTLE)
GOSO
WE AIN'T GOT TIME TO GO GETTIN' SIDE-TRACKED...
GU (GRAB)
BAN (SLAM)
A ROYAL PALACE, YOU SEE...
!!
...ALWAYS HAS ITS LESSER-KNOWN ENTRANCES AND EXITS.

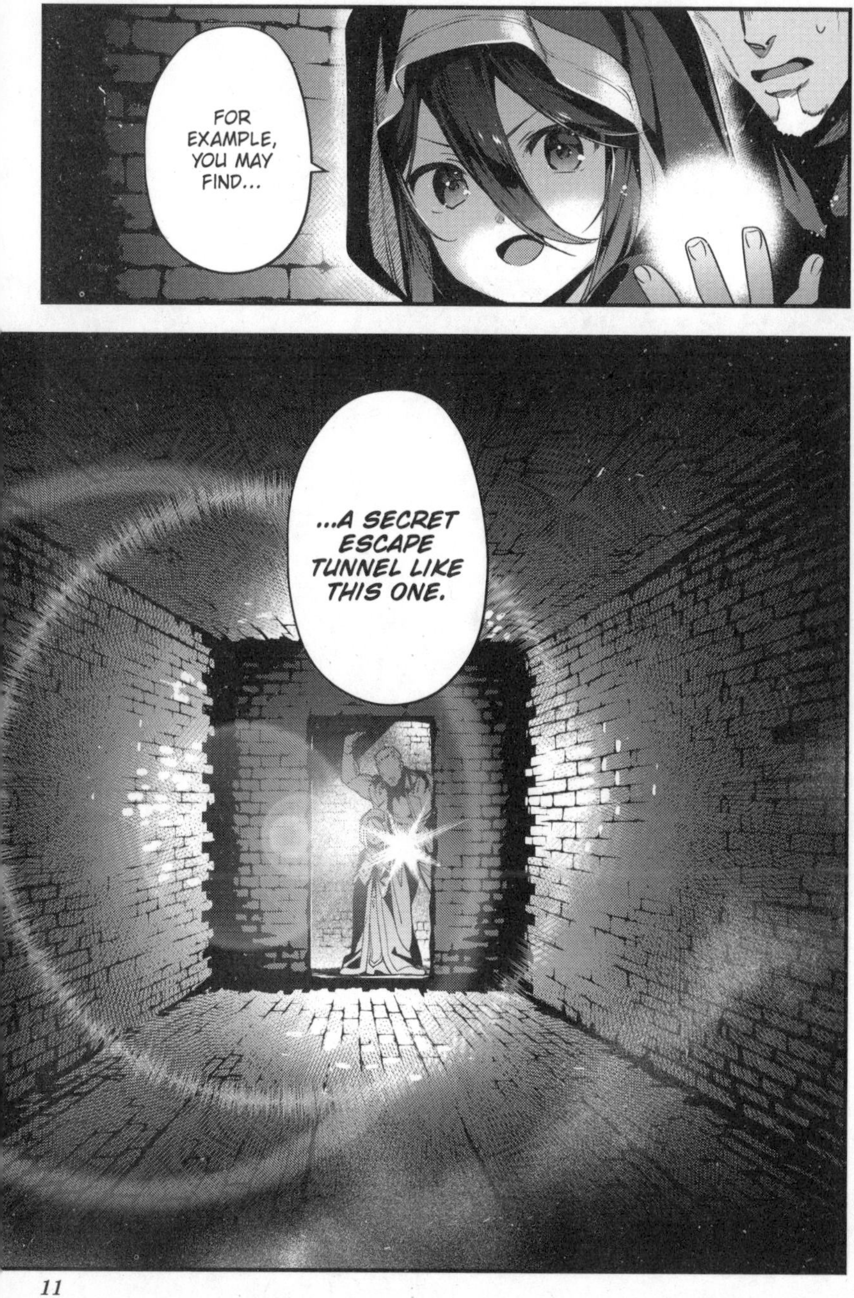
FOR EXAMPLE, YOU MAY FIND...
...A SECRET ESCAPE TUNNEL LIKE THIS ONE.

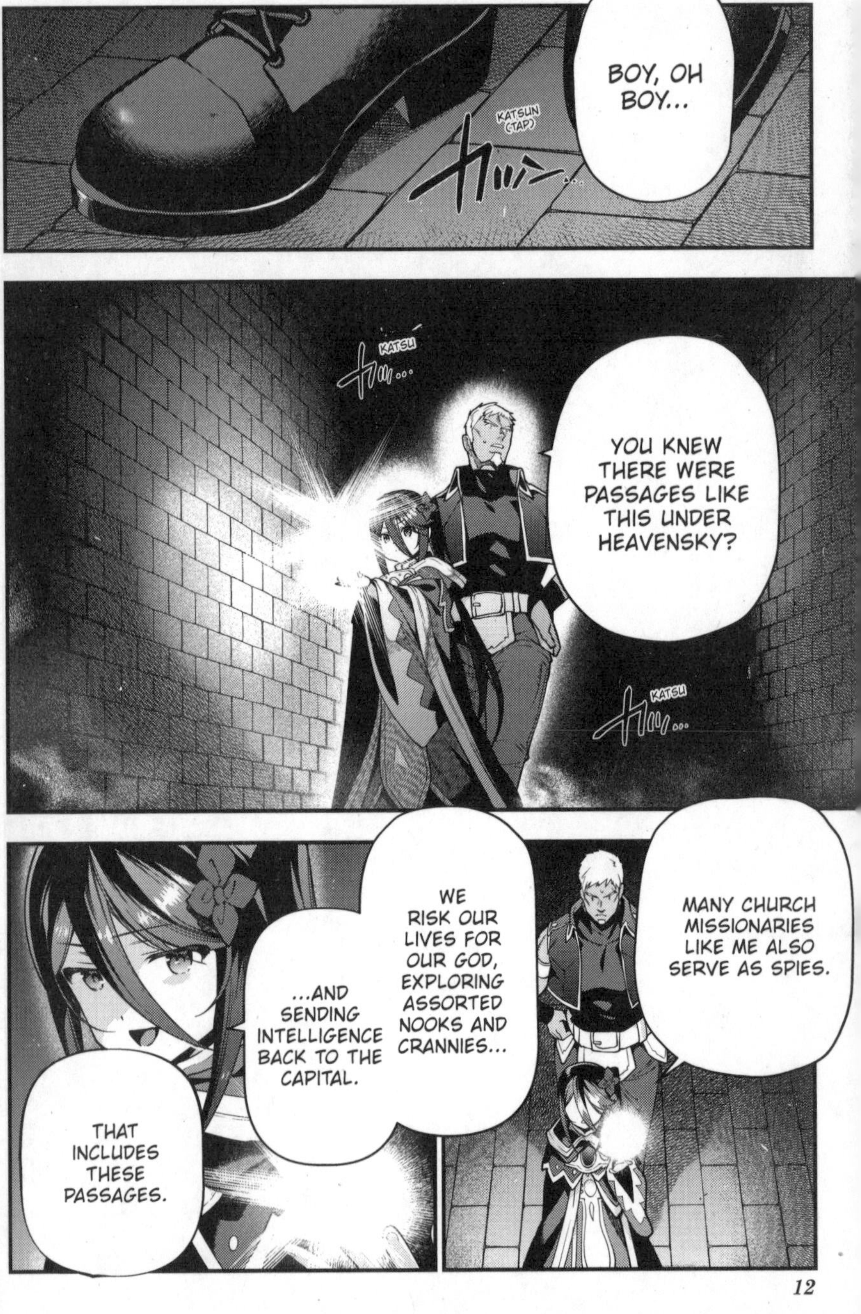
BOY, OH BOY...
KATSUN (TAP)
YOU KNEW THERE WERE PASSAGES LIKE THIS UNDER HEAVENSKY?
KATSU
KATSU
MANY CHURCH MISSIONARIES LIKE ME ALSO SERVE AS SPIES.
WE RISK OUR LIVES FOR OUR GOD, EXPLORING ASSORTED NOOKS AND CRANNIES...
...AND SENDING INTELLIGENCE BACK TO THE CAPITAL.
THAT INCLUDES THESE PASSAGES.

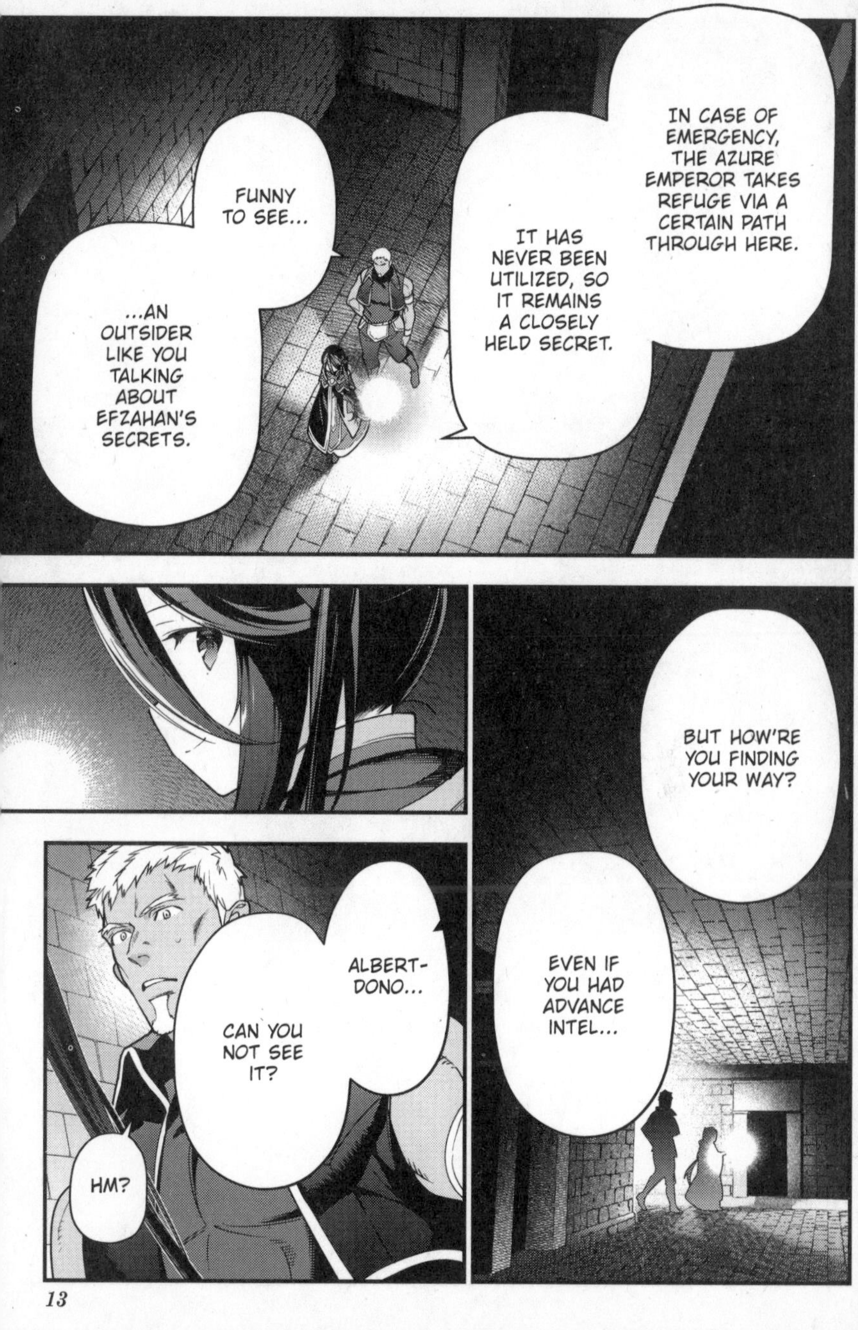
IN CASE OF EMERGENCY, THE AZURE EMPEROR TAKES REFUGE VIA A CERTAIN PATH THROUGH HERE.
IT HAS NEVER BEEN UTILIZED, SO IT REMAINS A CLOSELY HELD SECRET.
FUNNY TO SEE...
...AN OUTSIDER LIKE YOU TALKING ABOUT EFZAHAN'S SECRETS.
BUT HOW'RE YOU FINDING YOUR WAY?
EVEN IF YOU HAD ADVANCE INTEL...
ALBERT-DONO...
CAN YOU NOT SEE IT?
HM?

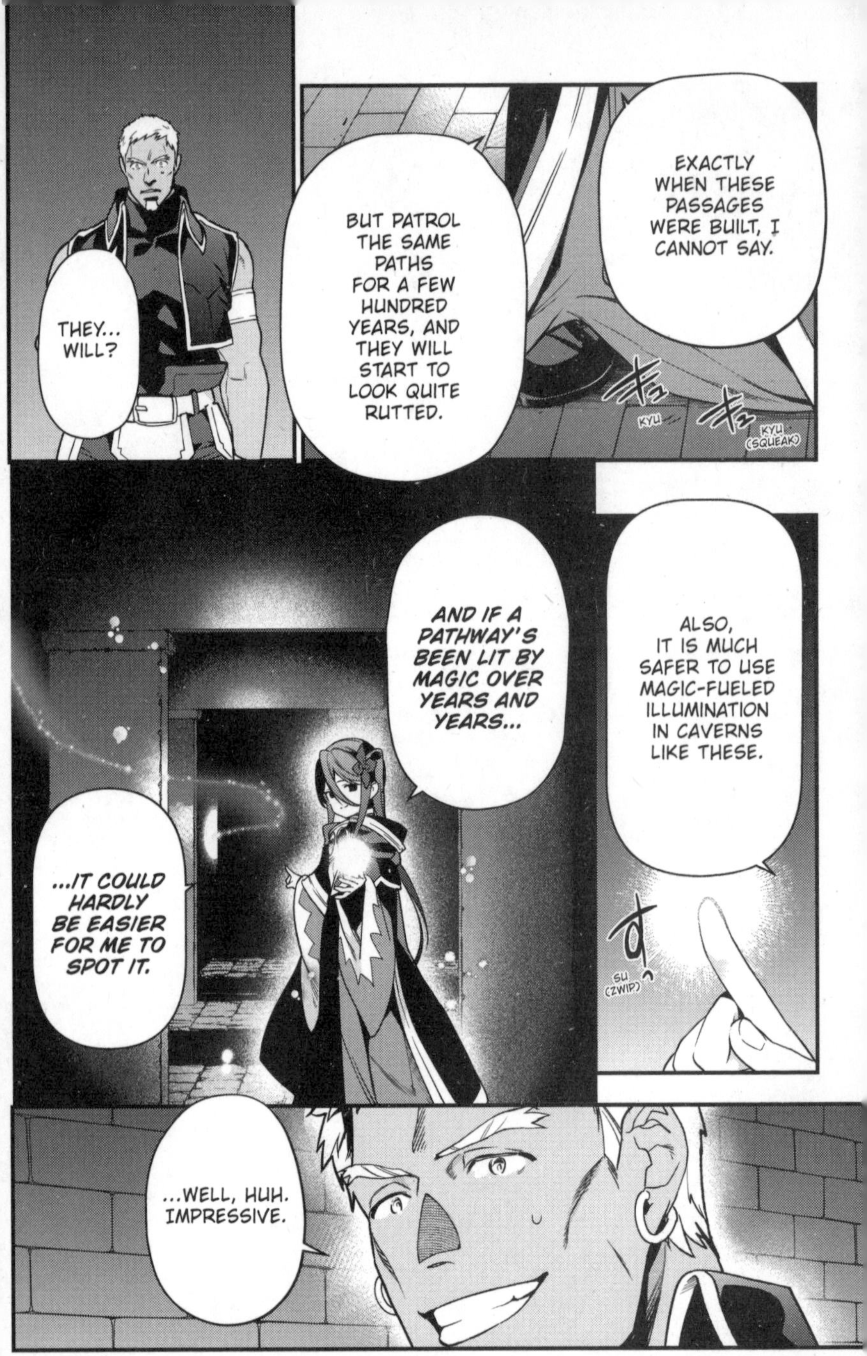
EXACTLY WHEN THESE PASSAGES WERE BUILT, I CANNOT SAY.
BUT PATROL THE SAME PATHS FOR A FEW HUNDRED YEARS, AND THEY WILL START TO LOOK QUITE RUTTED.
KYU
KYU (SQUEAK)
THEY... WILL?
ALSO, IT IS MUCH SAFER TO USE MAGIC-FUELED ILLUMINATION IN CAVERNS LIKE THESE.
SU (ZWIP)
AND IF A PATHWAY'S BEEN LIT BY MAGIC OVER YEARS AND YEARS...
...IT COULD HARDLY BE EASIER FOR ME TO SPOT IT.
...WELL, HUH. IMPRESSIVE.

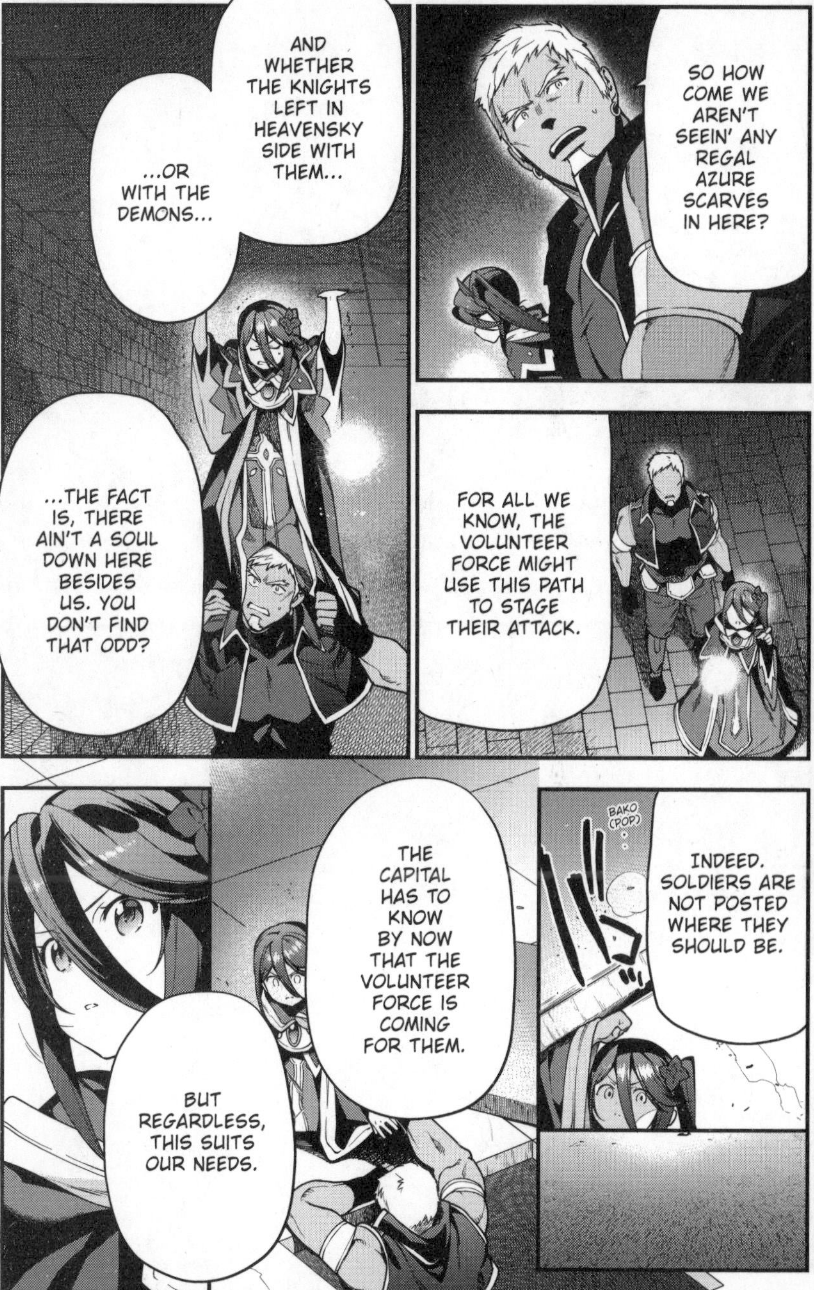
SO HOW COME WE AREN'T SEEIN' ANY REGAL AZURE SCARVES IN HERE?
FOR ALL WE KNOW, THE VOLUNTEER FORCE MIGHT USE THIS PATH TO STAGE THEIR ATTACK.
AND WHETHER THE KNIGHTS LEFT IN HEAVENSKY SIDE WITH THEM...
...OR WITH THE DEMONS...
...THE FACT IS, THERE AIN'T A SOUL DOWN HERE BESIDES US. YOU DON'T FIND THAT ODD?
BAKO (POP)
INDEED. SOLDIERS ARE NOT POSTED WHERE THEY SHOULD BE.
THE CAPITAL HAS TO KNOW BY NOW THAT THE VOLUNTEER FORCE IS COMING FOR THEM.
BUT REGARDLESS, THIS SUITS OUR NEEDS.

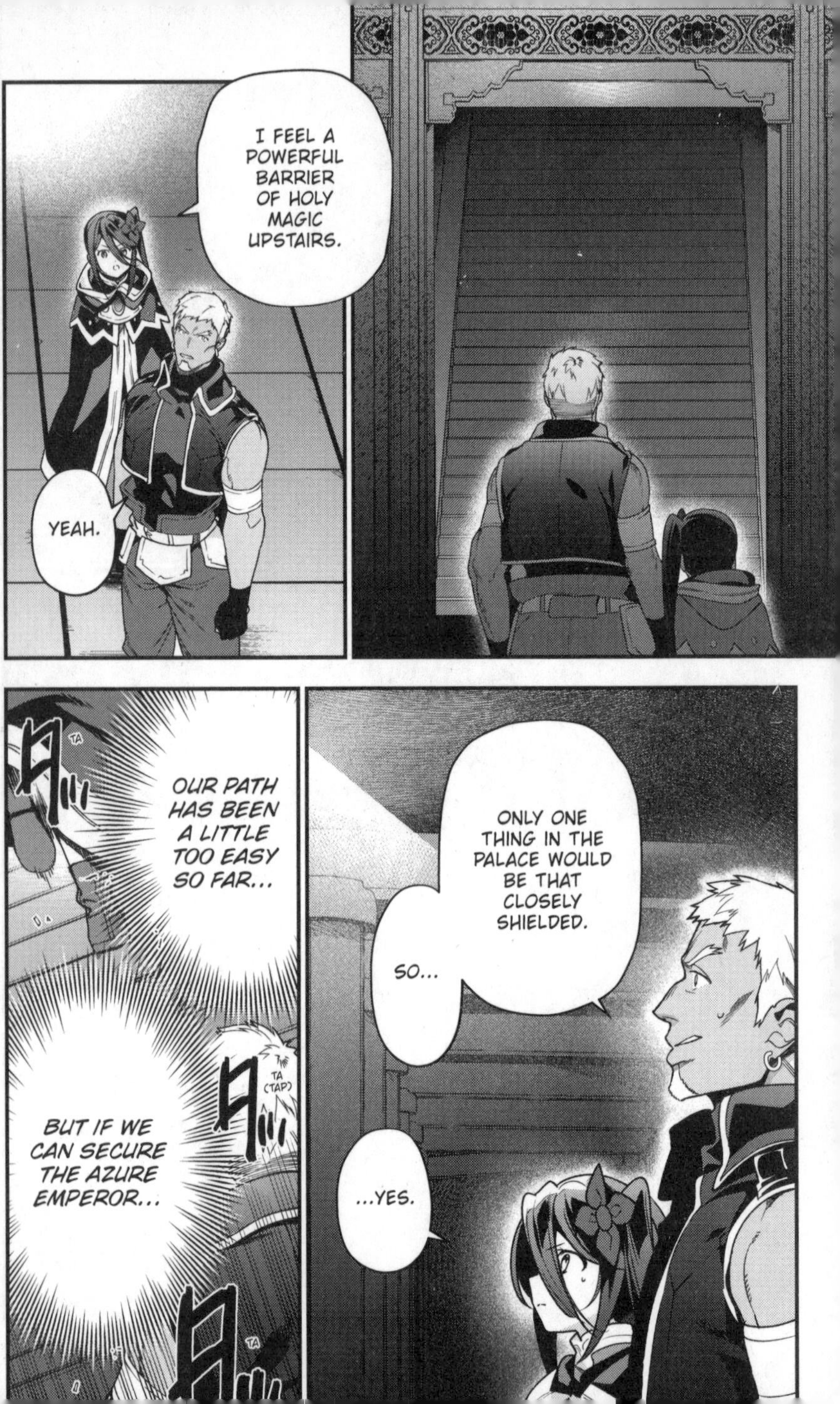
I FEEL A POWERFUL BARRIER OF HOLY MAGIC UPSTAIRS.
YEAH.
ONLY ONE THING IN THE PALACE WOULD BE THAT CLOSELY SHIELDED.
SO...
...YES.
TA
OUR PATH HAS BEEN A LITTLE TOO EASY SO FAR...
TA (TAP)
BUT IF WE CAN SECURE THE AZURE EMPEROR...
TA

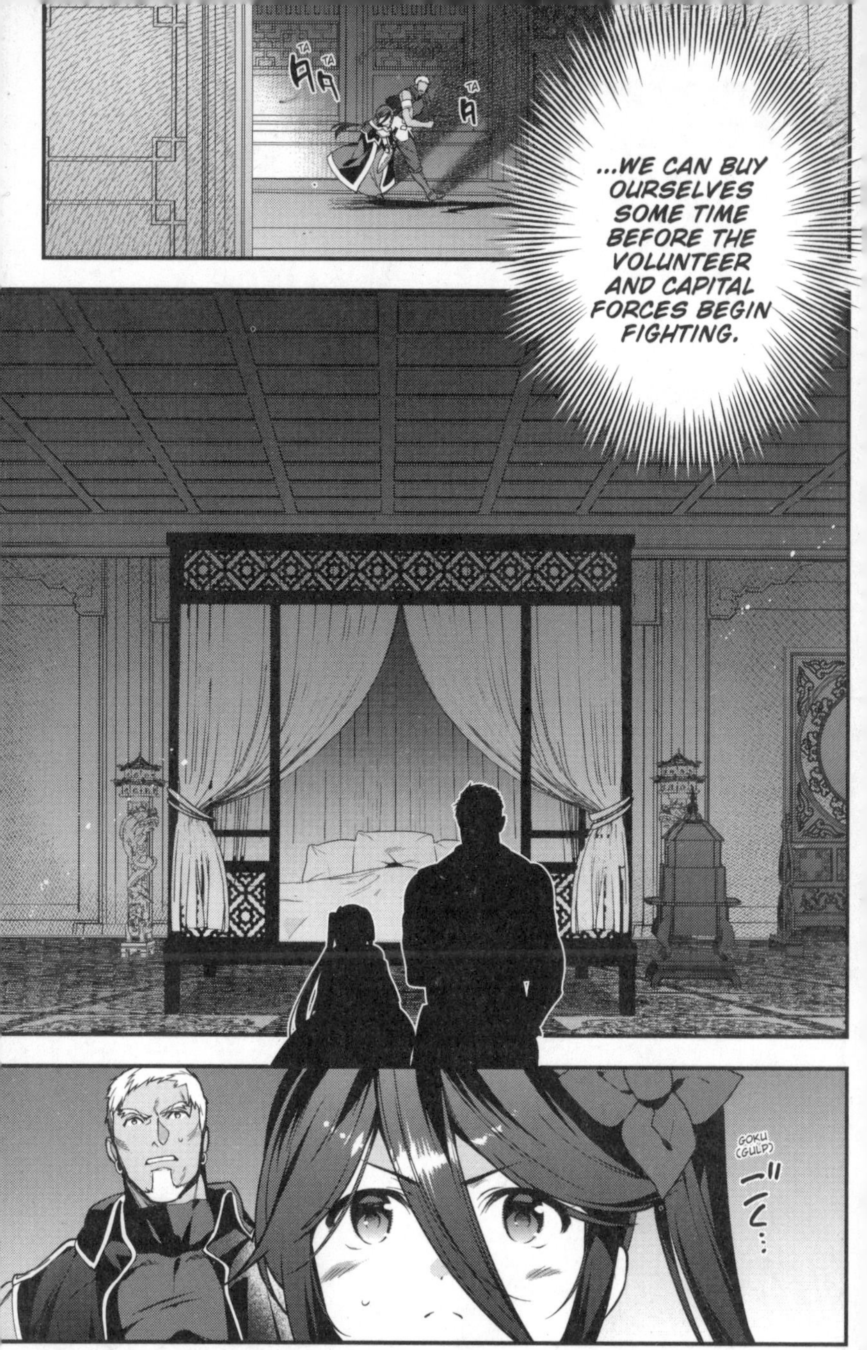

...WE CAN BUY OURSELVES SOME TIME BEFORE THE VOLUNTEER AND CAPITAL FORCES BEGIN FIGHTING.
TA
TA TA
GOKU (GULP)

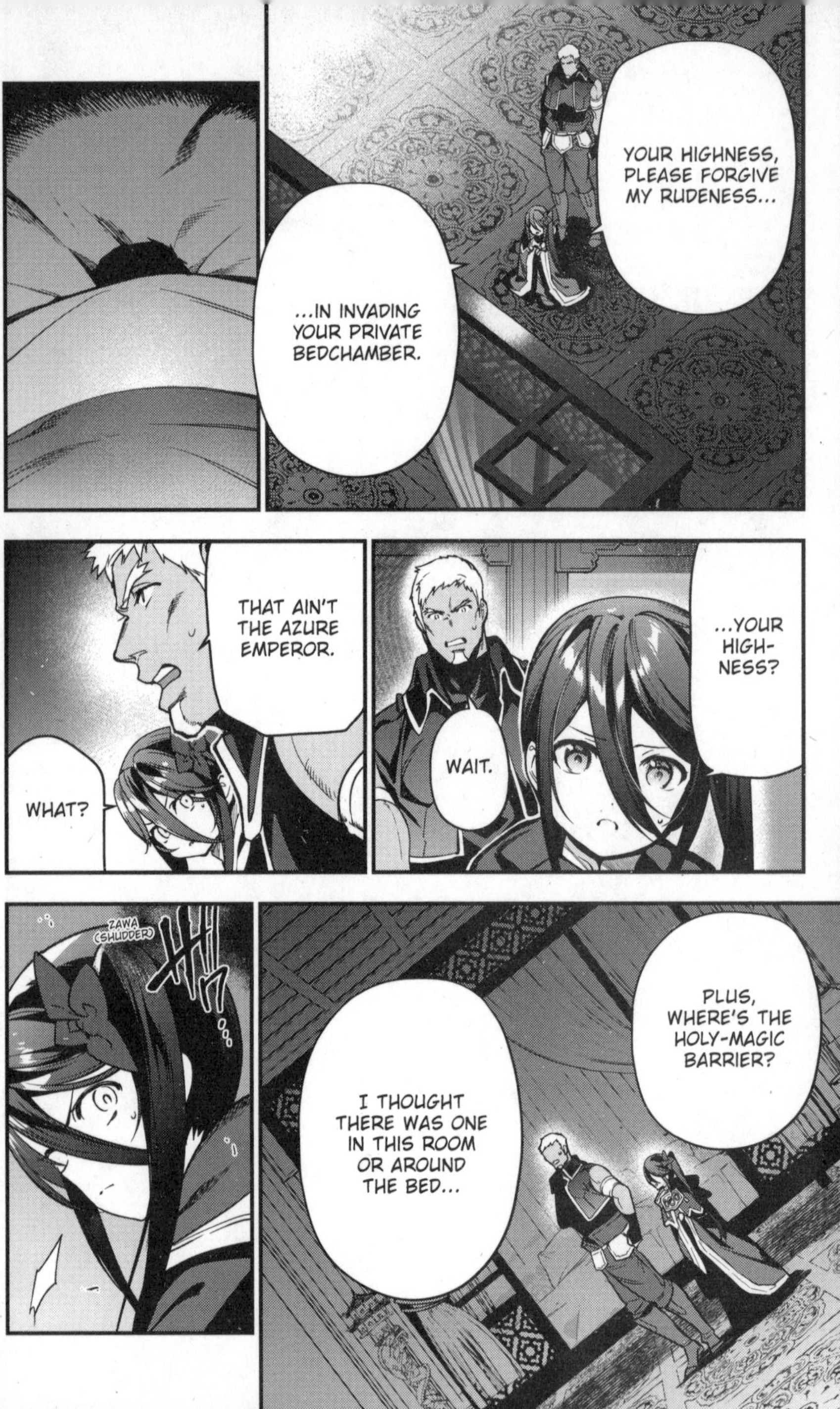
YOUR HIGHNESS, PLEASE FORGIVE MY RUDENESS...
...IN INVADING YOUR PRIVATE BEDCHAMBER.
...YOUR HIGH-NESS?
WAIT.
THAT AIN'T THE AZURE EMPEROR.
WHAT?
PLUS, WHERE'S THE HOLY-MAGIC BARRIER?
I THOUGHT THERE WAS ONE IN THIS ROOM OR AROUND THE BED...
ZAWA (SHUDDER)

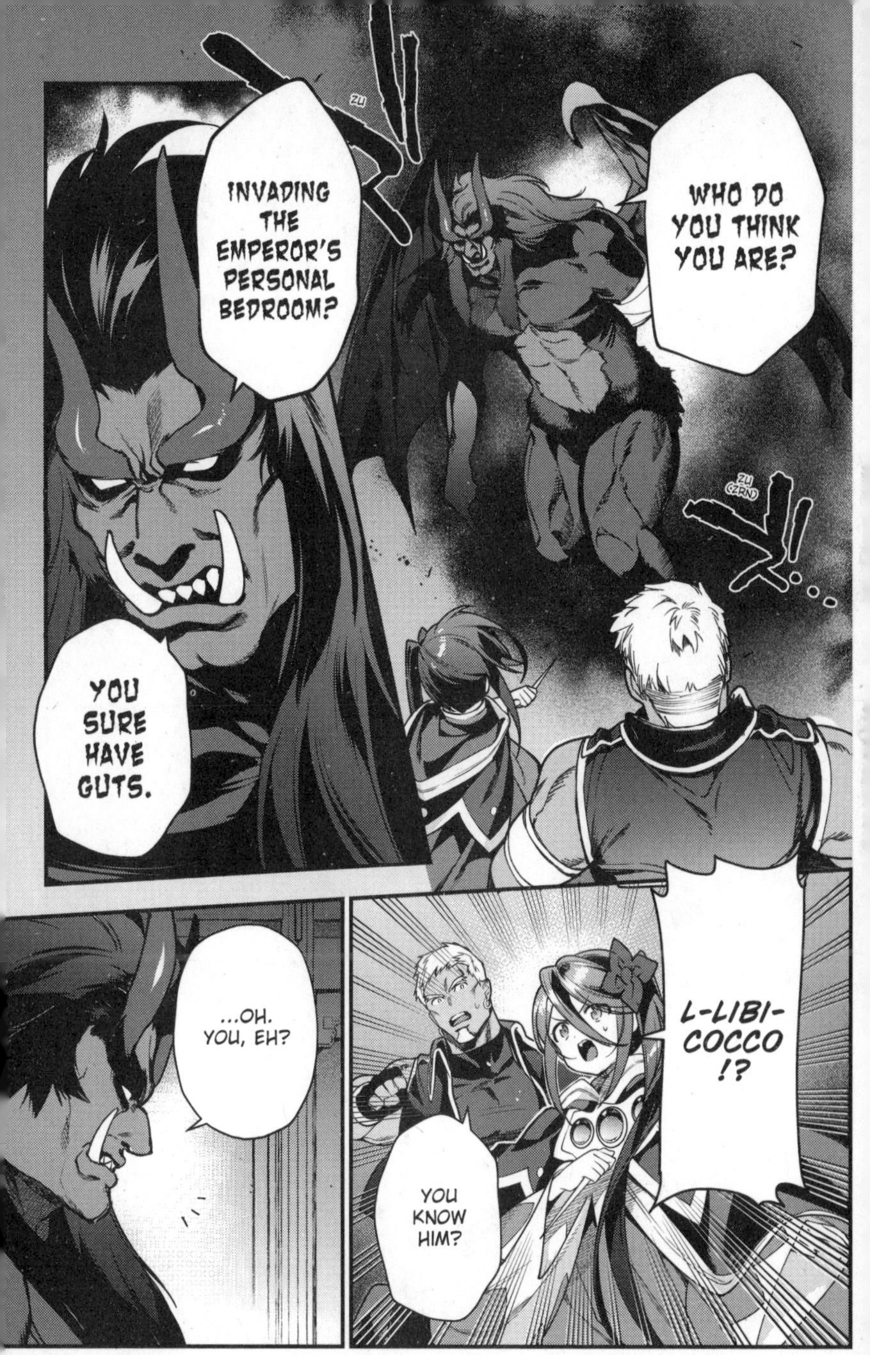
WHO DO YOU THINK YOU ARE?
INVADING THE EMPEROR'S PERSONAL BEDROOM?
ZU
ZU (ZRN)
YOU SURE HAVE GUTS.
L-LIBI-COCCO!?
YOU KNOW HIM?
...OH. YOU, EH?

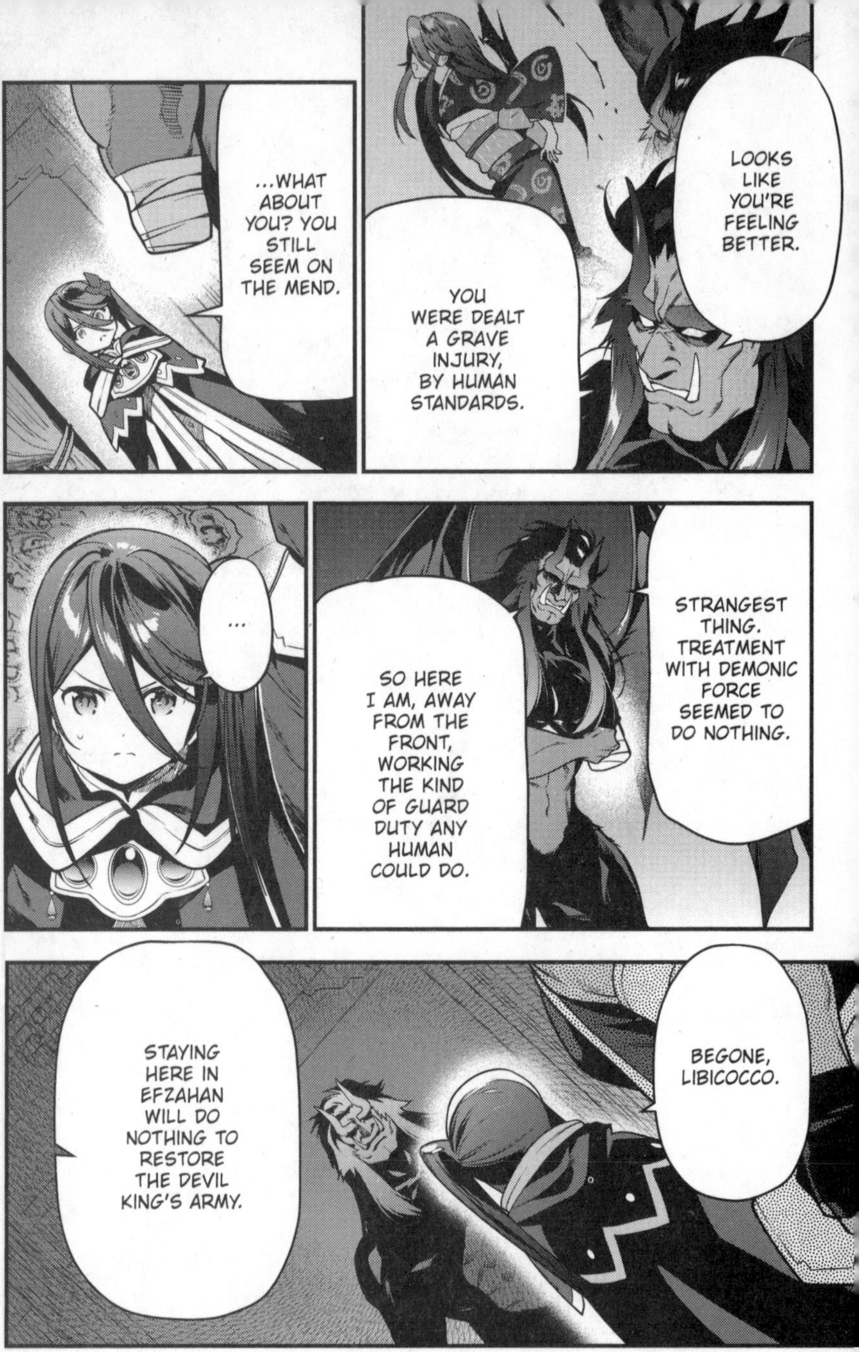
LOOKS LIKE YOU'RE FEELING BETTER.
YOU WERE DEALT A GRAVE INJURY, BY HUMAN STANDARDS.
...WHAT ABOUT YOU? YOU STILL SEEM ON THE MEND.
STRANGEST THING. TREATMENT WITH DEMONIC FORCE SEEMED TO DO NOTHING.
SO HERE I AM, AWAY FROM THE FRONT, WORKING THE KIND OF GUARD DUTY ANY HUMAN COULD DO.
...
BEGONE, LIBICOCCO.
STAYING HERE IN EFZAHAN WILL DO NOTHING TO RESTORE THE DEVIL KING'S ARMY.

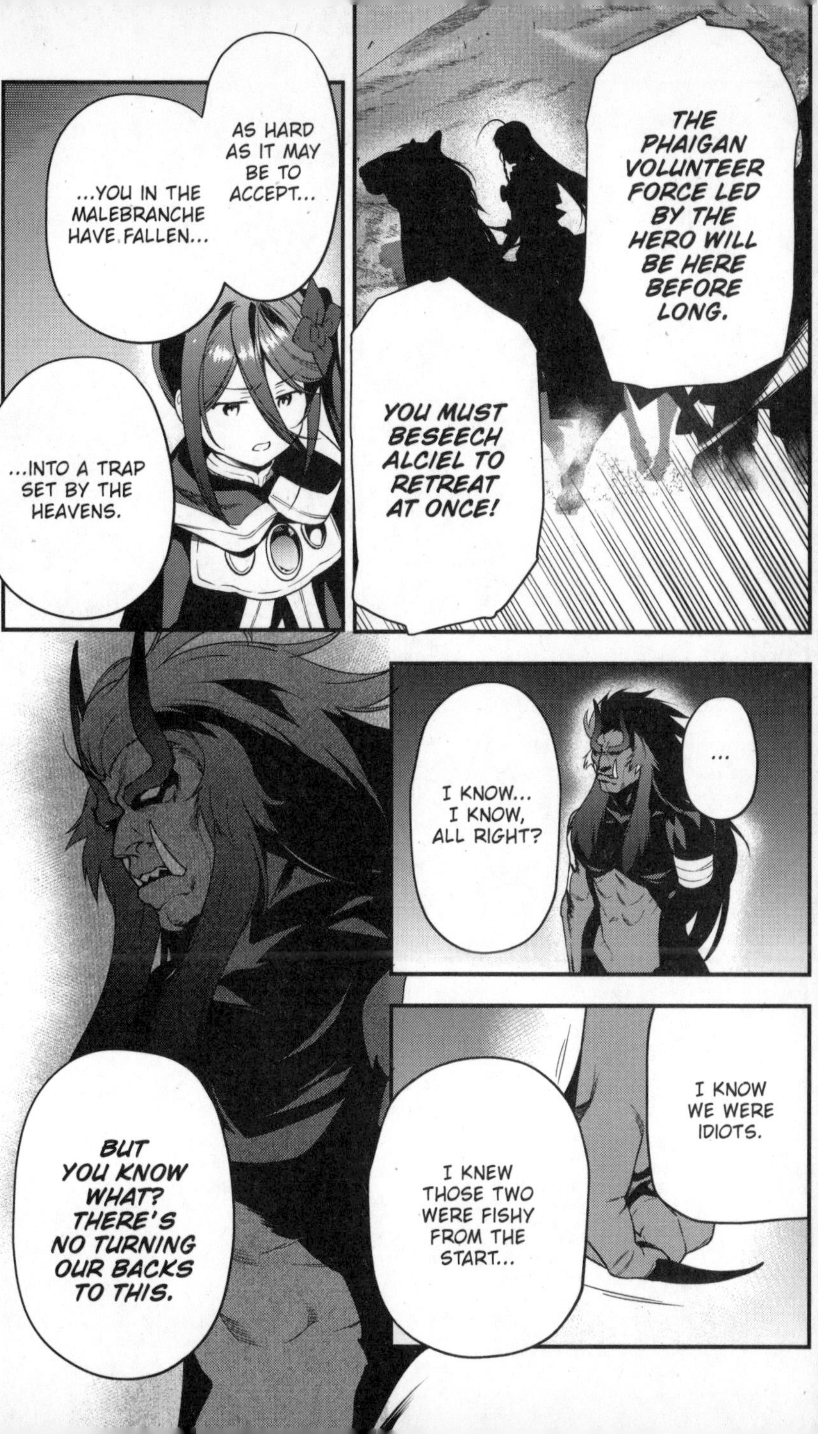
THE PHAIGAN VOLUNTEER FORCE LED BY THE HERO WILL BE HERE BEFORE LONG.
YOU MUST BESEECH ALCIEL TO RETREAT AT ONCE!
AS HARD AS IT MAY BE TO ACCEPT...
...YOU IN THE MALEBRANCHE HAVE FALLEN...
...INTO A TRAP SET BY THE HEAVENS.
...
I KNOW... I KNOW, ALL RIGHT?
I KNOW WE WERE IDIOTS.
I KNEW THOSE TWO WERE FISHY FROM THE START...
BUT YOU KNOW WHAT? THERE'S NO TURNING OUR BACKS TO THIS.

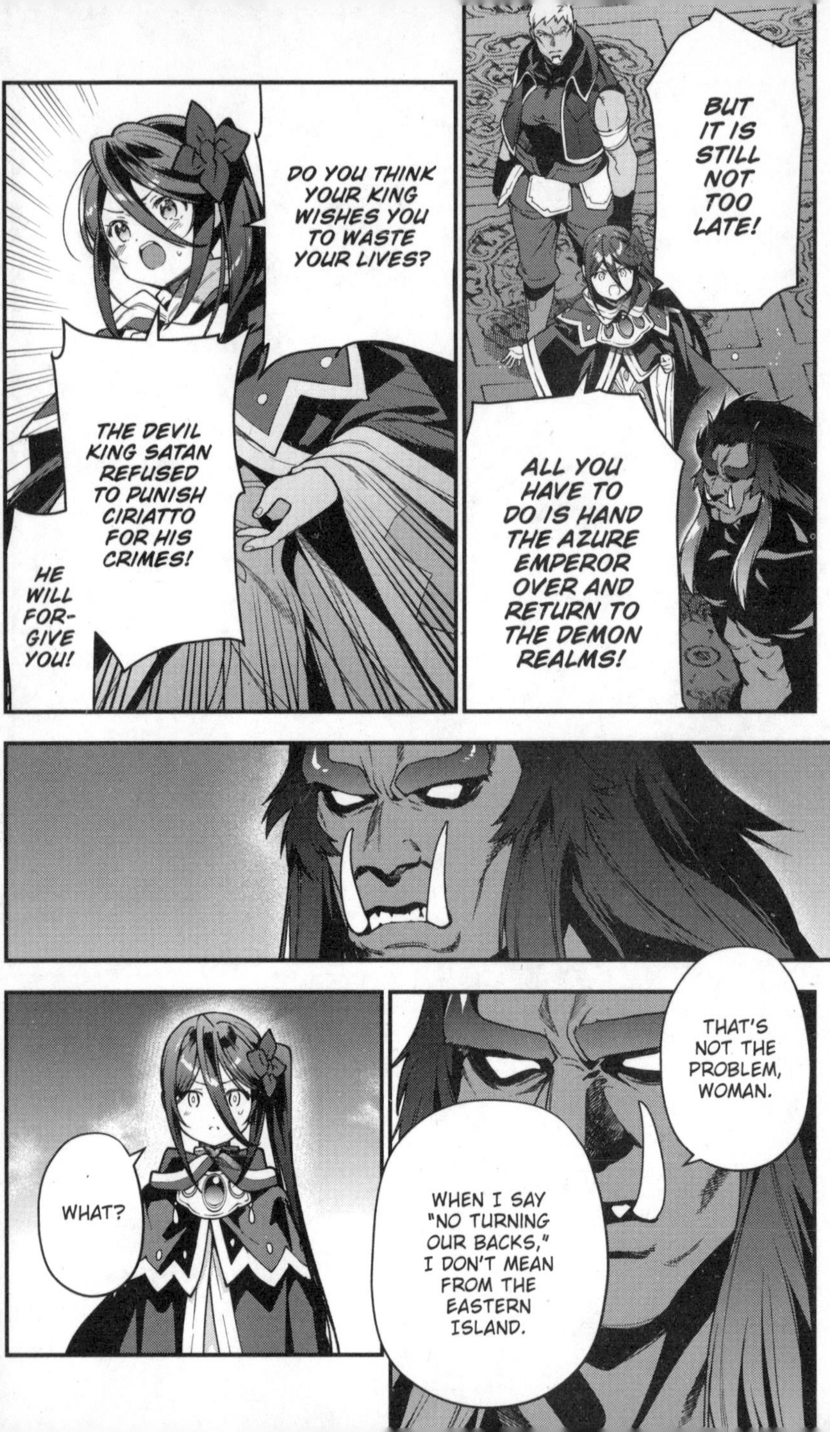
BUT IT IS STILL NOT TOO LATE!
ALL YOU HAVE TO DO IS HAND THE AZURE EMPEROR OVER AND RETURN TO THE DEMON REALMS!
DO YOU THINK YOUR KING WISHES YOU TO WASTE YOUR LIVES?
THE DEVIL KING SATAN REFUSED TO PUNISH CIRIATTO FOR HIS CRIMES!
HE WILL FOR-GIVE YOU!
THAT'S NOT THE PROBLEM, WOMAN.
WHEN I SAY "NO TURNING OUR BACKS," I DON'T MEAN FROM THE EASTERN ISLAND.
WHAT?

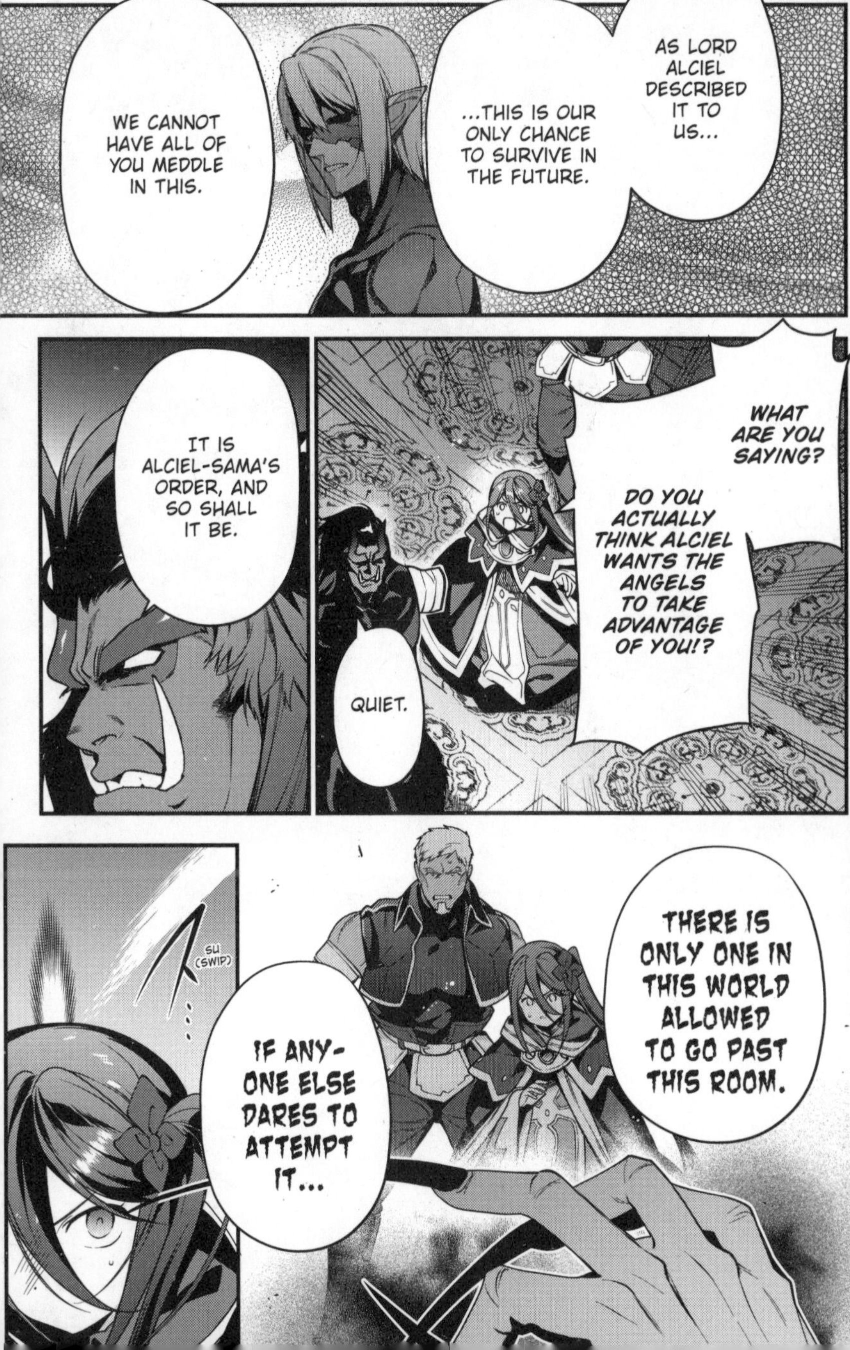
AS LORD ALCIEL DESCRIBED IT TO US...
...THIS IS OUR ONLY CHANCE TO SURVIVE IN THE FUTURE.
WE CANNOT HAVE ALL OF YOU MEDDLE IN THIS.
WHAT ARE YOU SAYING?
DO YOU ACTUALLY THINK ALCIEL WANTS THE ANGELS TO TAKE ADVANTAGE OF YOU!?
QUIET.
IT IS ALCIEL-SAMA'S ORDER, AND SO SHALL IT BE.
THERE IS ONLY ONE IN THIS WORLD ALLOWED TO GO PAST THIS ROOM.
IF ANY-ONE ELSE DARES TO ATTEMPT IT...
SU (SWIP)
...

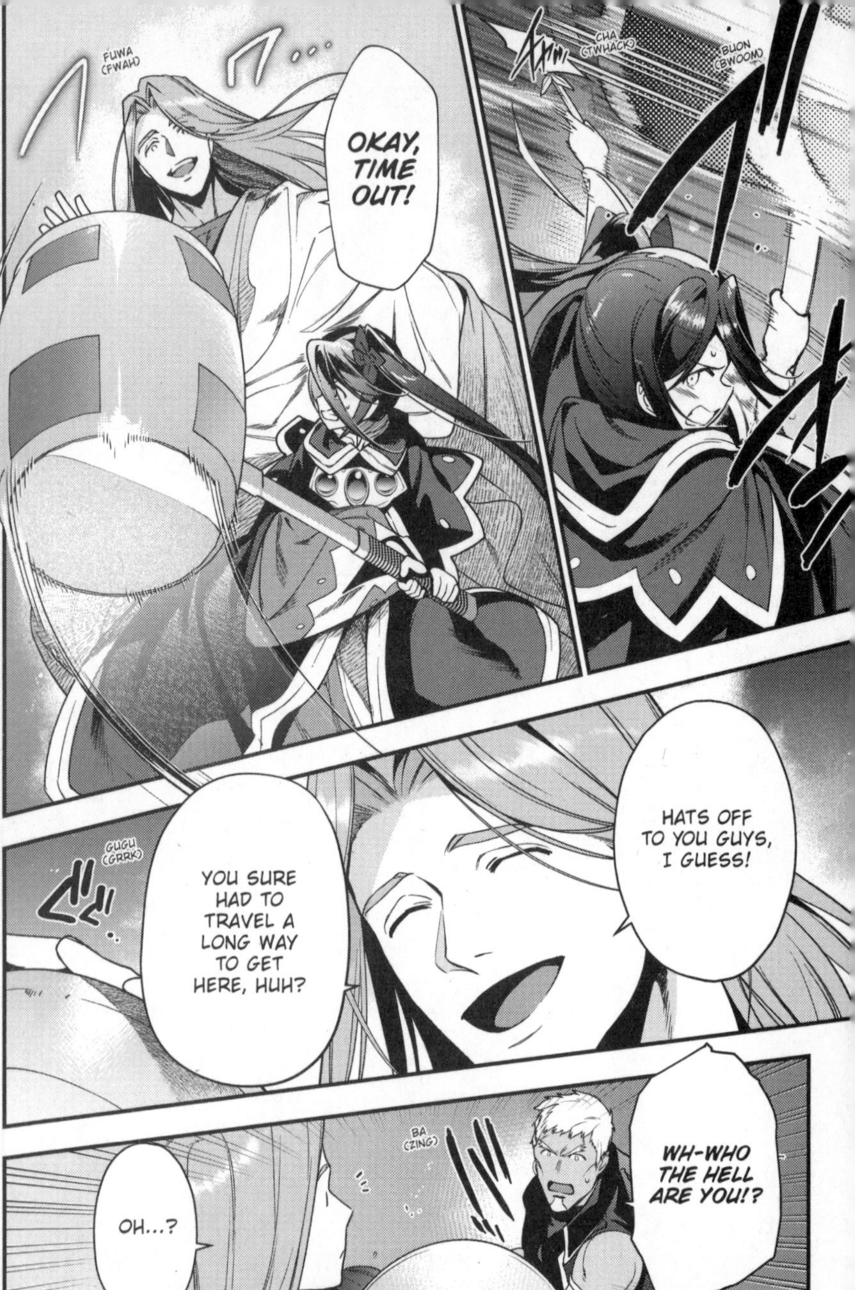
CHA (TWHACK)
BUON (BWOOM)
FUWA (FWAH)
OKAY, TIME OUT!
HATS OFF TO YOU GUYS, I GUESS!
YOU SURE HAD TO TRAVEL A LONG WAY TO GET HERE, HUH?
GUGU (GRRK)
WH-WHO THE HELL ARE YOU!?
BA (ZING)
OH...?

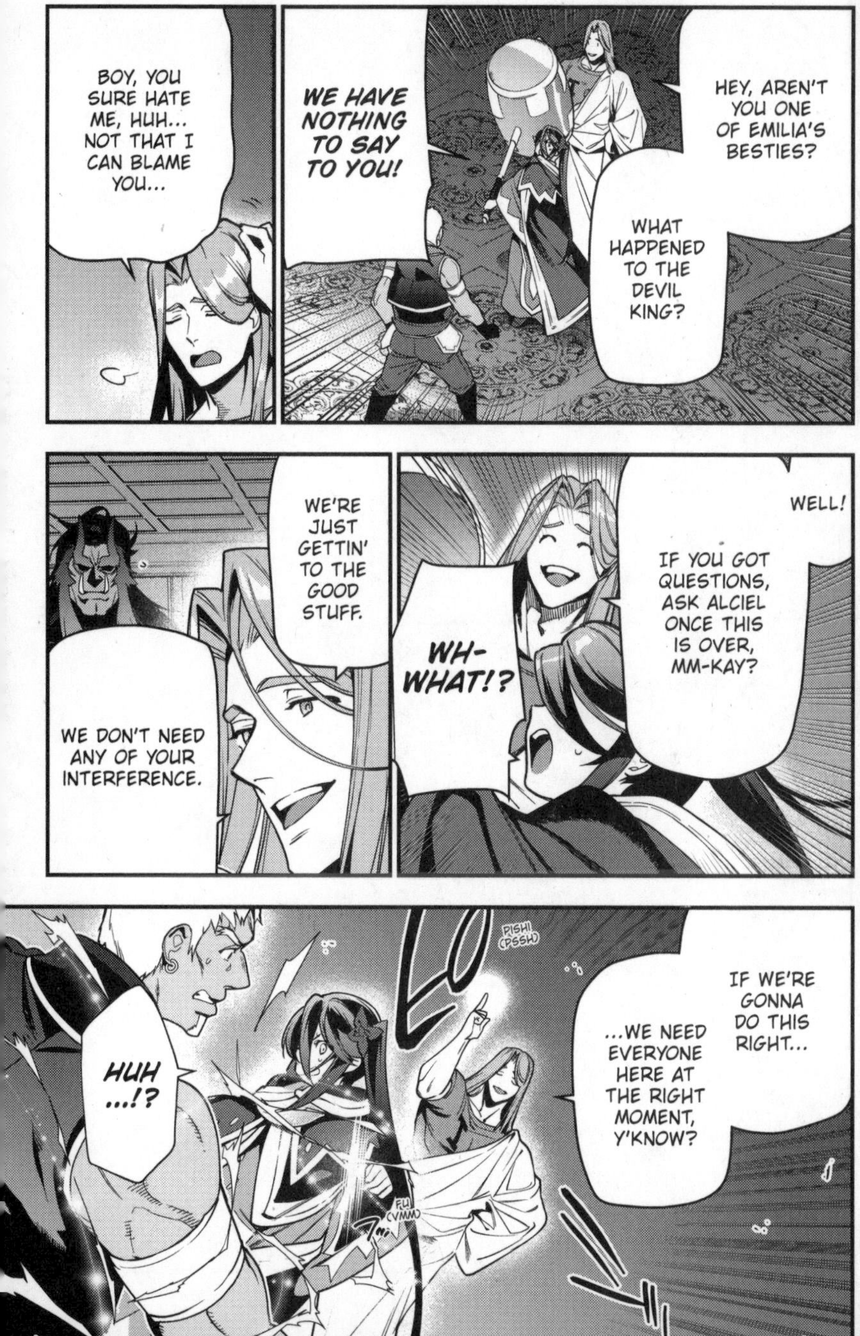
HEY, AREN'T YOU ONE OF EMILIA'S BESTIES?
WHAT HAPPENED TO THE DEVIL KING?
WE HAVE NOTHING TO SAY TO YOU!
BOY, YOU SURE HATE ME, HUH... NOT THAT I CAN BLAME YOU...
WELL!
IF YOU GOT QUESTIONS, ASK ALCIEL ONCE THIS IS OVER, MM-KAY?
WH-WHAT!?
WE'RE JUST GETTIN' TO THE GOOD STUFF.
WE DON'T NEED ANY OF YOUR INTERFERENCE.
IF WE'RE GONNA DO THIS RIGHT...
...WE NEED EVERYONE HERE AT THE RIGHT MOMENT, Y'KNOW?
PISHI (PSSSH)
HUH ...!?
FU (VMM)

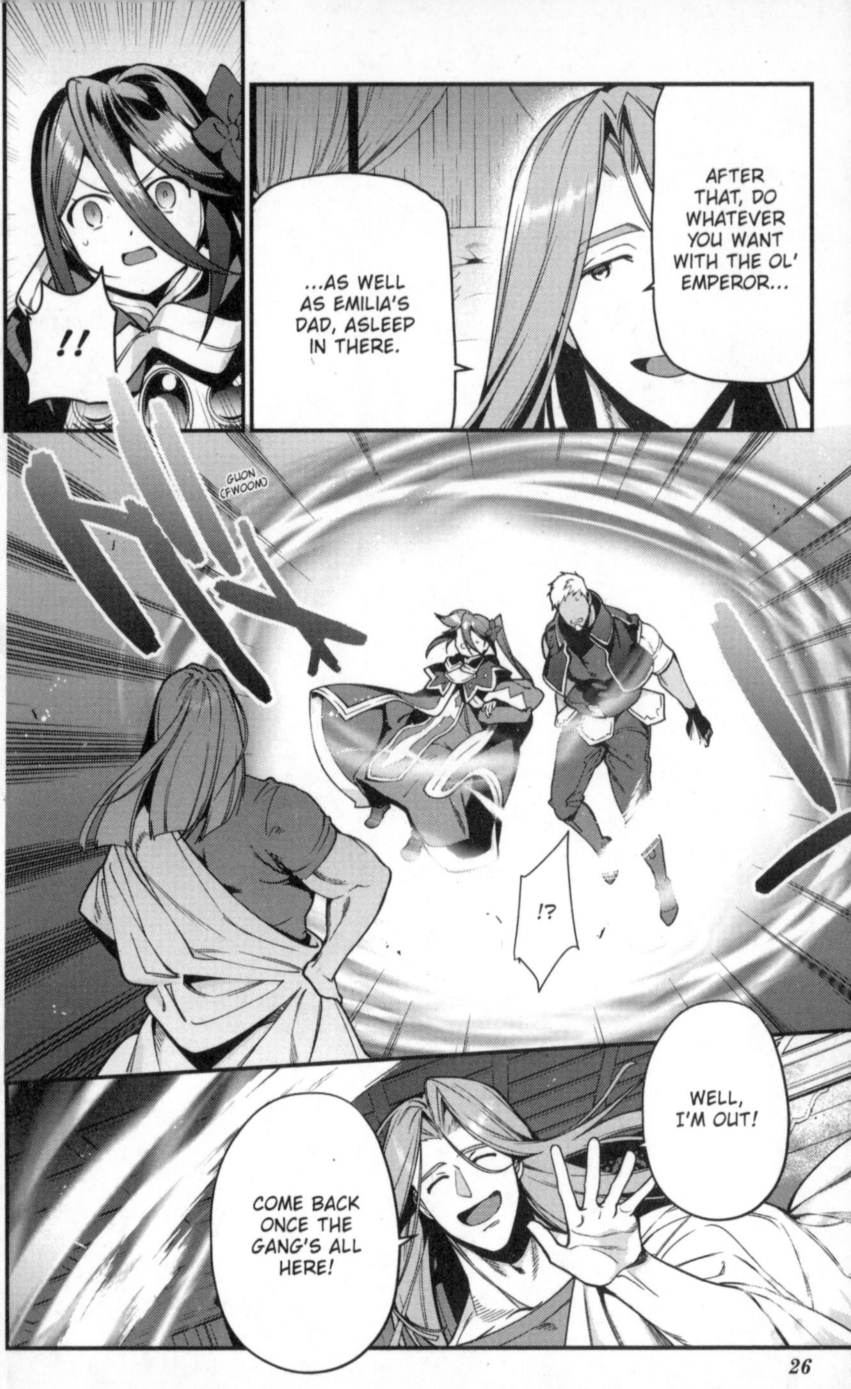
AFTER THAT, DO WHATEVER YOU WANT WITH THE OL' EMPEROR...
...AS WELL AS EMILIA'S DAD, ASLEEP IN THERE.
!!
GUON (FWOOM)
!?
WELL, I'M OUT!
COME BACK ONCE THE GANG'S ALL HERE!

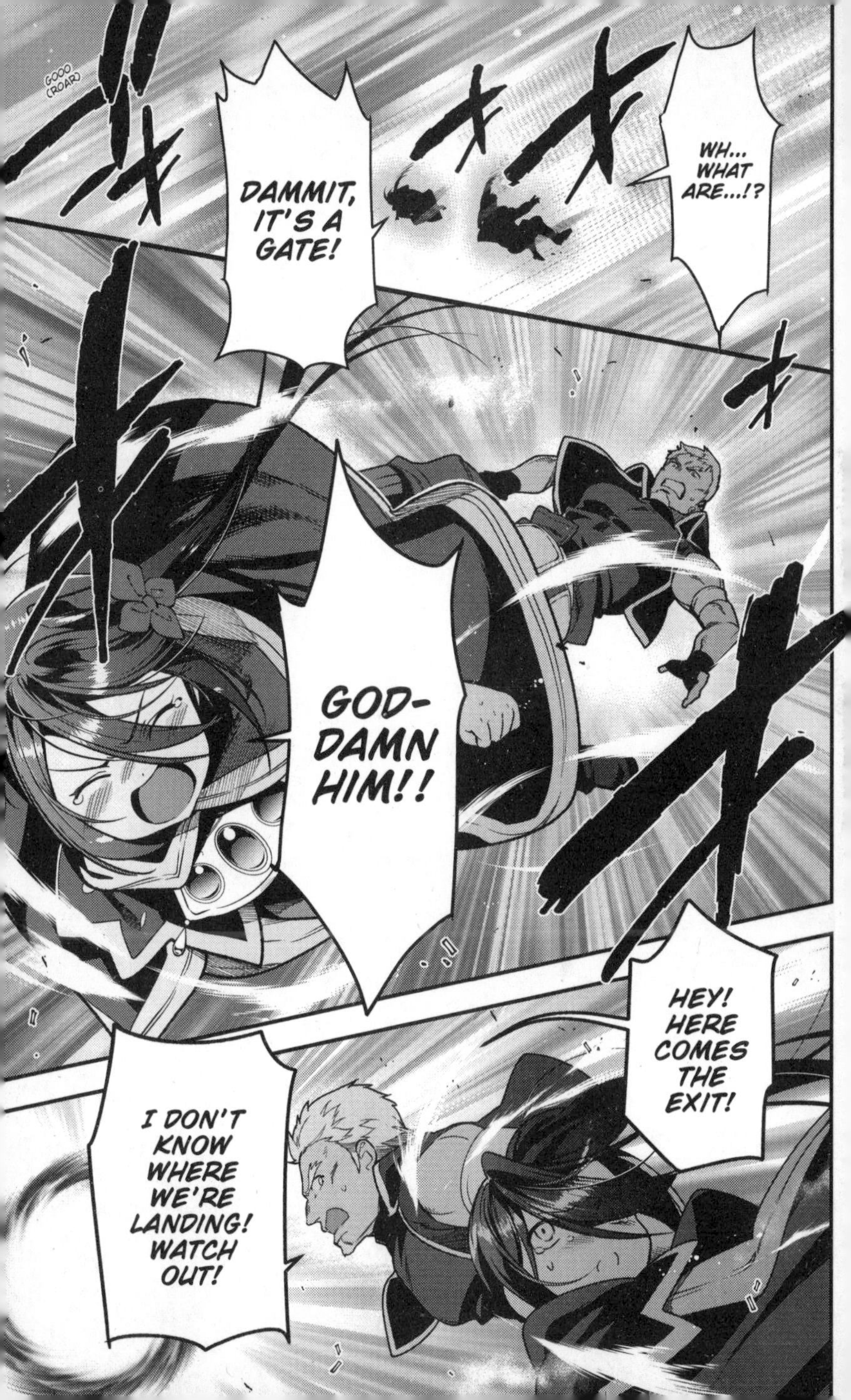
WH... WHAT ARE...!?
DAMMIT, IT'S A GATE!
GOOO (ROAR)
GOD-DAMN HIM!!
HEY! HERE COMES THE EXIT!
I DON'T KNOW WHERE WE'RE LANDING! WATCH OUT!

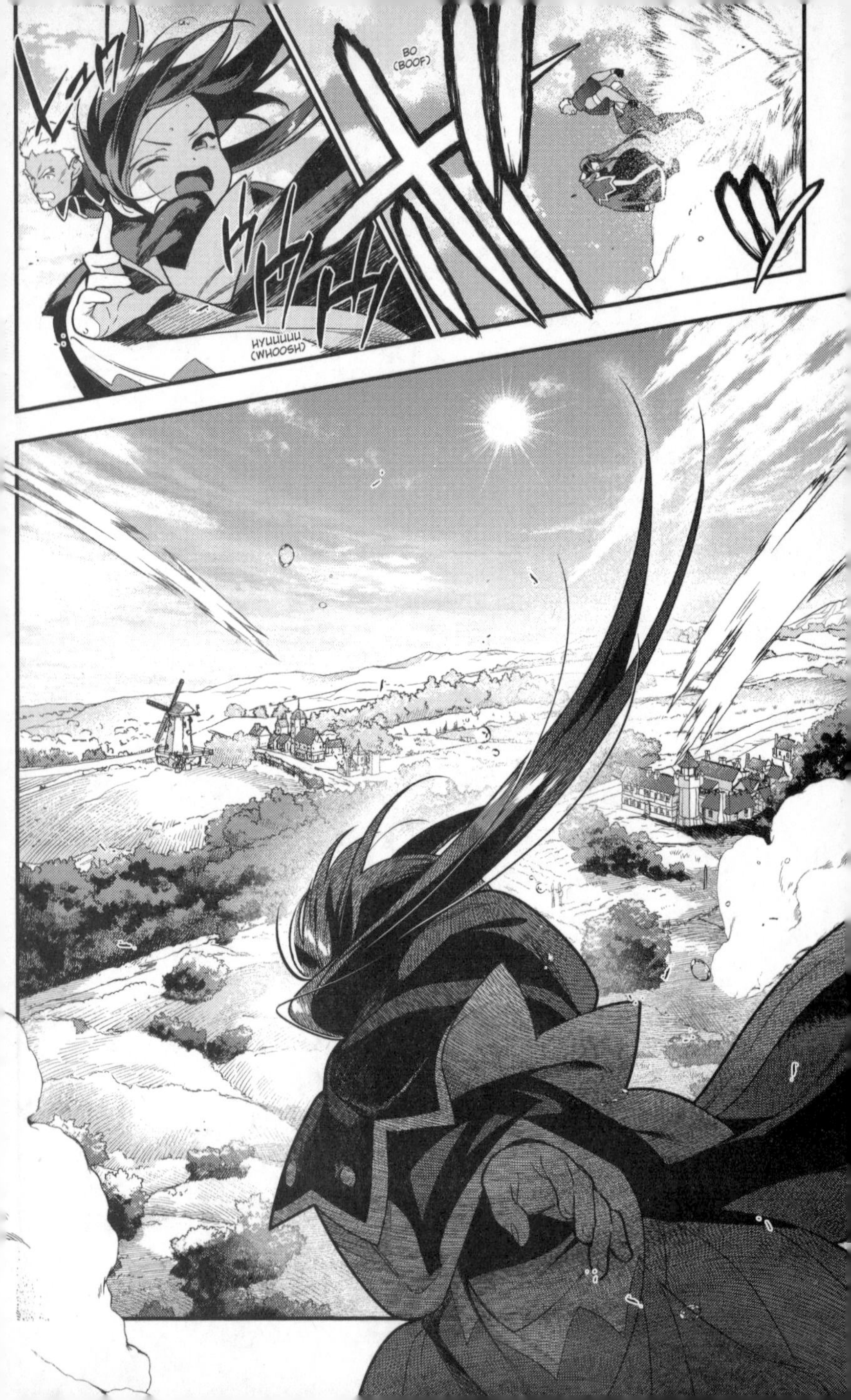
BO
(BOOF)
HYUUUUU
(WHOOSH)

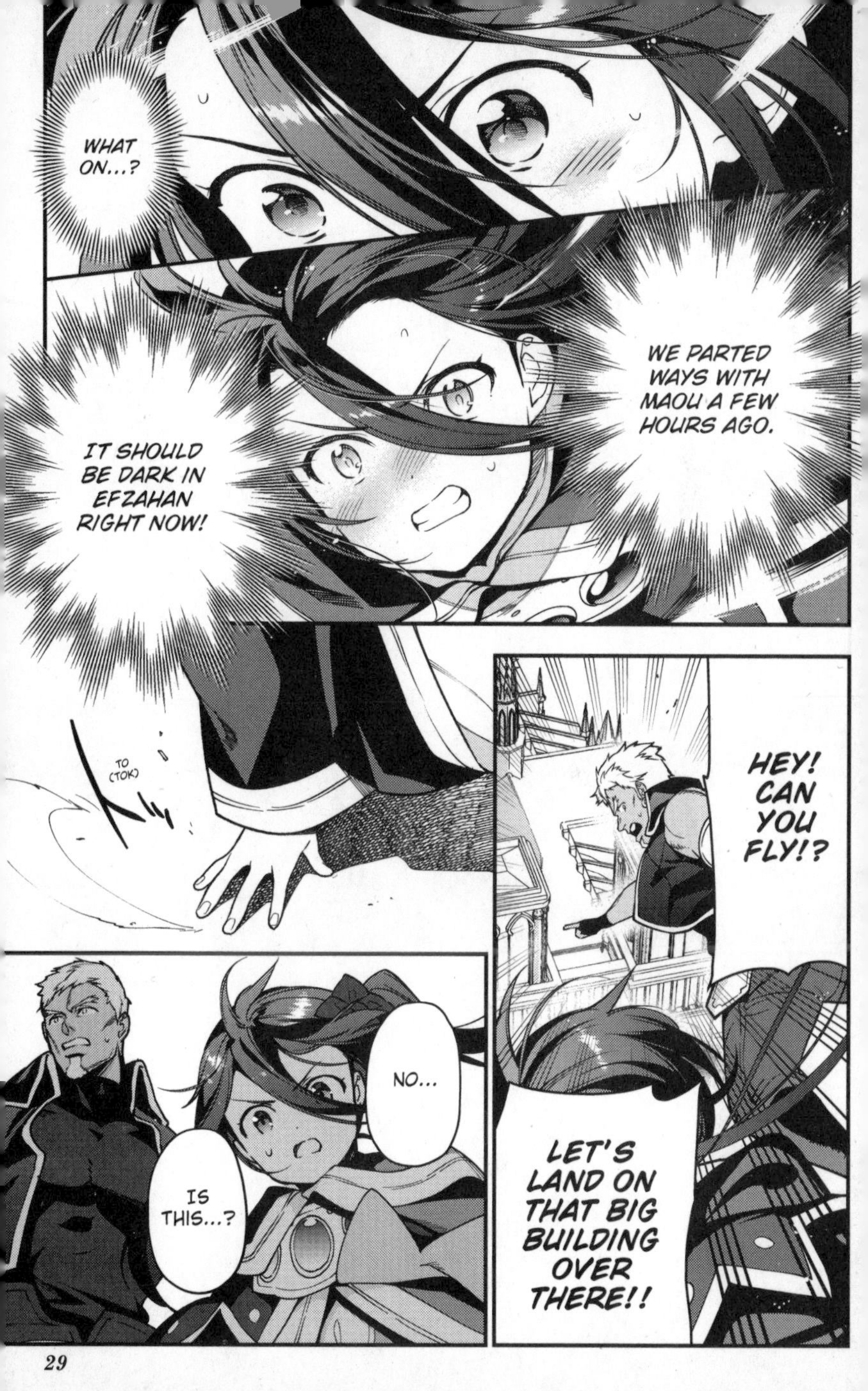
WHAT ON...?
WE PARTED WAYS WITH MAOU A FEW HOURS AGO.
IT SHOULD BE DARK IN EFZAHAN RIGHT NOW!
HEY! CAN YOU FLY!?
LET'S LAND ON THAT BIG BUILDING OVER THERE!!
TO (TOK)
NO...
IS THIS...?

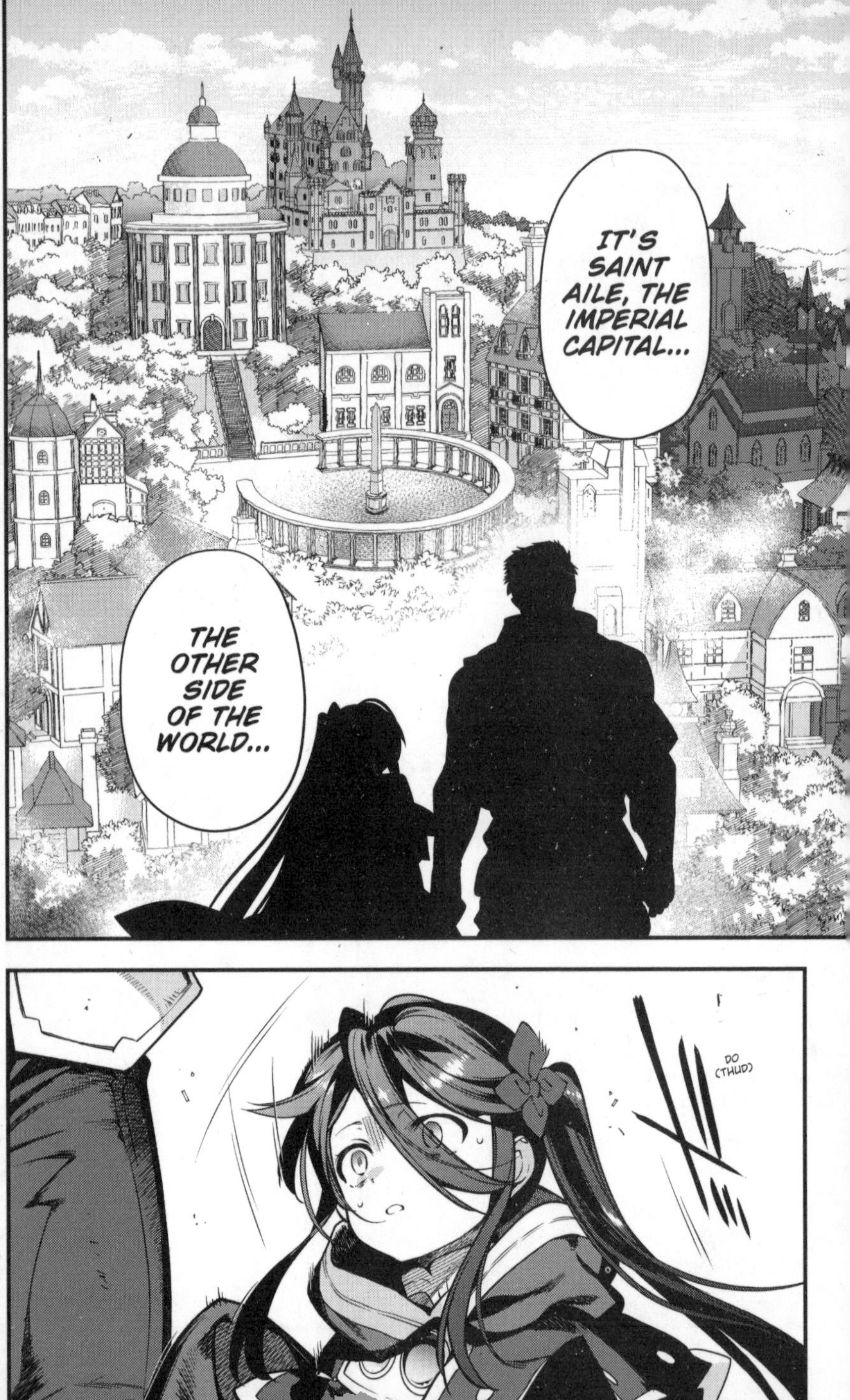
IT'S SAINT AILE, THE IMPERIAL CAPITAL...
THE OTHER SIDE OF THE WORLD...
DO (THUD)

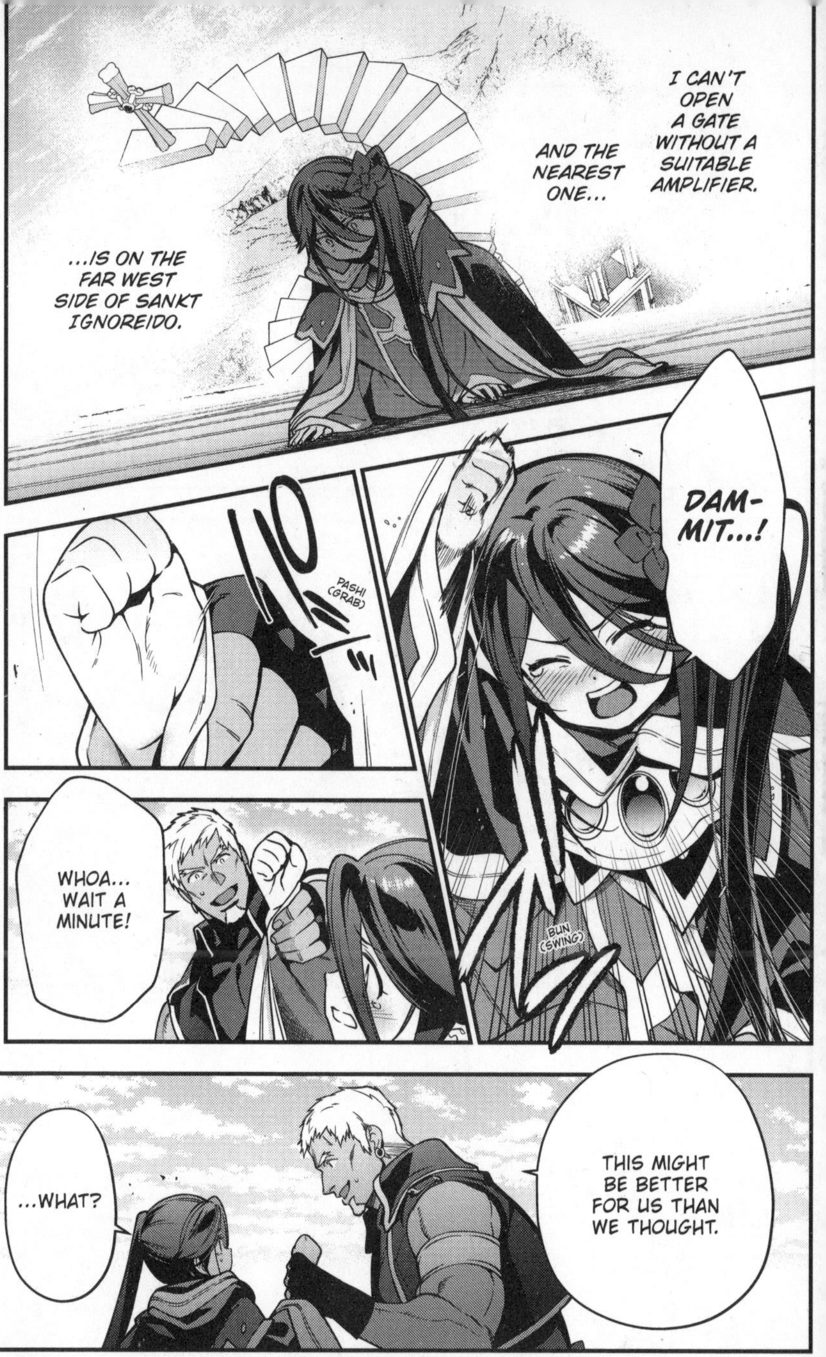
I CAN'T OPEN A GATE WITHOUT A SUITABLE AMPLIFIER.
AND THE NEAREST ONE...
...IS ON THE FAR WEST SIDE OF SANKT IGNOREIDO.
DAM-MIT...!
BUN (SWING)
PASHI (GRAB)
WHOA... WAIT A MINUTE!
THIS MIGHT BE BETTER FOR US THAN WE THOUGHT.
...WHAT?

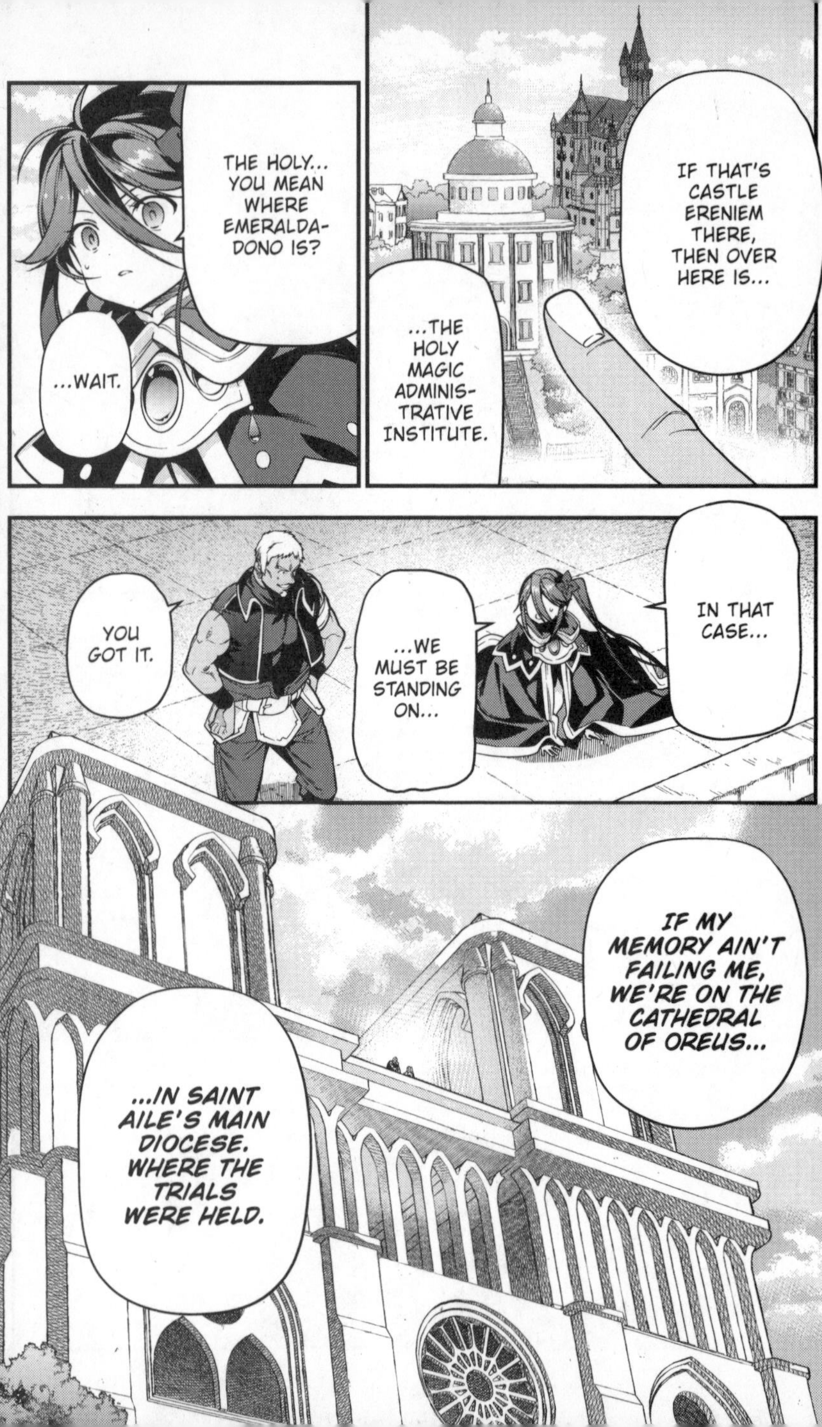
IF THAT'S CASTLE ERENIEM THERE, THEN OVER HERE IS...
...THE HOLY MAGIC ADMINISTRATIVE INSTITUTE.
THE HOLY... YOU MEAN WHERE EMERALDA-DONO IS?
...WAIT.
IN THAT CASE...
...WE MUST BE STANDING ON...
YOU GOT IT.
IF MY MEMORY AIN'T FAILING ME, WE'RE ON THE CATHEDRAL OF OREUS...
...IN SAINT AILE'S MAIN DIOCESE. WHERE THE TRIALS WERE HELD.

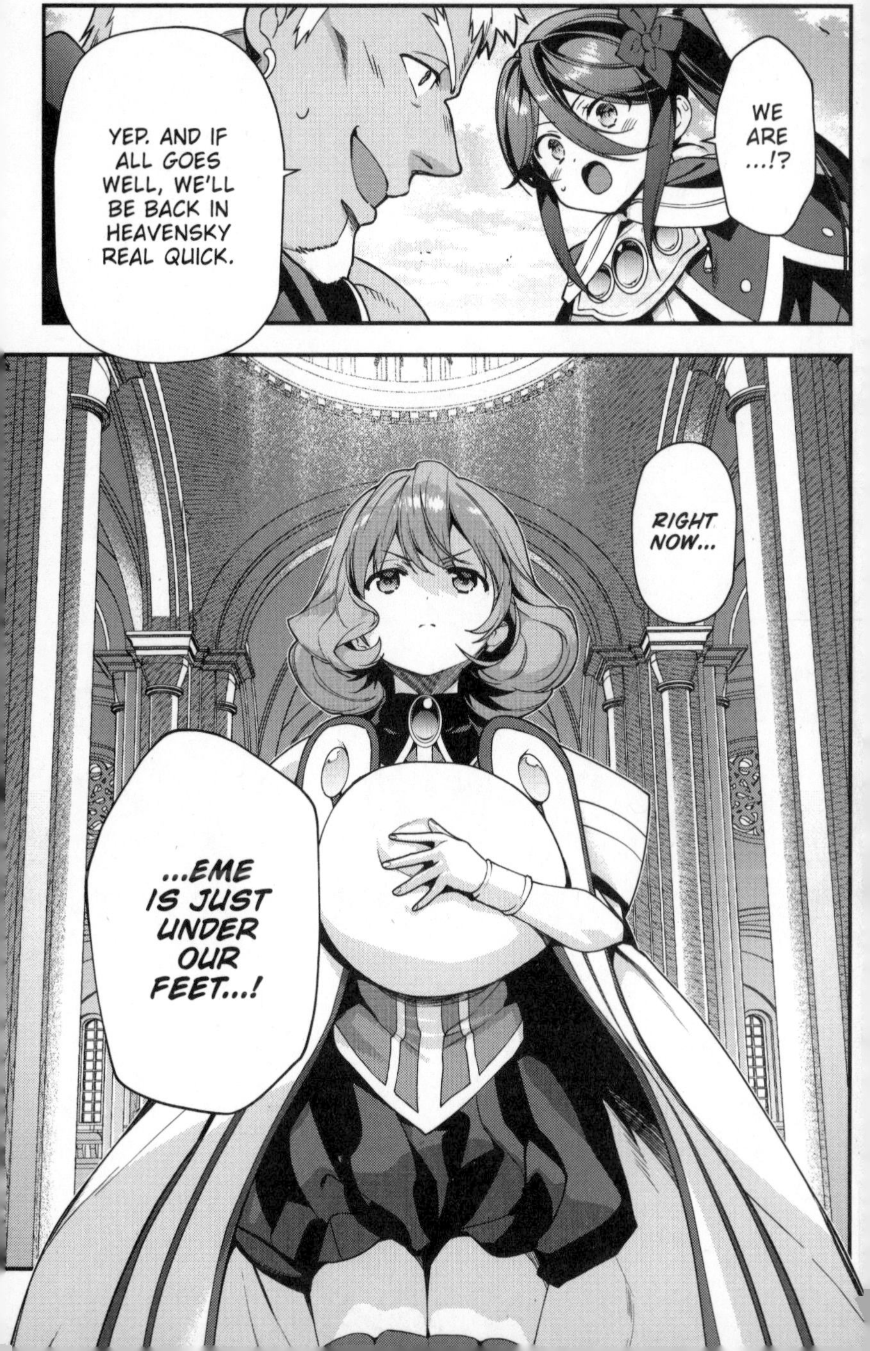
WE ARE ...!?
YEP. AND IF ALL GOES WELL, WE'LL BE BACK IN HEAVENSKY REAL QUICK.
RIGHT NOW...
...EME IS JUST UNDER OUR FEET...!

THE DEVIL IS A PART-TIMER!

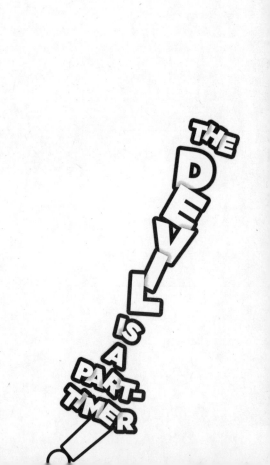

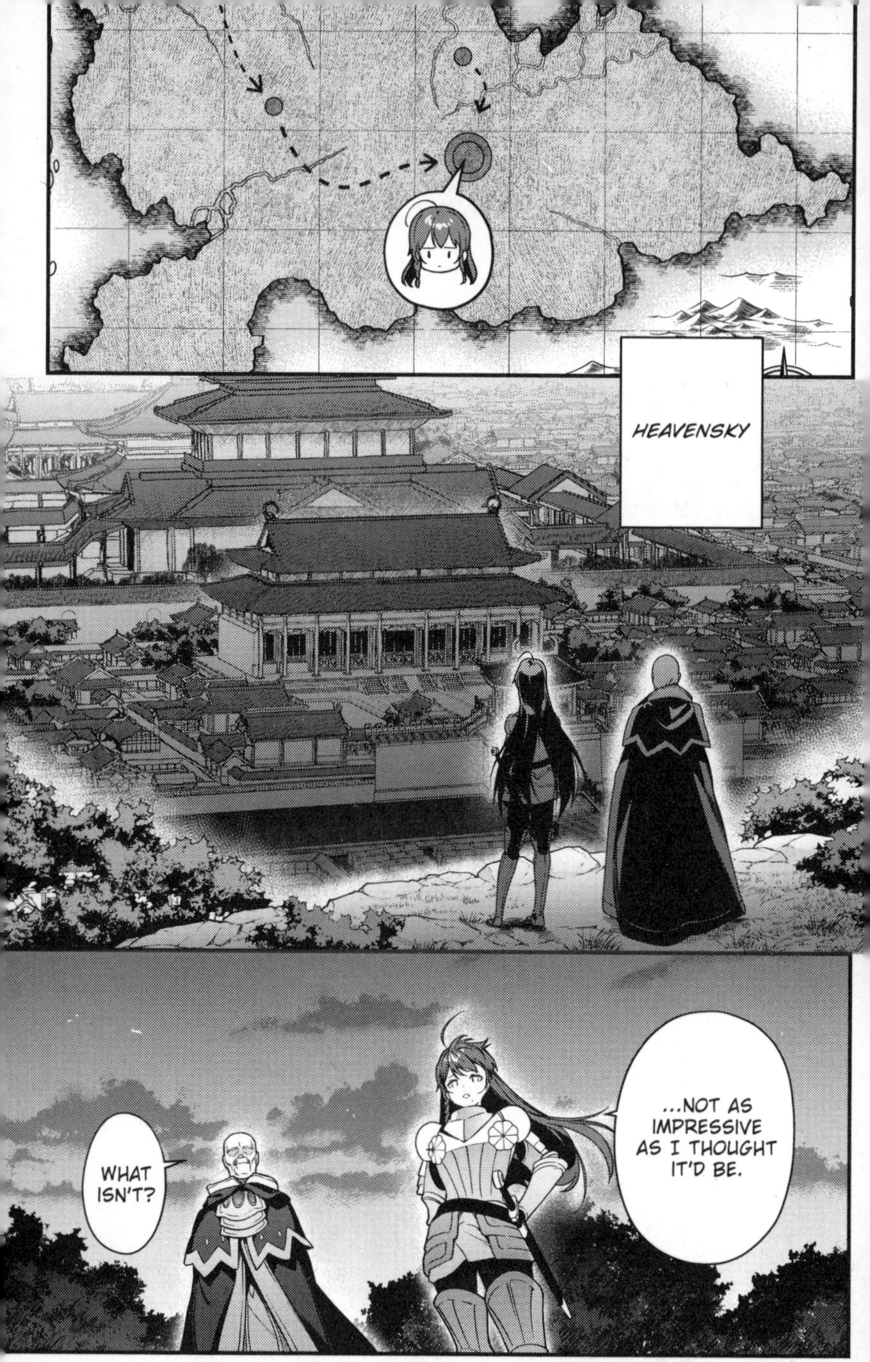
HEAVENSKY
...NOT AS IMPRESSIVE AS I THOUGHT IT'D BE.
WHAT ISN'T?

CHAPTER 91: THE HERO IS CHEERED BY A CRYPTIC MISSIVE

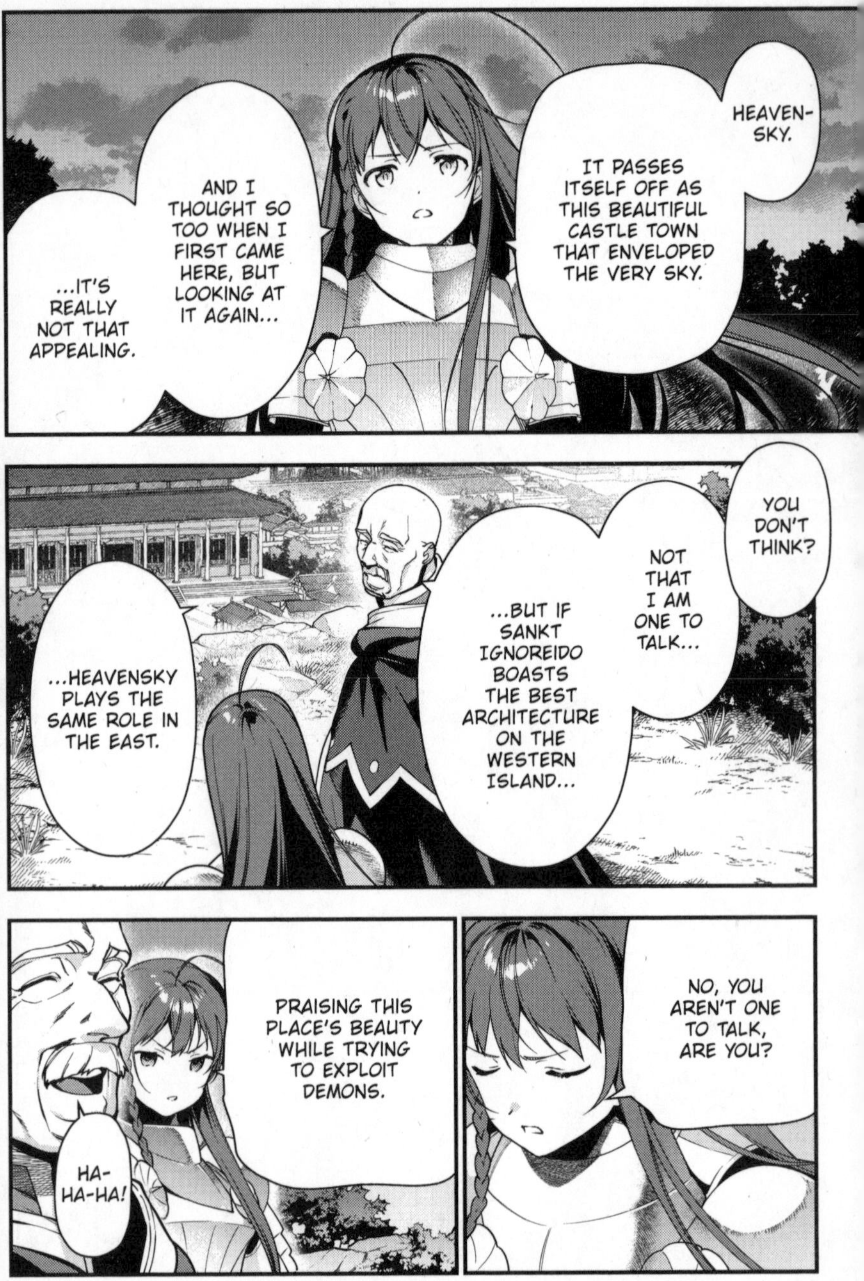
HEAVEN-SKY.
IT PASSES ITSELF OFF AS THIS BEAUTIFUL CASTLE TOWN THAT ENVELOPED THE VERY SKY.
AND I THOUGHT SO TOO WHEN I FIRST CAME HERE, BUT LOOKING AT IT AGAIN...
...IT'S REALLY NOT THAT APPEALING.
YOU DON'T THINK?
NOT THAT I AM ONE TO TALK...
...BUT IF SANKT IGNOREIDO BOASTS THE BEST ARCHITECTURE ON THE WESTERN ISLAND...
...HEAVENSKY PLAYS THE SAME ROLE IN THE EAST.
NO, YOU AREN'T ONE TO TALK, ARE YOU?
PRAISING THIS PLACE'S BEAUTY WHILE TRYING TO EXPLOIT DEMONS.
HA-HA-HA!

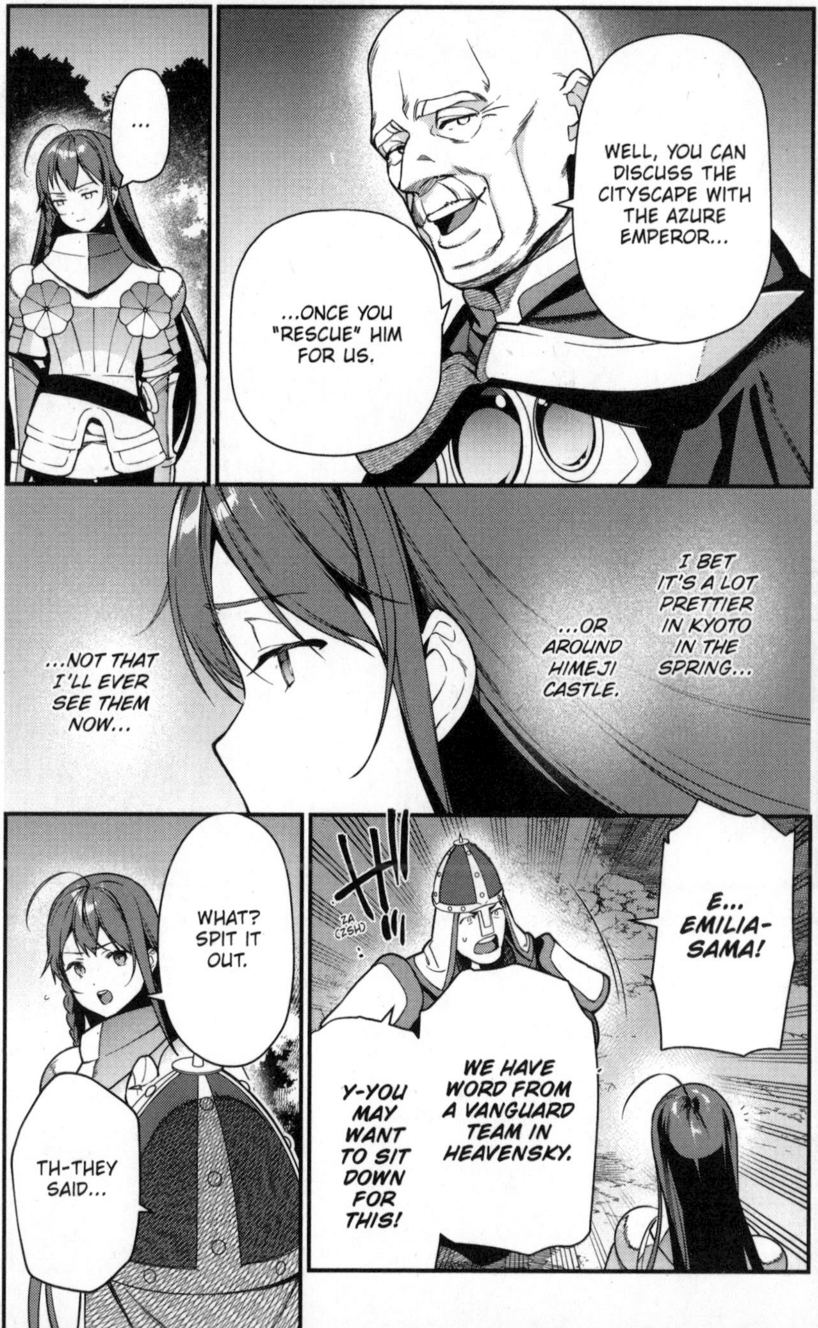
WELL, YOU CAN DISCUSS THE CITYSCAPE WITH THE AZURE EMPEROR...
...ONCE YOU "RESCUE" HIM FOR US.
...
I BET IT'S A LOT PRETTIER IN KYOTO IN THE SPRING...
...OR AROUND HIMEJI CASTLE.
...NOT THAT I'LL EVER SEE THEM NOW...
ZA (ZSH)
E... EMILIA-SAMA!
WE HAVE WORD FROM A VANGUARD TEAM IN HEAVENSKY.
Y-YOU MAY WANT TO SIT DOWN FOR THIS!
WHAT? SPIT IT OUT.
TH-THEY SAID...

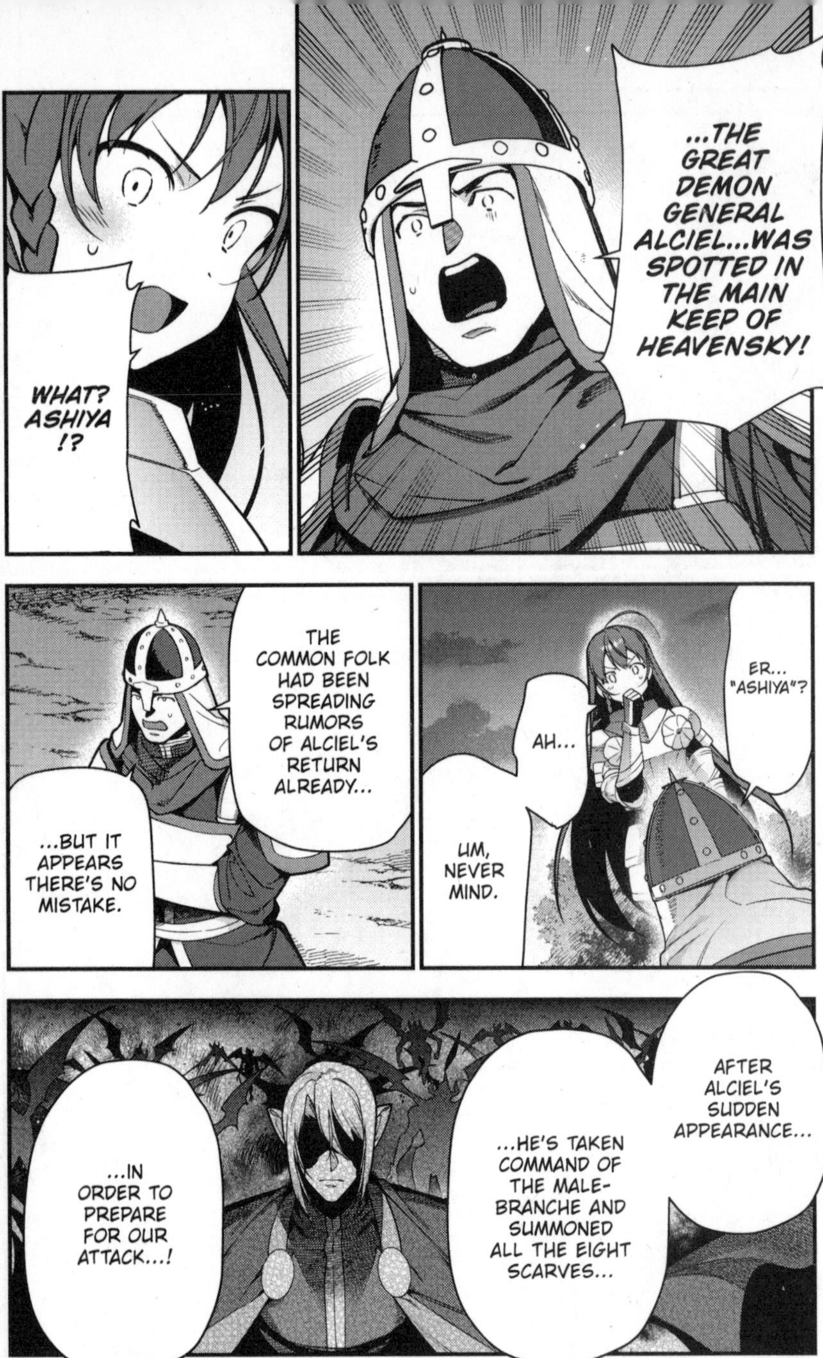
...THE GREAT DEMON GENERAL ALCIEL...WAS SPOTTED IN THE MAIN KEEP OF HEAVENSKY!
WHAT? ASHIYA!?
ER... "ASHIYA"?
AH...
UM, NEVER MIND.
THE COMMON FOLK HAD BEEN SPREADING RUMORS OF ALCIEL'S RETURN ALREADY...
...BUT IT APPEARS THERE'S NO MISTAKE.
AFTER ALCIEL'S SUDDEN APPEARANCE...
...HE'S TAKEN COMMAND OF THE MALE-BRANCHE AND SUMMONED ALL THE EIGHT SCARVES...
...IN ORDER TO PREPARE FOR OUR ATTACK...!

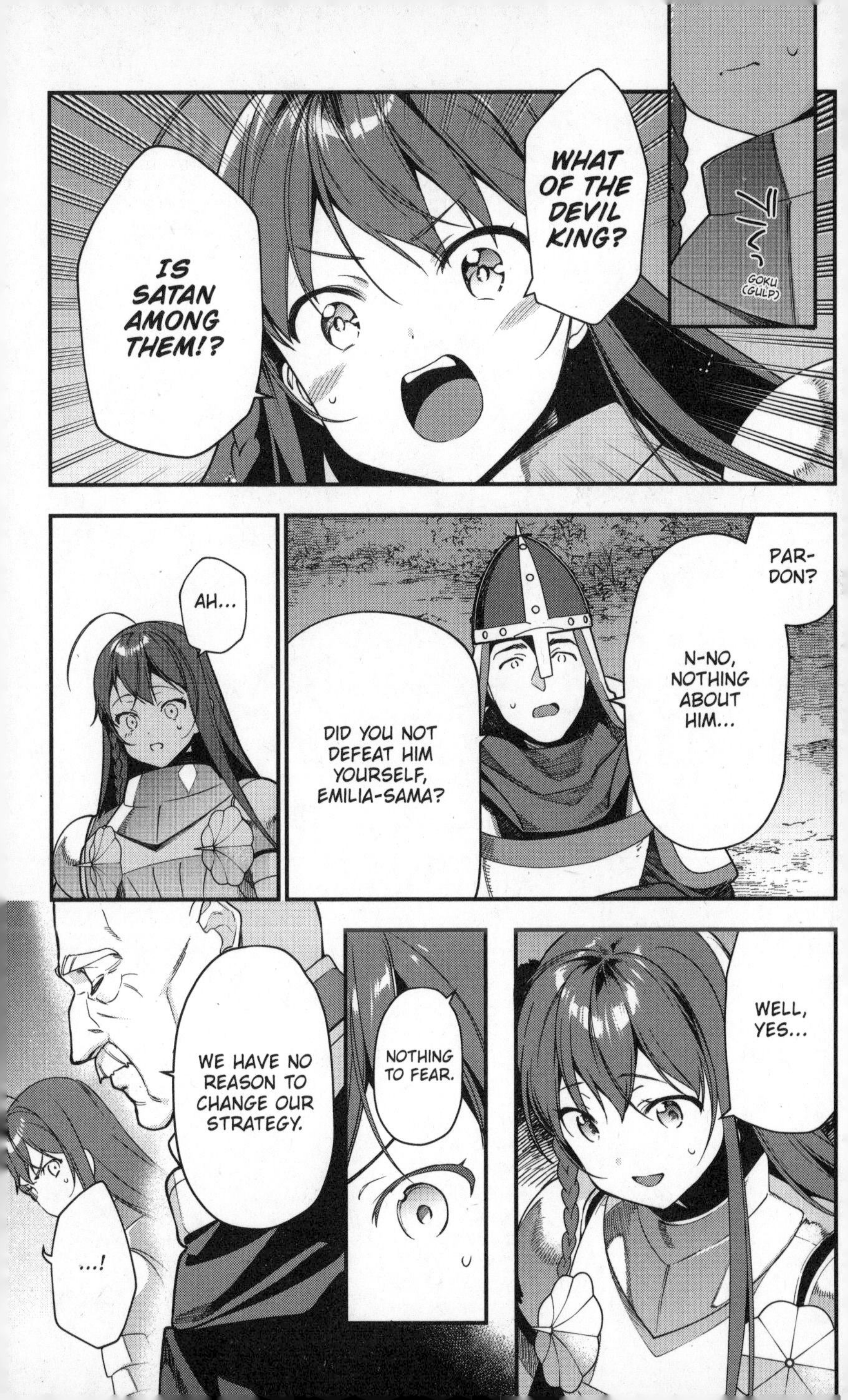
GOKU (GULP)
WHAT OF THE DEVIL KING?
IS SATAN AMONG THEM!?
PARDON?
N-NO, NOTHING ABOUT HIM...
DID YOU NOT DEFEAT HIM YOURSELF, EMILIA-SAMA?
AH...
WELL, YES...
NOTHING TO FEAR.
WE HAVE NO REASON TO CHANGE OUR STRATEGY.
...!

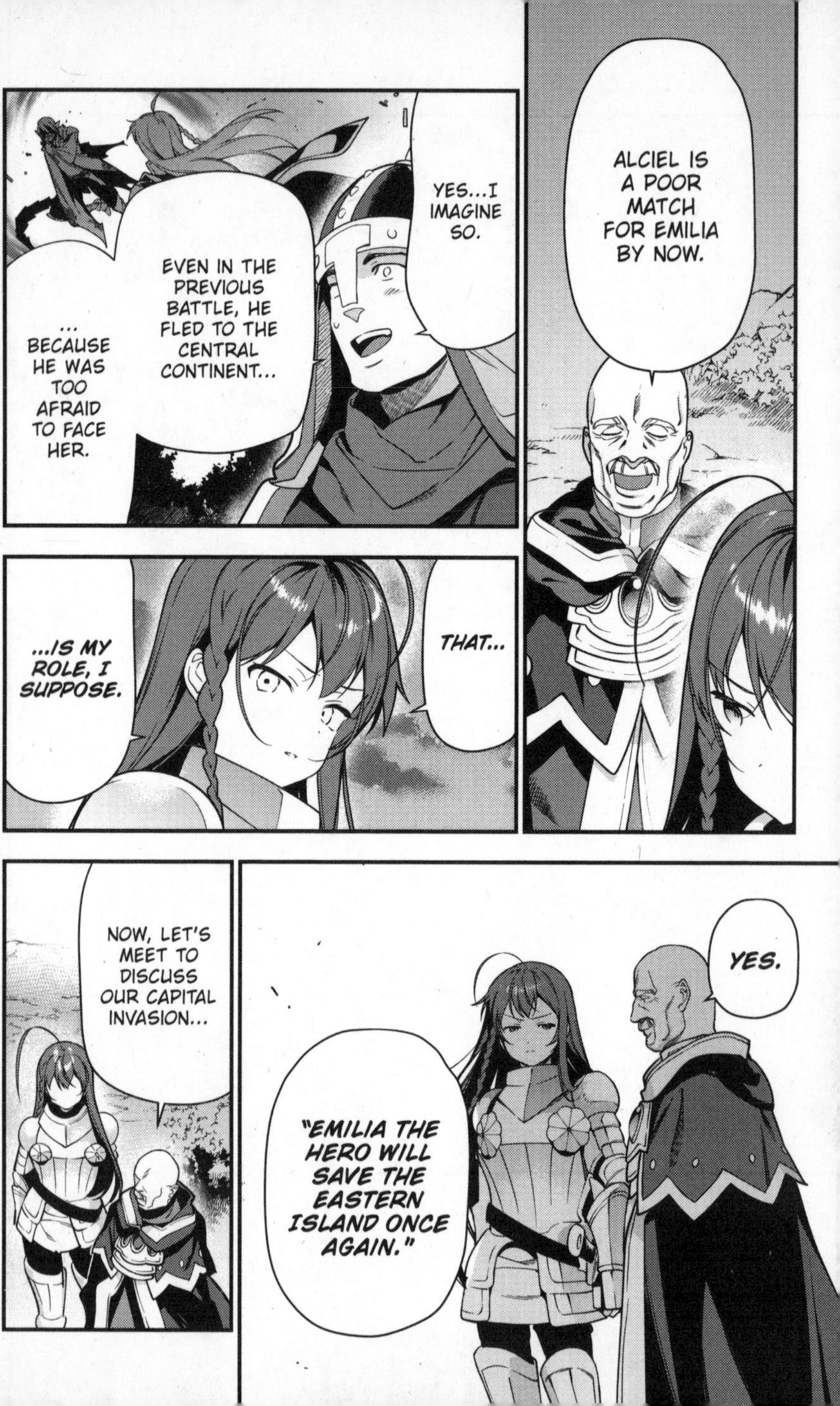
ALCIEL IS A POOR MATCH FOR EMILIA BY NOW.
YES…I IMAGINE SO.
EVEN IN THE PREVIOUS BATTLE, HE FLED TO THE CENTRAL CONTINENT…
…BECAUSE HE WAS TOO AFRAID TO FACE HER.
THAT…
…IS MY ROLE, I SUPPOSE.
YES.
"EMILIA THE HERO WILL SAVE THE EASTERN ISLAND ONCE AGAIN."
NOW, LET'S MEET TO DISCUSS OUR CAPITAL INVASION…

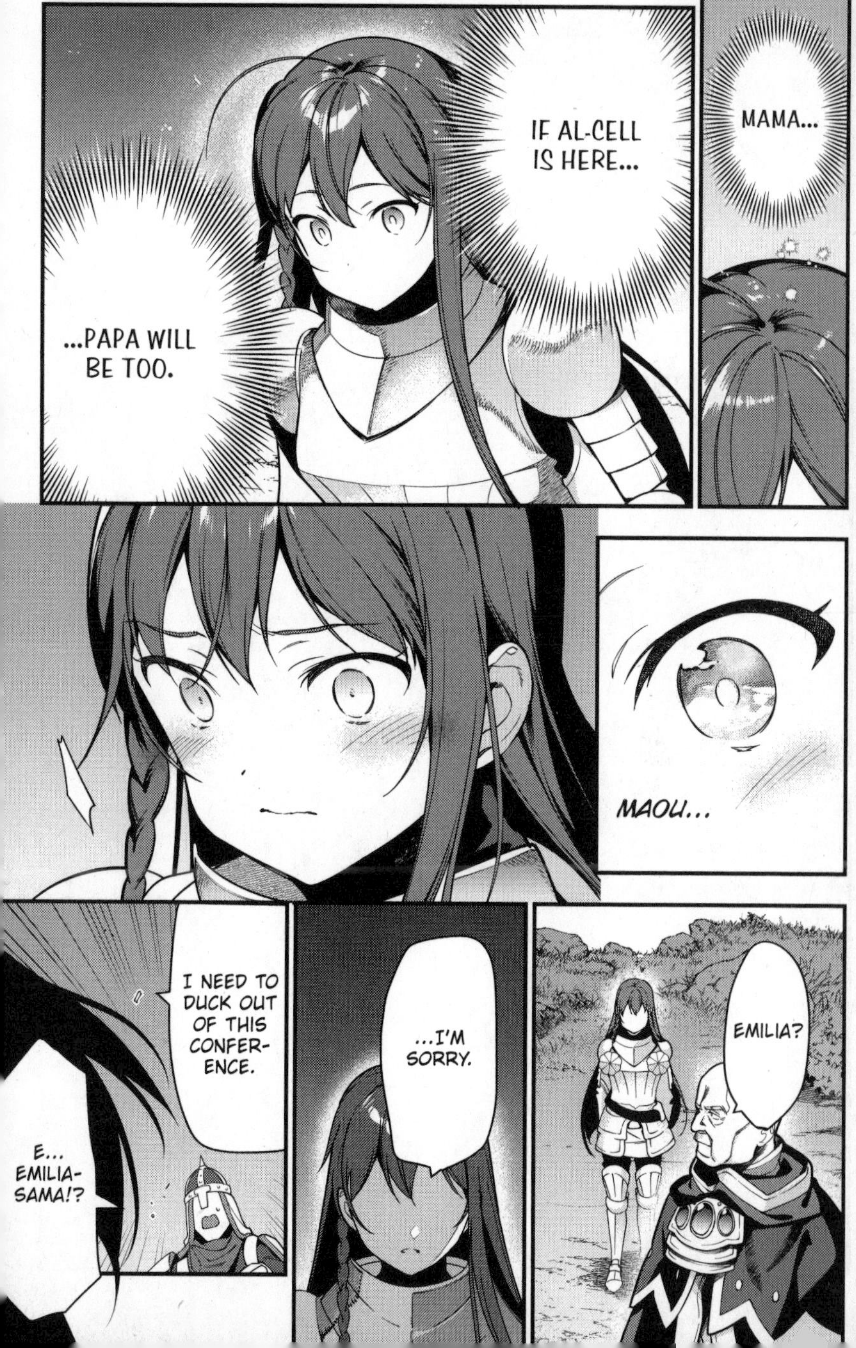
MAMA...
IF AL-CELL IS HERE...
...PAPA WILL BE TOO.
MAOU...
EMILIA?
...I'M SORRY.
I NEED TO DUCK OUT OF THIS CONFER-ENCE.
E... EMILIA-SAMA!?

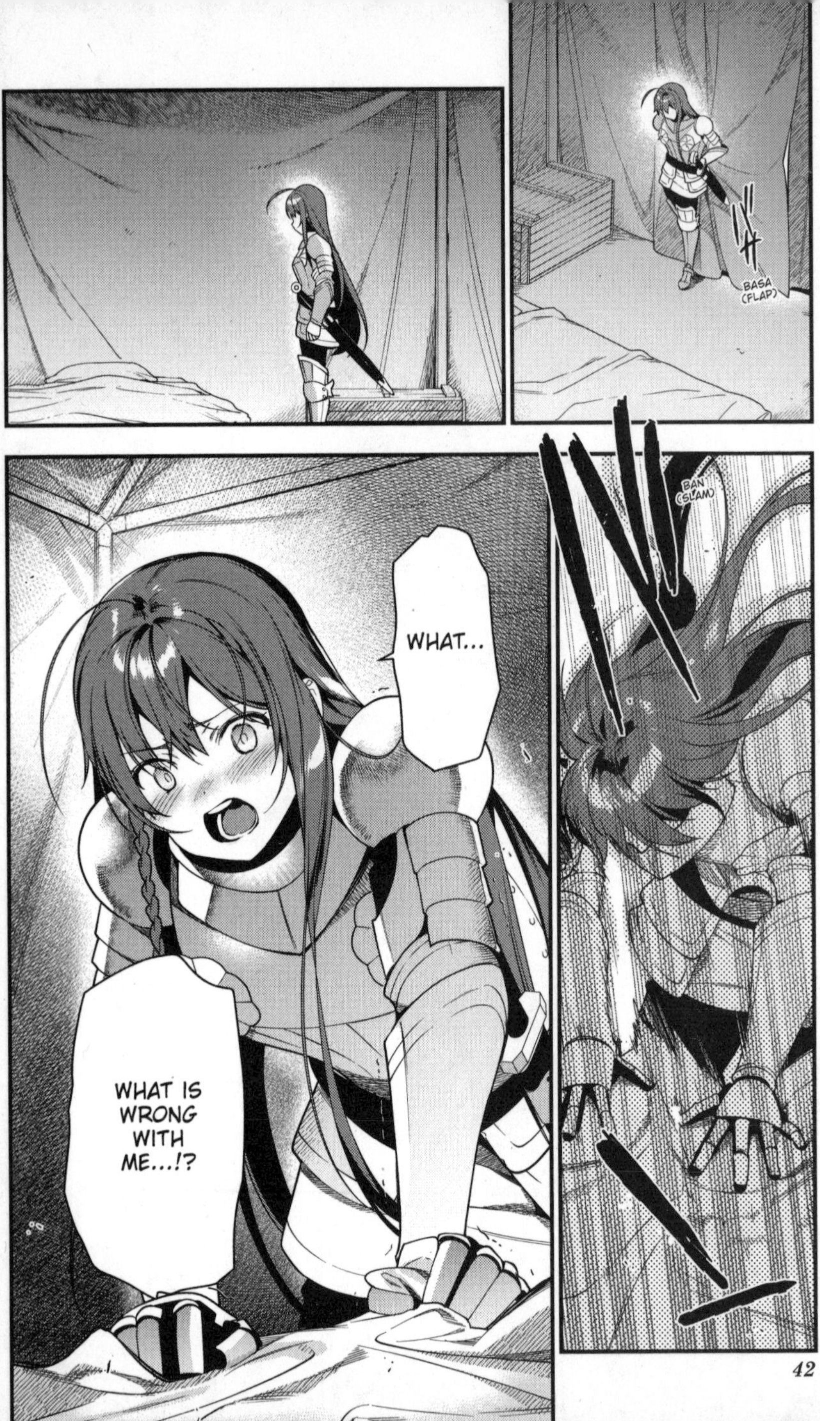
BASA (FLAP)
BAN (SLAM)
WHAT...
WHAT IS WRONG WITH ME...!?

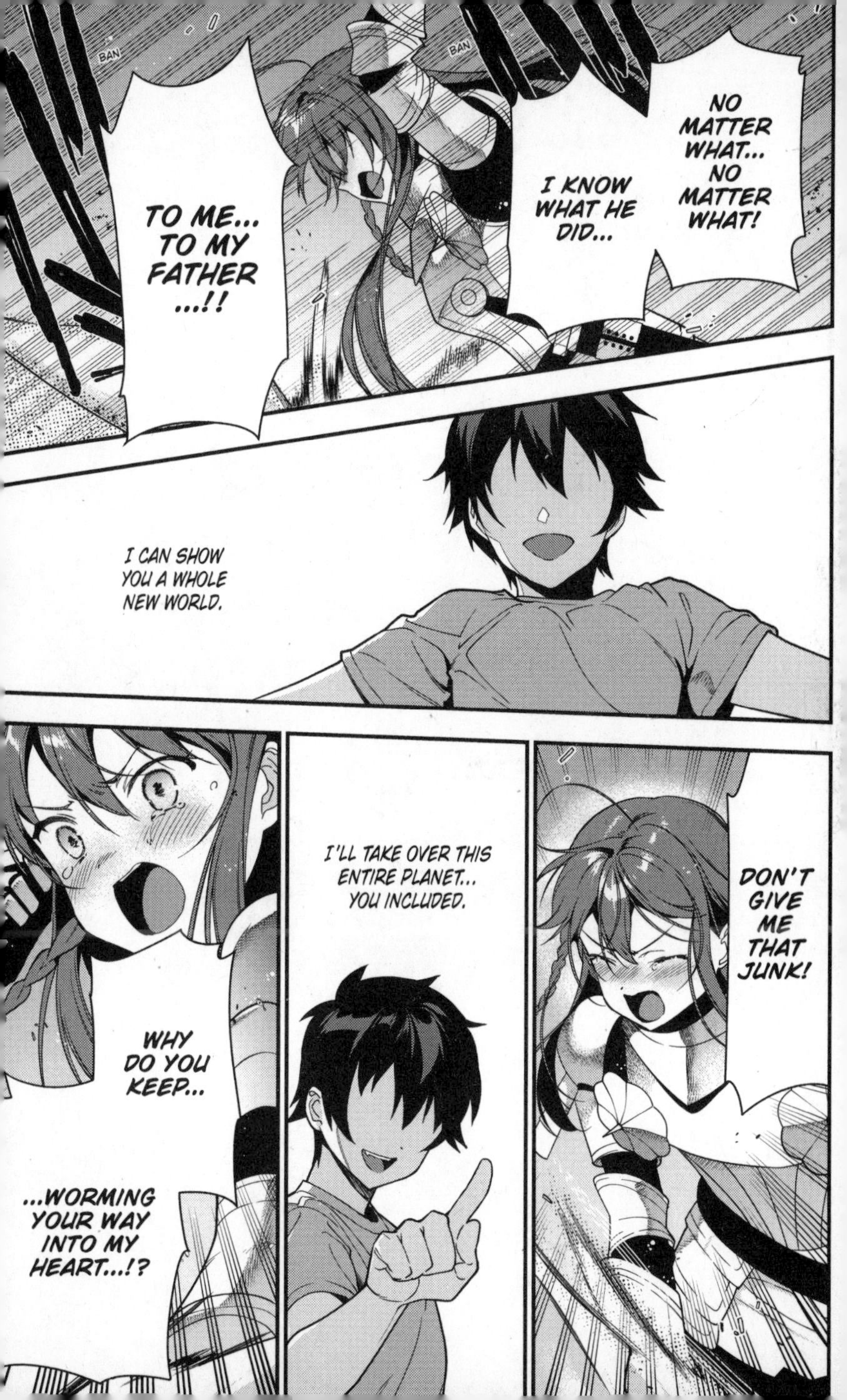
BAN
BAN
NO MATTER WHAT... NO MATTER WHAT!
I KNOW WHAT HE DID...
TO ME... TO MY FATHER ...!!
I CAN SHOW YOU A WHOLE NEW WORLD.
DON'T GIVE ME THAT JUNK!
I'LL TAKE OVER THIS ENTIRE PLANET... YOU INCLUDED.
WHY DO YOU KEEP...
...WORMING YOUR WAY INTO MY HEART...!?

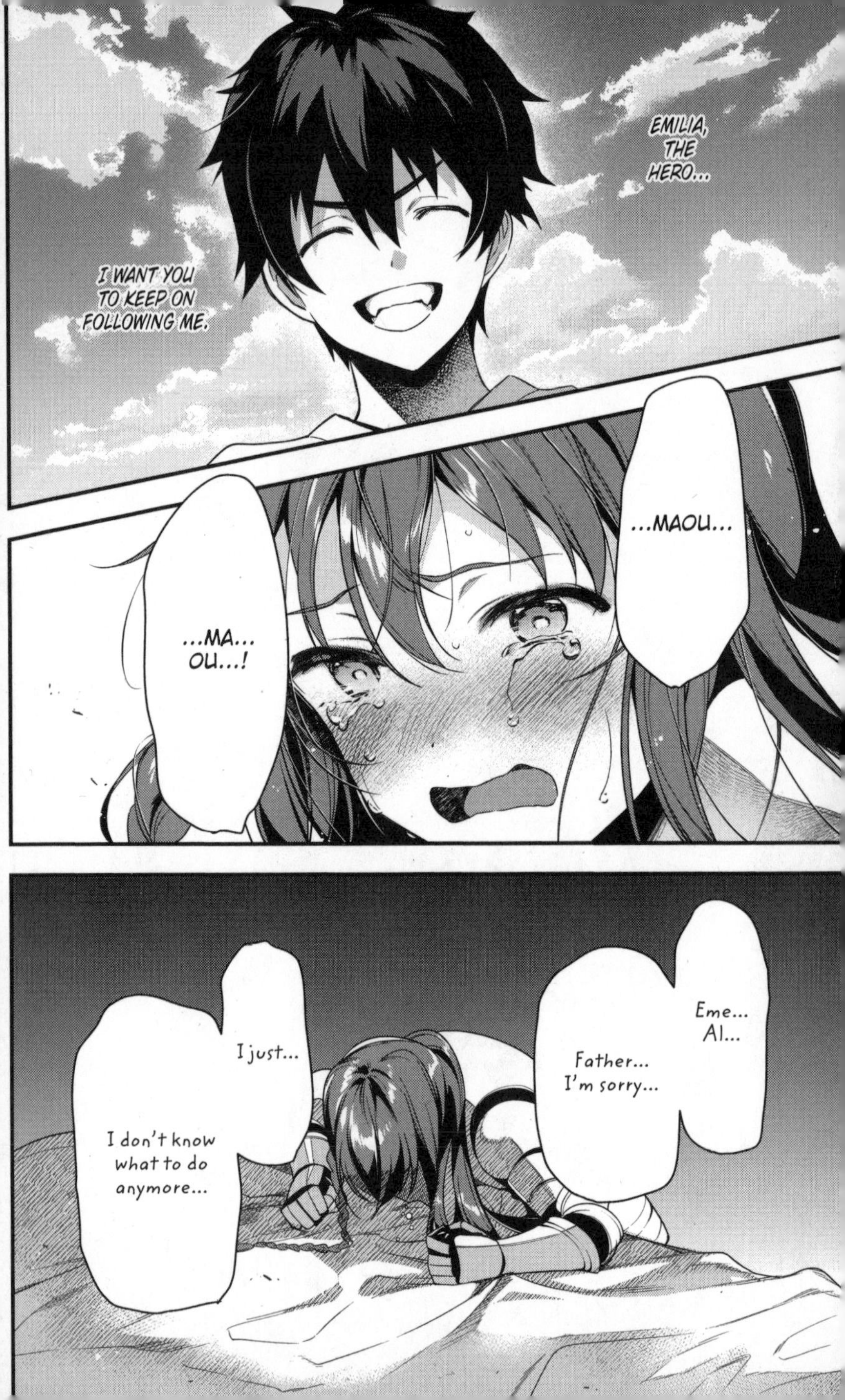
EMILIA, THE HERO...
I WANT YOU TO KEEP ON FOLLOWING ME.
...MAOU...
...MA... OU...!
Eme... Al...
Father... I'm sorry...
I just...
I don't know what to do anymore...

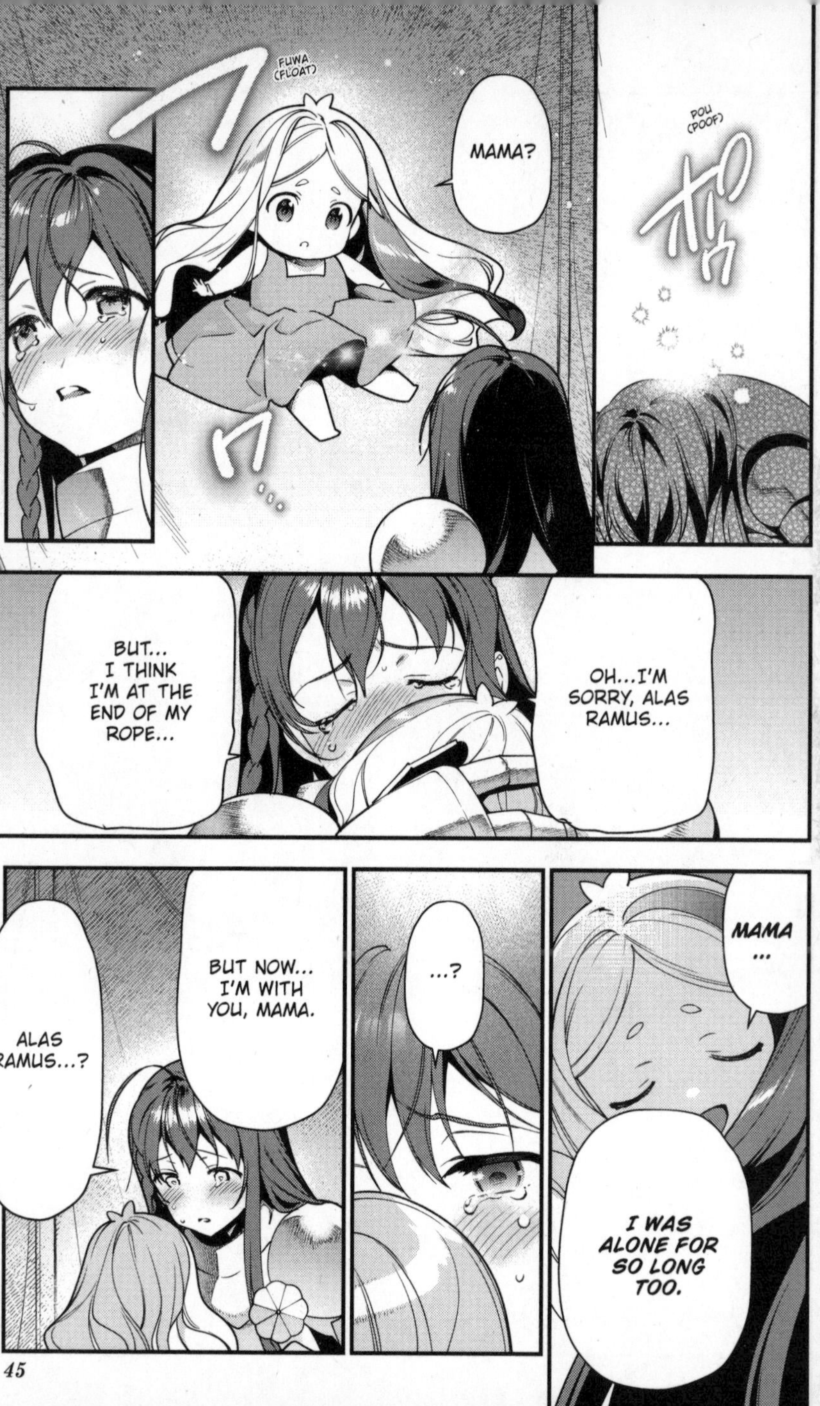
POU (POOF)
MAMA?
FUWA (FLOAT)
OH...I'M SORRY, ALAS RAMUS...
BUT... I THINK I'M AT THE END OF MY ROPE...
MAMA...
I WAS ALONE FOR SO LONG TOO.
...?
BUT NOW... I'M WITH YOU, MAMA.
ALAS RAMUS...?

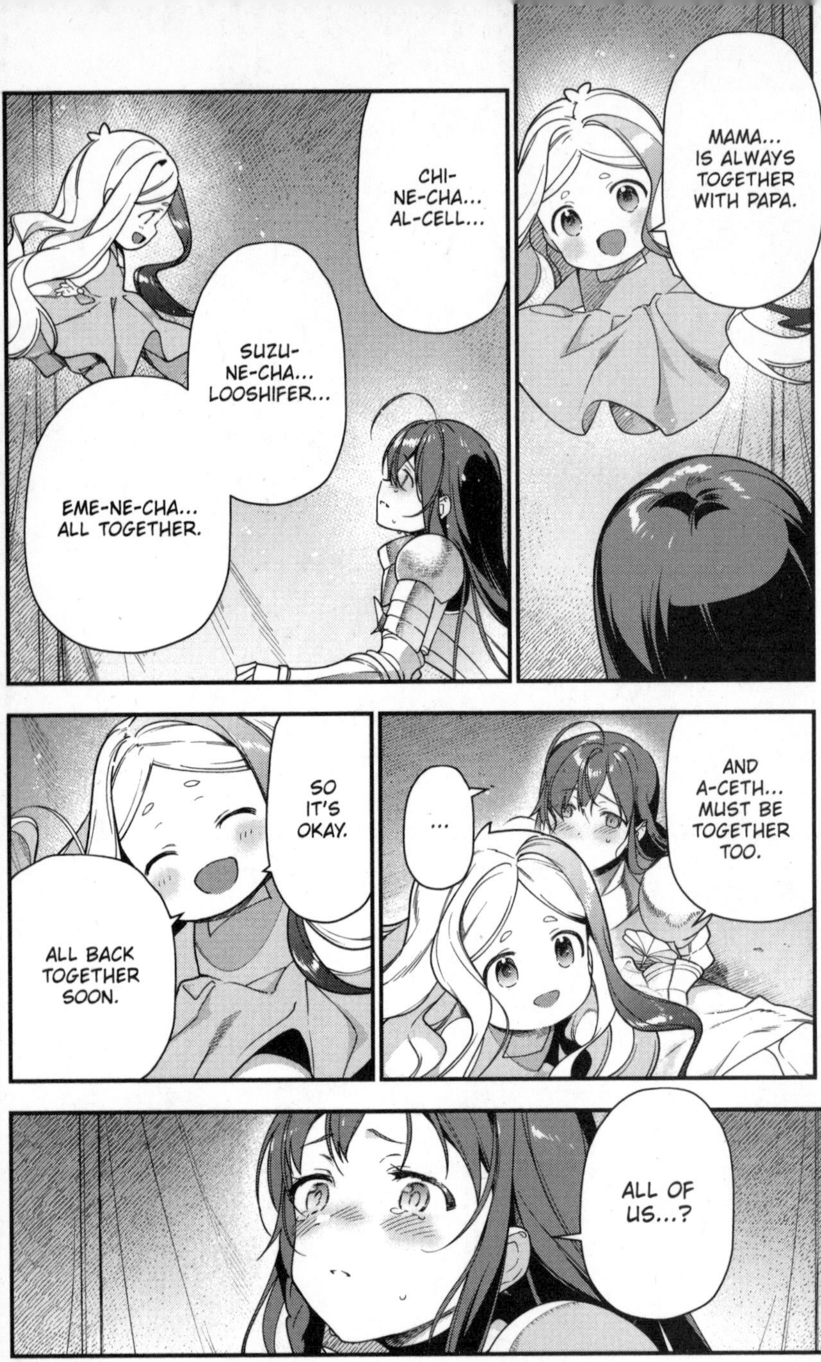
MAMA... IS ALWAYS TOGETHER WITH PAPA.
CHI-NE-CHA... AL-CELL...
SUZU-NE-CHA... LOOSHIFER...
EME-NE-CHA... ALL TOGETHER.
AND A-CETH... MUST BE TOGETHER TOO.
...
SO IT'S OKAY.
ALL BACK TOGETHER SOON.
ALL OF US...?

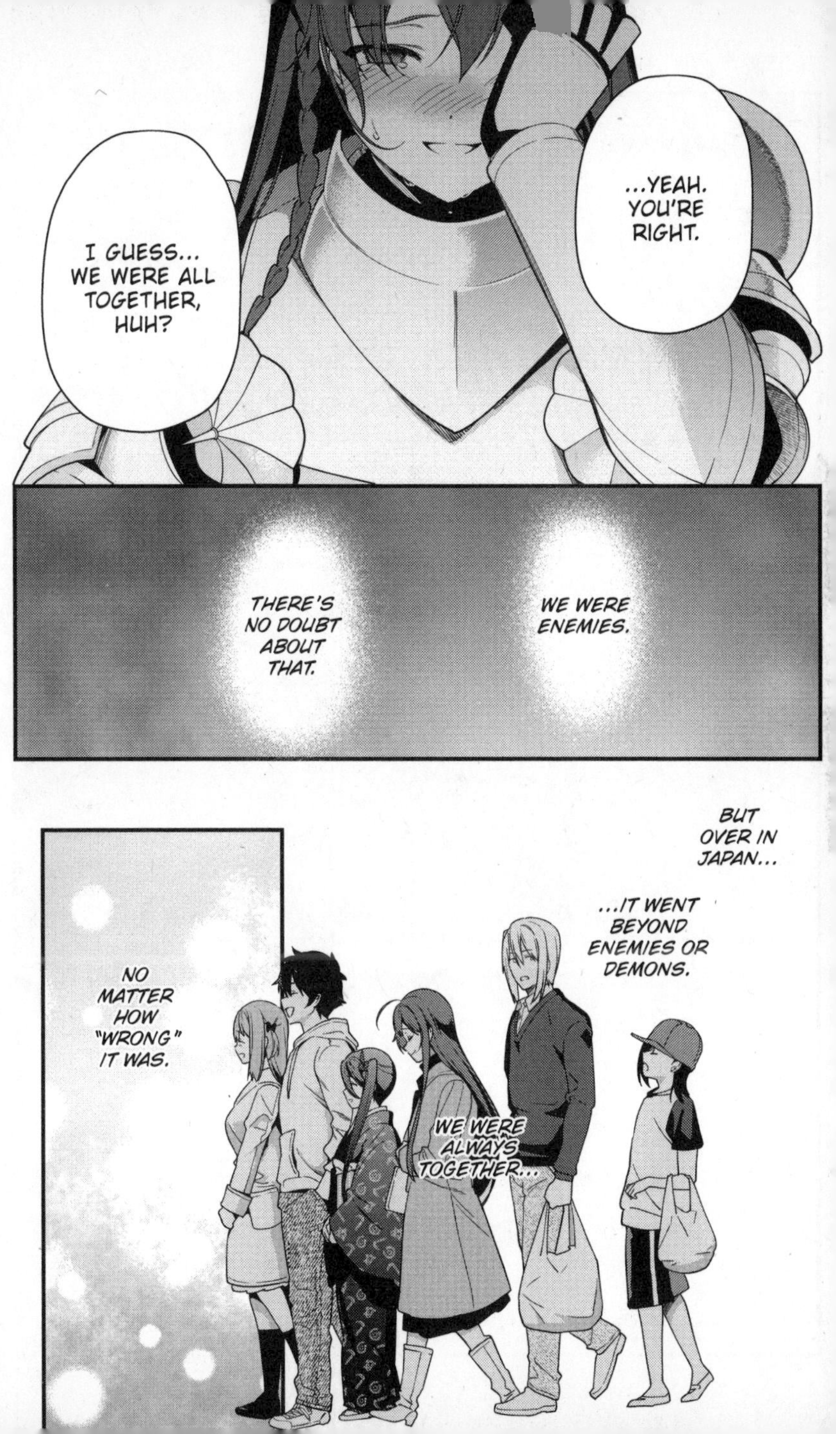
...YEAH. YOU'RE RIGHT.
I GUESS... WE WERE ALL TOGETHER, HUH?
WE WERE ENEMIES.
THERE'S NO DOUBT ABOUT THAT.
BUT OVER IN JAPAN...
...IT WENT BEYOND ENEMIES OR DEMONS.
NO MATTER HOW "WRONG" IT WAS.
WE WERE ALWAYS TOGETHER...

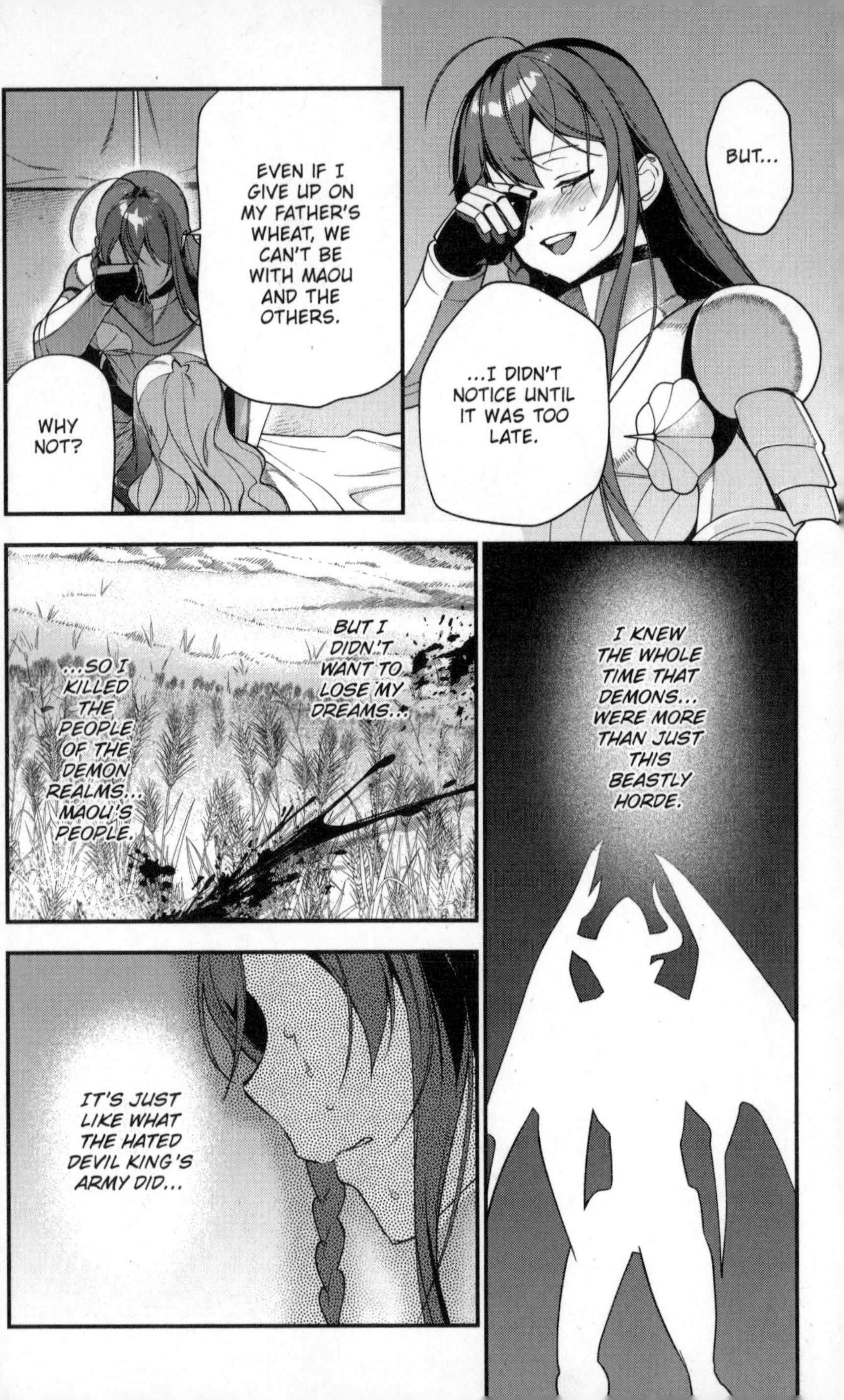
BUT...
...I DIDN'T NOTICE UNTIL IT WAS TOO LATE.
EVEN IF I GIVE UP ON MY FATHER'S WHEAT, WE CAN'T BE WITH MAOU AND THE OTHERS.
WHY NOT?
I KNEW THE WHOLE TIME THAT DEMONS... WERE MORE THAN JUST THIS BEASTLY HORDE.
BUT I DIDN'T WANT TO LOSE MY DREAMS...
...SO I KILLED THE PEOPLE OF THE DEMON REALMS... MAOU'S PEOPLE.
IT'S JUST LIKE WHAT THE HATED DEVIL KING'S ARMY DID...

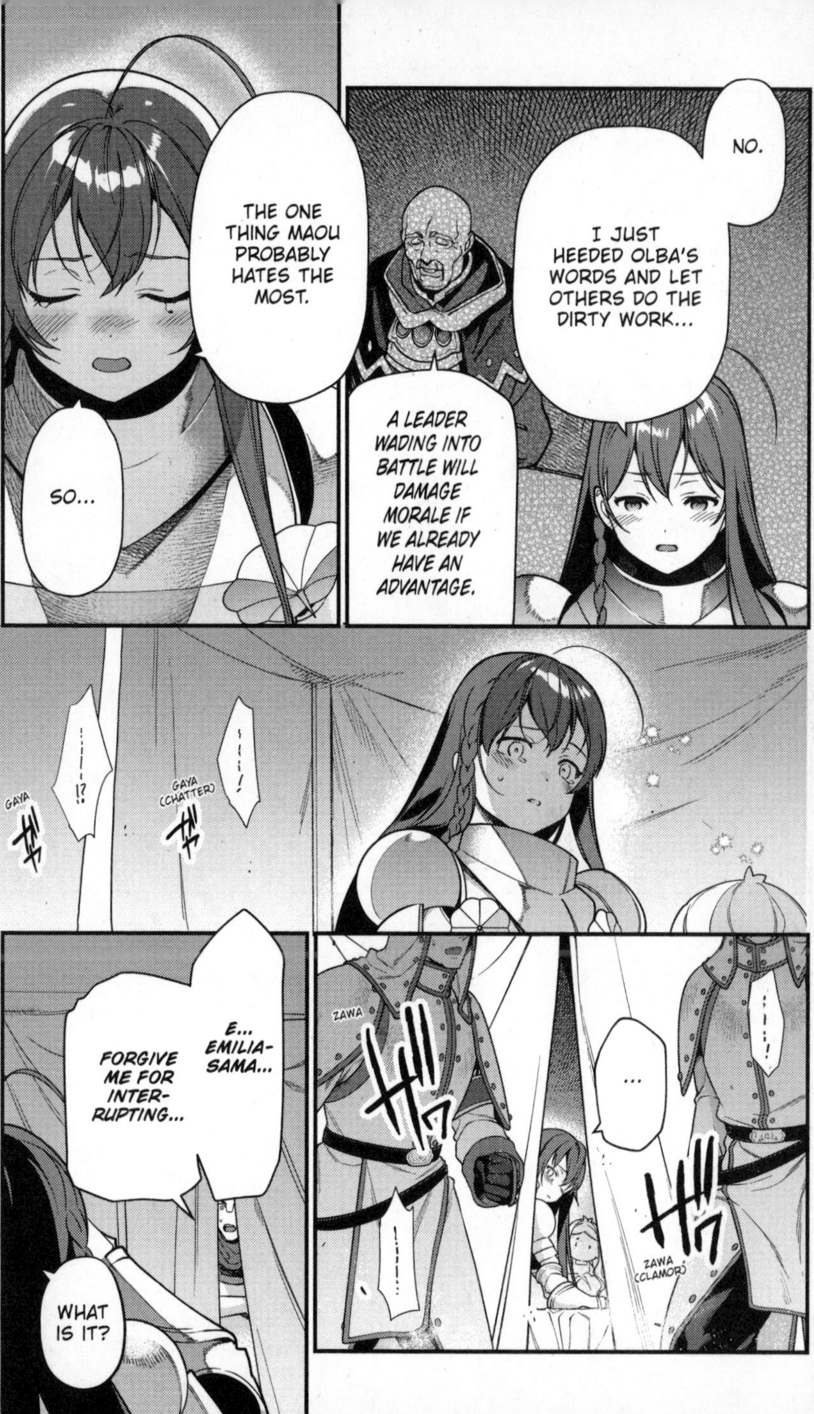
NO.
I JUST HEEDED OLBA'S WORDS AND LET OTHERS DO THE DIRTY WORK...
A LEADER WADING INTO BATTLE WILL DAMAGE MORALE IF WE ALREADY HAVE AN ADVANTAGE.
THE ONE THING MAOU PROBABLY HATES THE MOST.
SO...
......!
......!?
GAYA (CHATTER)
GAYA
......!
...
......
ZAWA
ZAWA (CLAMOR)
E... EMILIA-SAMA...
FORGIVE ME FOR INTER-RUPTING...
WHAT IS IT?

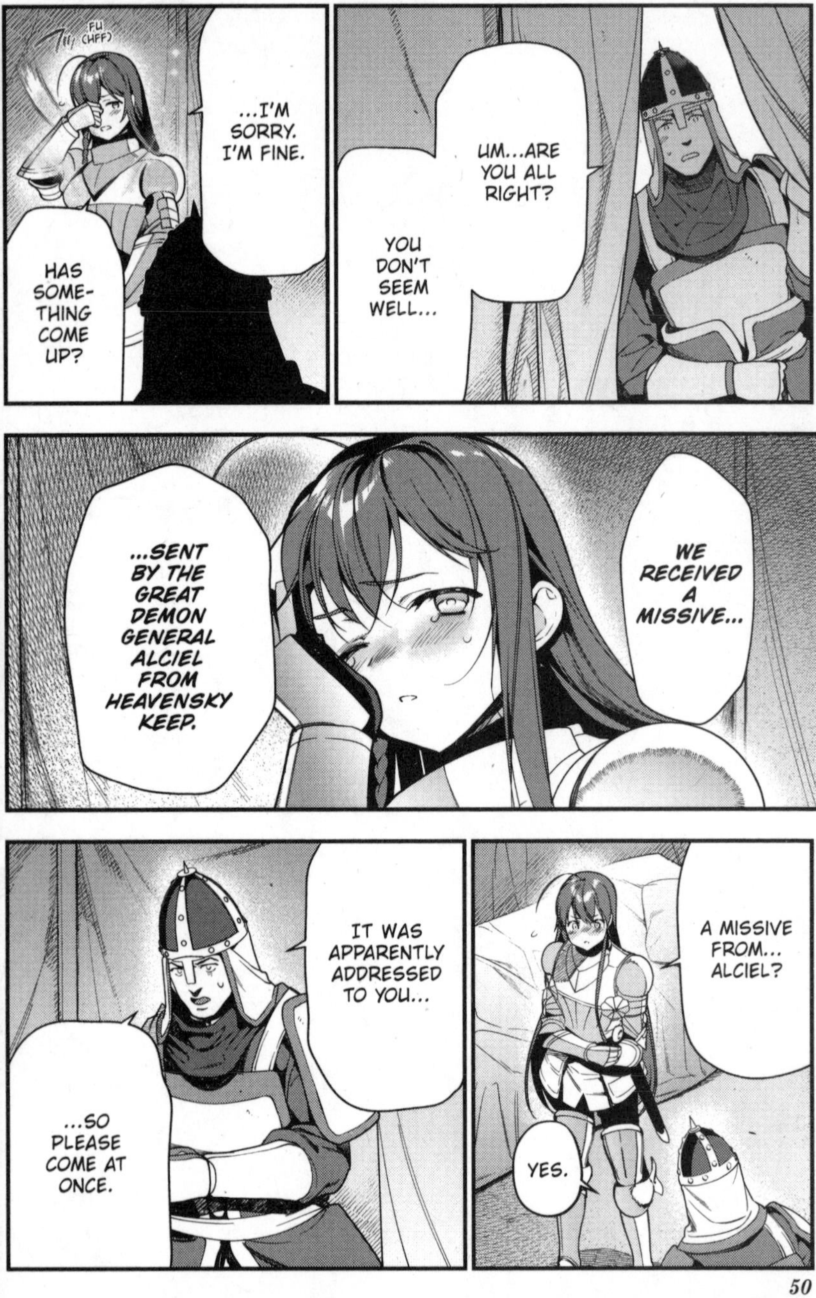
UM...ARE YOU ALL RIGHT?
YOU DON'T SEEM WELL...
FU (HFF)
...I'M SORRY. I'M FINE.
HAS SOME-THING COME UP?
WE RECEIVED A MISSIVE...
...SENT BY THE GREAT DEMON GENERAL ALCIEL FROM HEAVENSKY KEEP.
A MISSIVE FROM... ALCIEL?
YES.
IT WAS APPARENTLY ADDRESSED TO YOU...
...SO PLEASE COME AT ONCE.

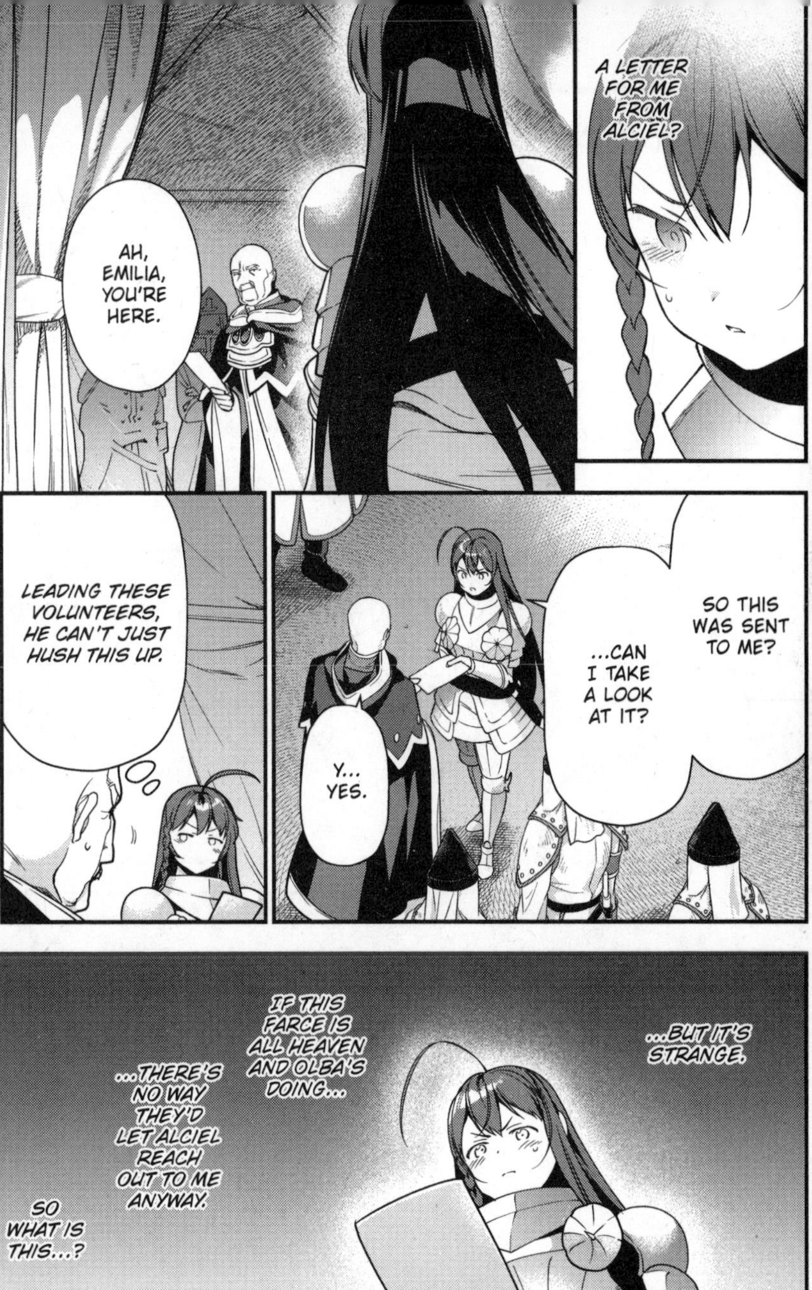
A LETTER FOR ME FROM ALCIEL?
AH, EMILIA, YOU'RE HERE.
SO THIS WAS SENT TO ME?
...CAN I TAKE A LOOK AT IT?
Y... YES.
LEADING THESE VOLUNTEERS, HE CAN'T JUST HUSH THIS UP.
...BUT IT'S STRANGE.
IF THIS FARCE IS ALL HEAVEN AND OLBA'S DOING...
...THERE'S NO WAY THEY'D LET ALCIEL REACH OUT TO ME ANYWAY.
SO WHAT IS THIS...?

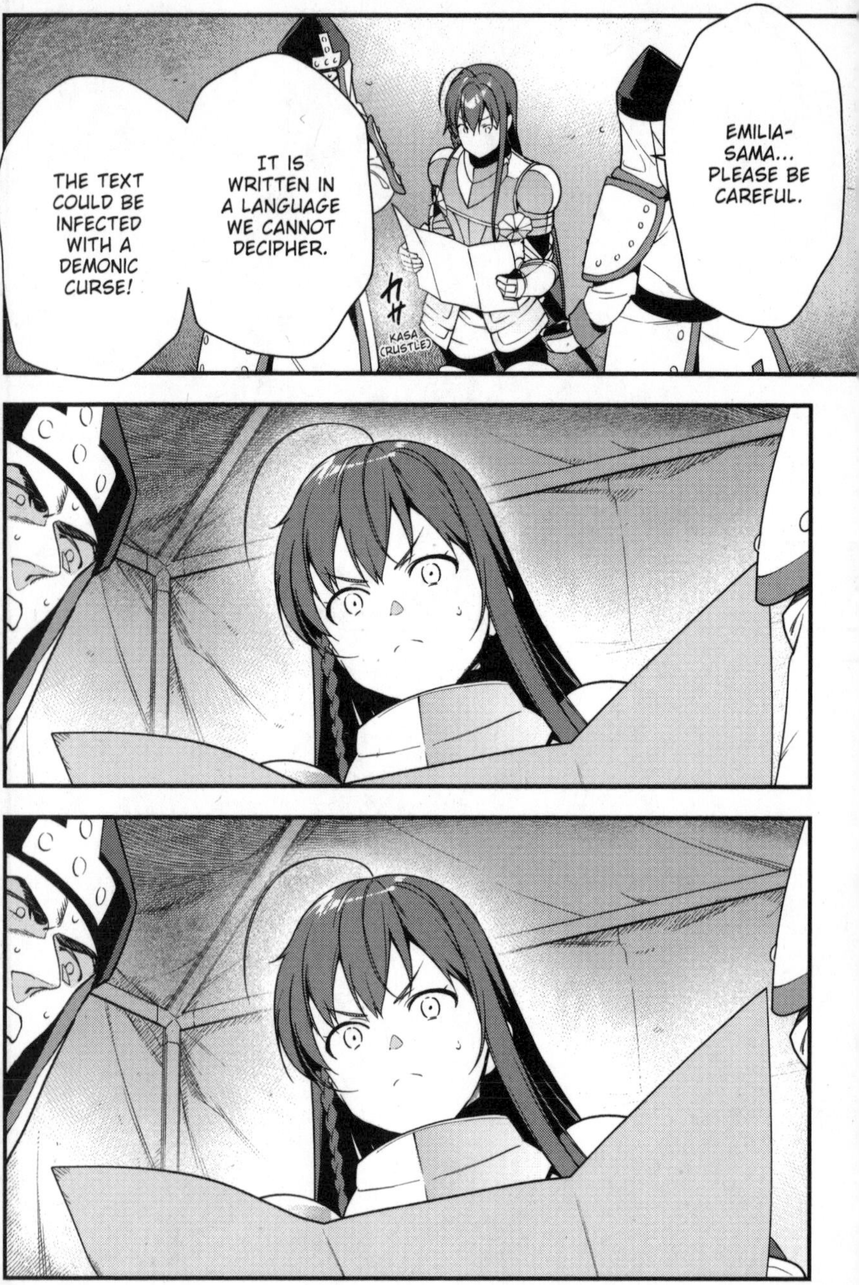
EMILIA-SAMA... PLEASE BE CAREFUL.
IT IS WRITTEN IN A LANGUAGE WE CANNOT DECIPHER.
カサ
KASA (RUSTLE)
THE TEXT COULD BE INFECTED WITH A DEMONIC CURSE!

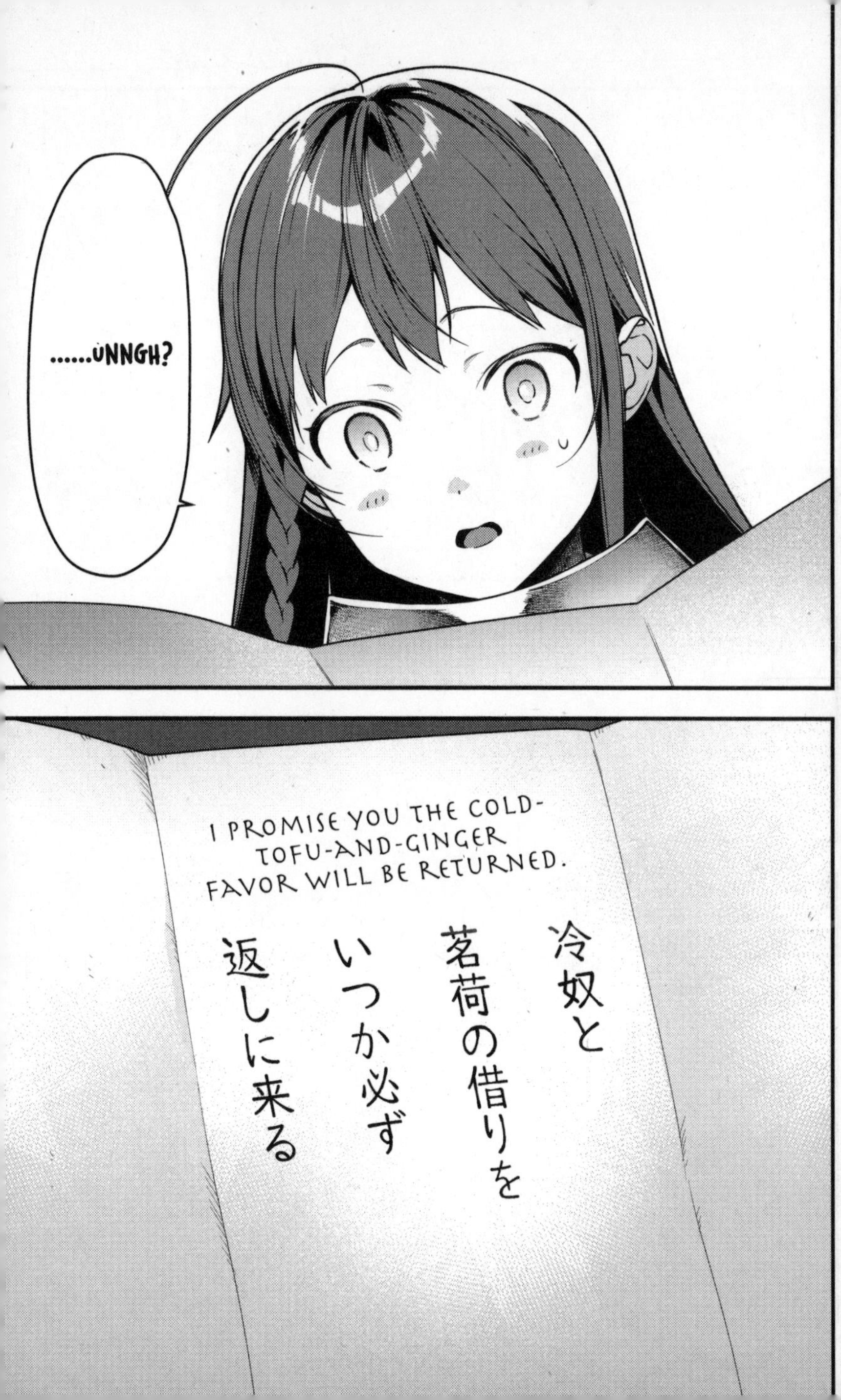
......UNNGH?
I PROMISE YOU THE COLD-TOFU-AND-GINGER FAVOR WILL BE RETURNED.
冷奴と茗荷の借りをいつか必ず返しに来る

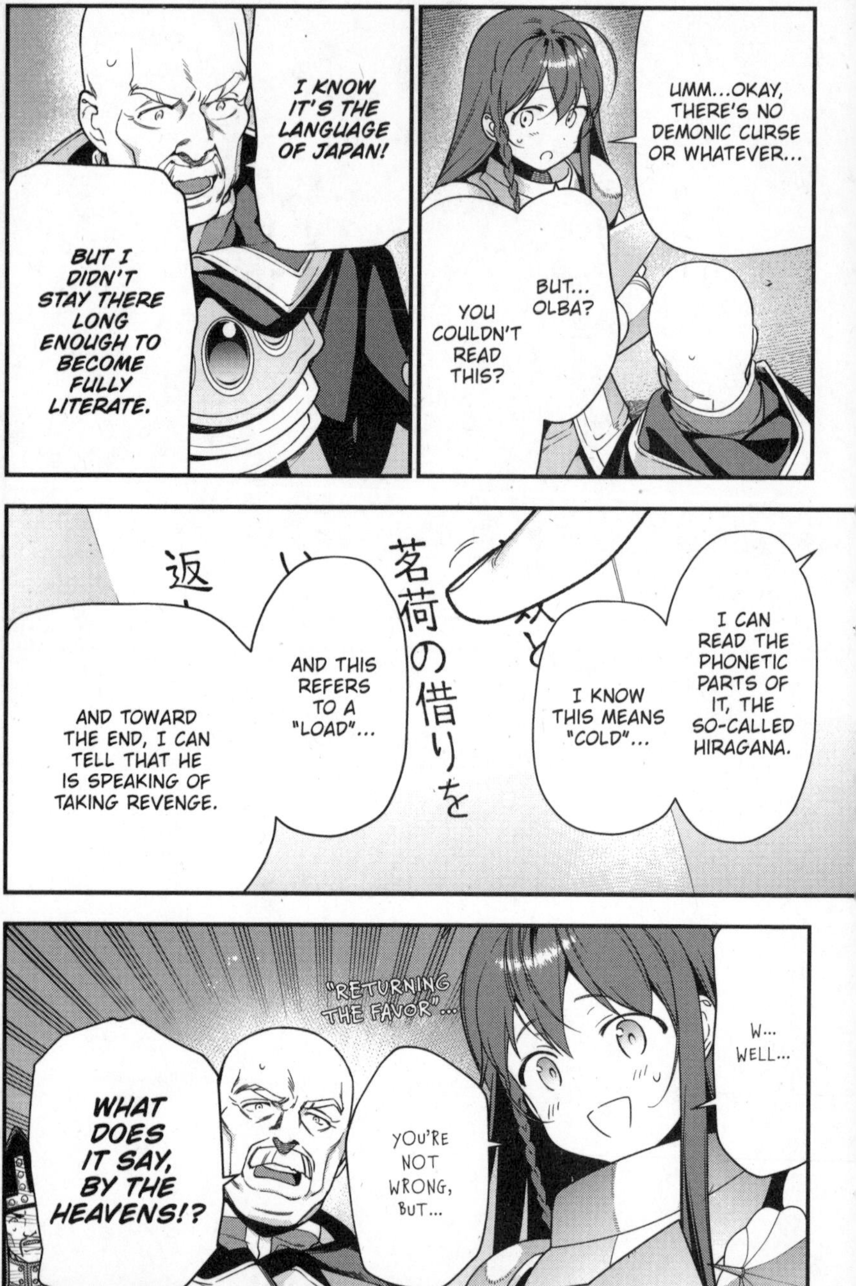
UMM...OKAY, THERE'S NO DEMONIC CURSE OR WHATEVER...
BUT... OLBA?
YOU COULDN'T READ THIS?
I KNOW IT'S THE LANGUAGE OF JAPAN!
BUT I DIDN'T STAY THERE LONG ENOUGH TO BECOME FULLY LITERATE.
I CAN READ THE PHONETIC PARTS OF IT, THE SO-CALLED HIRAGANA.
I KNOW THIS MEANS "COLD"...
茗荷の借りを
AND THIS REFERS TO A "LOAD"...
返
AND TOWARD THE END, I CAN TELL THAT HE IS SPEAKING OF TAKING REVENGE.
W... WELL...
YOU'RE NOT WRONG, BUT...
"RETURNING THE FAVOR"...
WHAT DOES IT SAY, BY THE HEAVENS!?

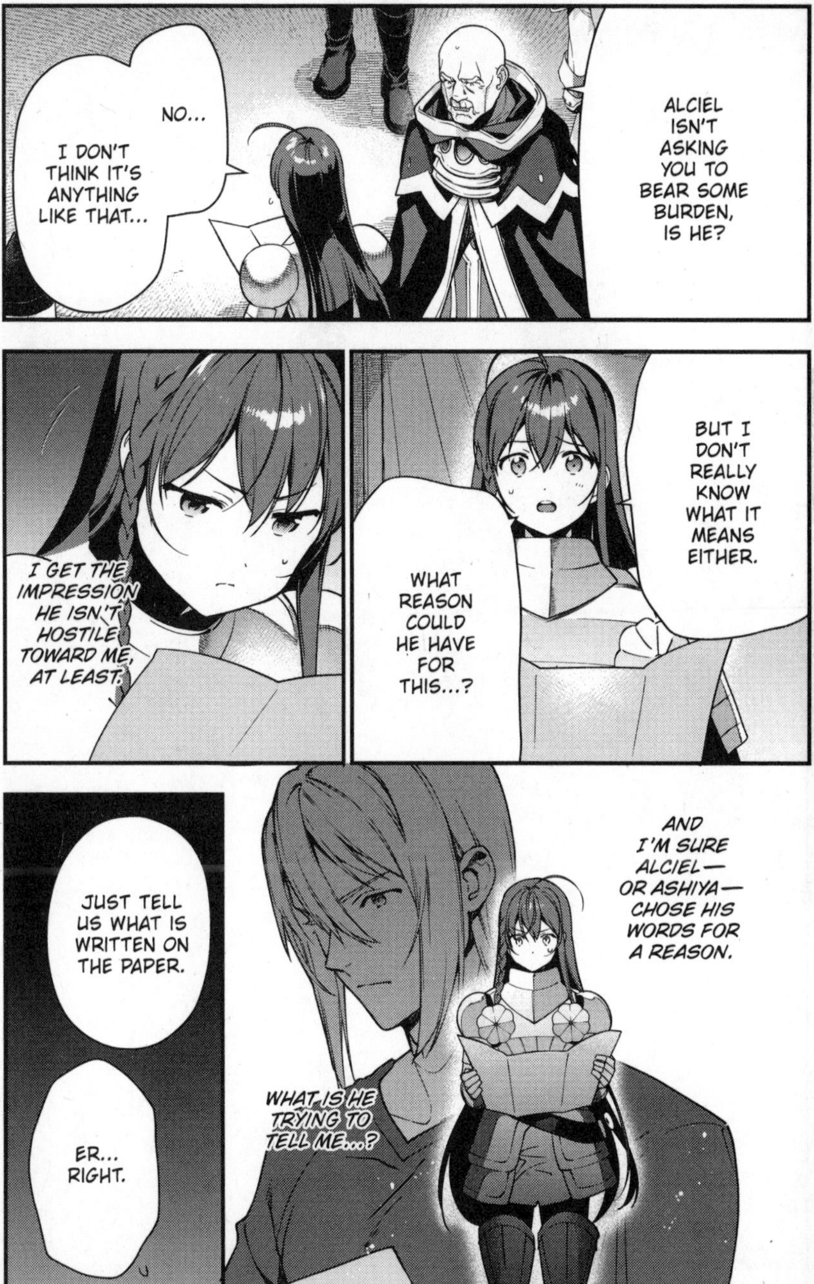
ALCIEL ISN'T ASKING YOU TO BEAR SOME BURDEN, IS HE?
NO...
I DON'T THINK IT'S ANYTHING LIKE THAT...
BUT I DON'T REALLY KNOW WHAT IT MEANS EITHER.
WHAT REASON COULD HE HAVE FOR THIS...?
I GET THE IMPRESSION HE ISN'T HOSTILE TOWARD ME, AT LEAST.
AND I'M SURE ALCIEL— OR ASHIYA— CHOSE HIS WORDS FOR A REASON.
WHAT IS HE TRYING TO TELL ME...?
JUST TELL US WHAT IS WRITTEN ON THE PAPER.
ER... RIGHT.

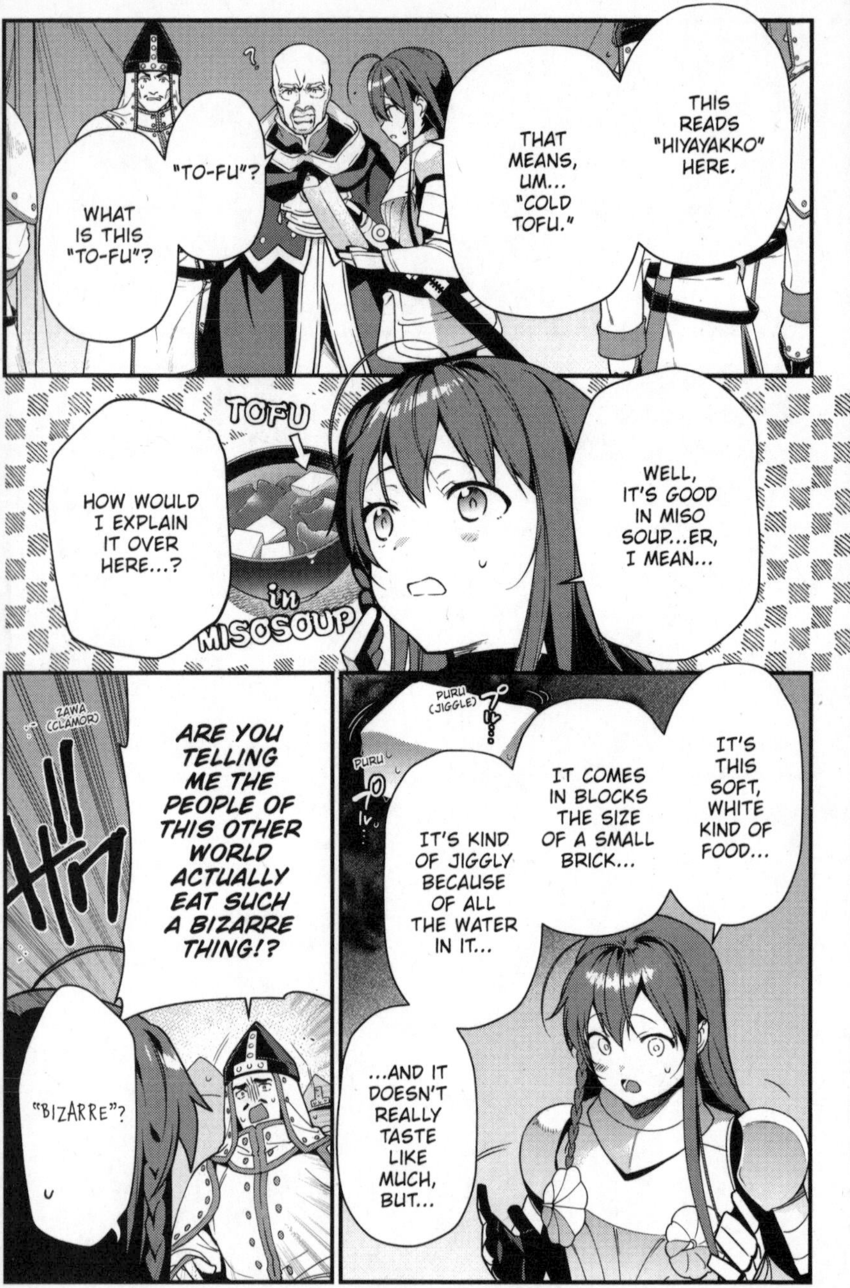
THIS READS "HIYAYAKKO" HERE.
THAT MEANS, UM... "COLD TOFU."
"TO-FU"?
WHAT IS THIS "TO-FU"?
WELL, IT'S GOOD IN MISO SOUP...ER, I MEAN...
TOFU
in MISOSOUP
HOW WOULD I EXPLAIN IT OVER HERE...?
PURU (JIGGLE)
PURU
IT'S THIS SOFT, WHITE KIND OF FOOD...
IT COMES IN BLOCKS THE SIZE OF A SMALL BRICK...
IT'S KIND OF JIGGLY BECAUSE OF ALL THE WATER IN IT...
...AND IT DOESN'T REALLY TASTE LIKE MUCH, BUT...
ZAWA (CLAMOR)
ARE YOU TELLING ME THE PEOPLE OF THIS OTHER WORLD ACTUALLY EAT SUCH A BIZARRE THING!?
"BIZARRE"?

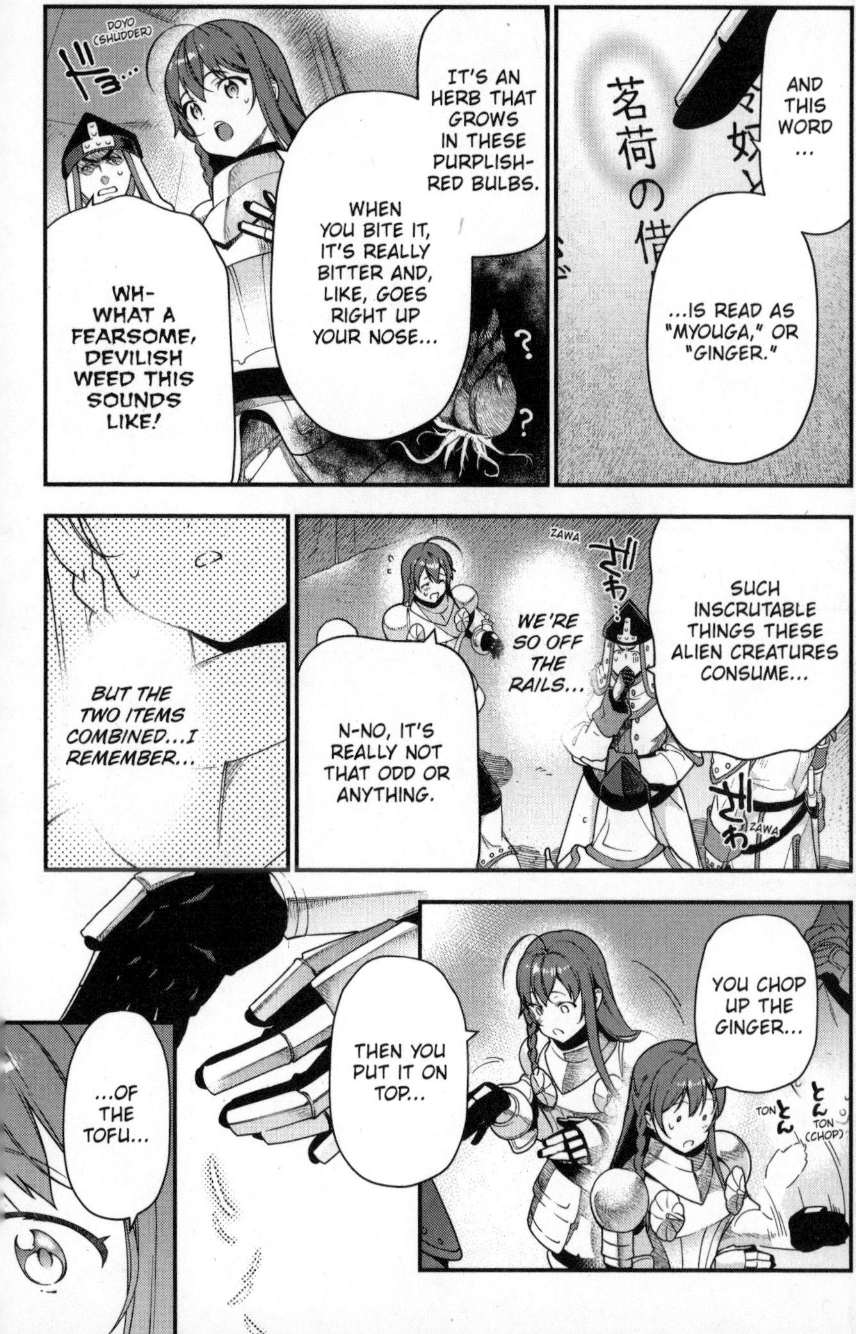
AND THIS WORD...
茗荷の
...IS READ AS "MYOUGA," OR "GINGER."
IT'S AN HERB THAT GROWS IN THESE PURPLISH-RED BULBS.
WHEN YOU BITE IT, IT'S REALLY BITTER AND, LIKE, GOES RIGHT UP YOUR NOSE...
DOYO (SHUDDER)
WH-WHAT A FEARSOME, DEVILISH WEED THIS SOUNDS LIKE!
SUCH INSCRUTABLE THINGS THESE ALIEN CREATURES CONSUME...
ZAWA
WE'RE SO OFF THE RAILS...
N-NO, IT'S REALLY NOT THAT ODD OR ANYTHING.
ZAWA
BUT THE TWO ITEMS COMBINED...I REMEMBER...
YOU CHOP UP THE GINGER...
TON TON (CHOP)
THEN YOU PUT IT ON TOP...
...OF THE TOFU...

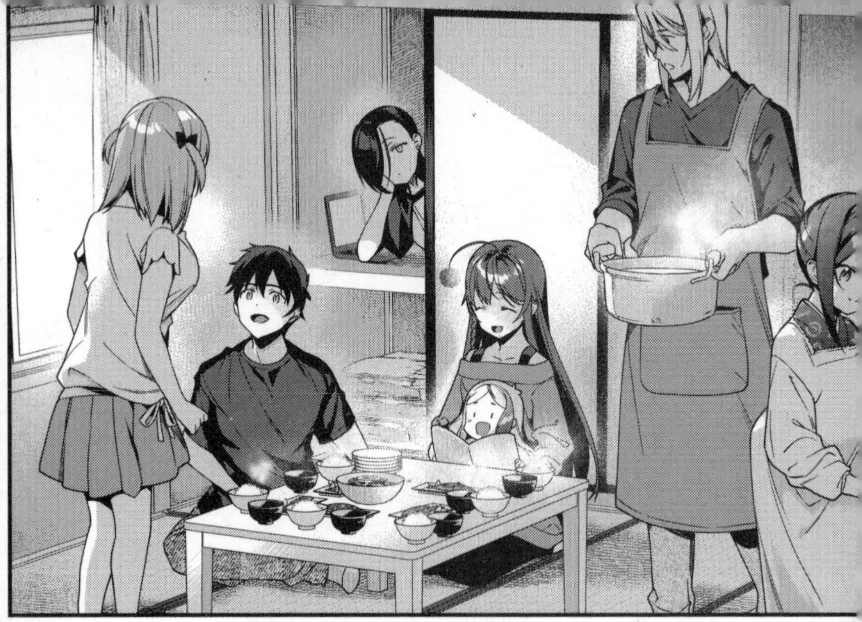
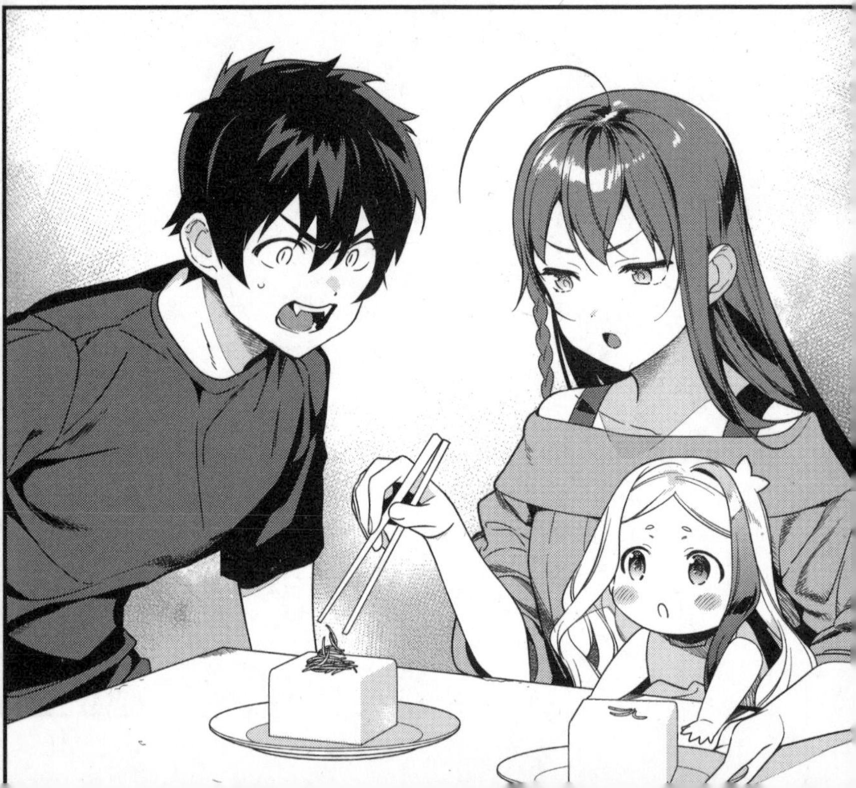

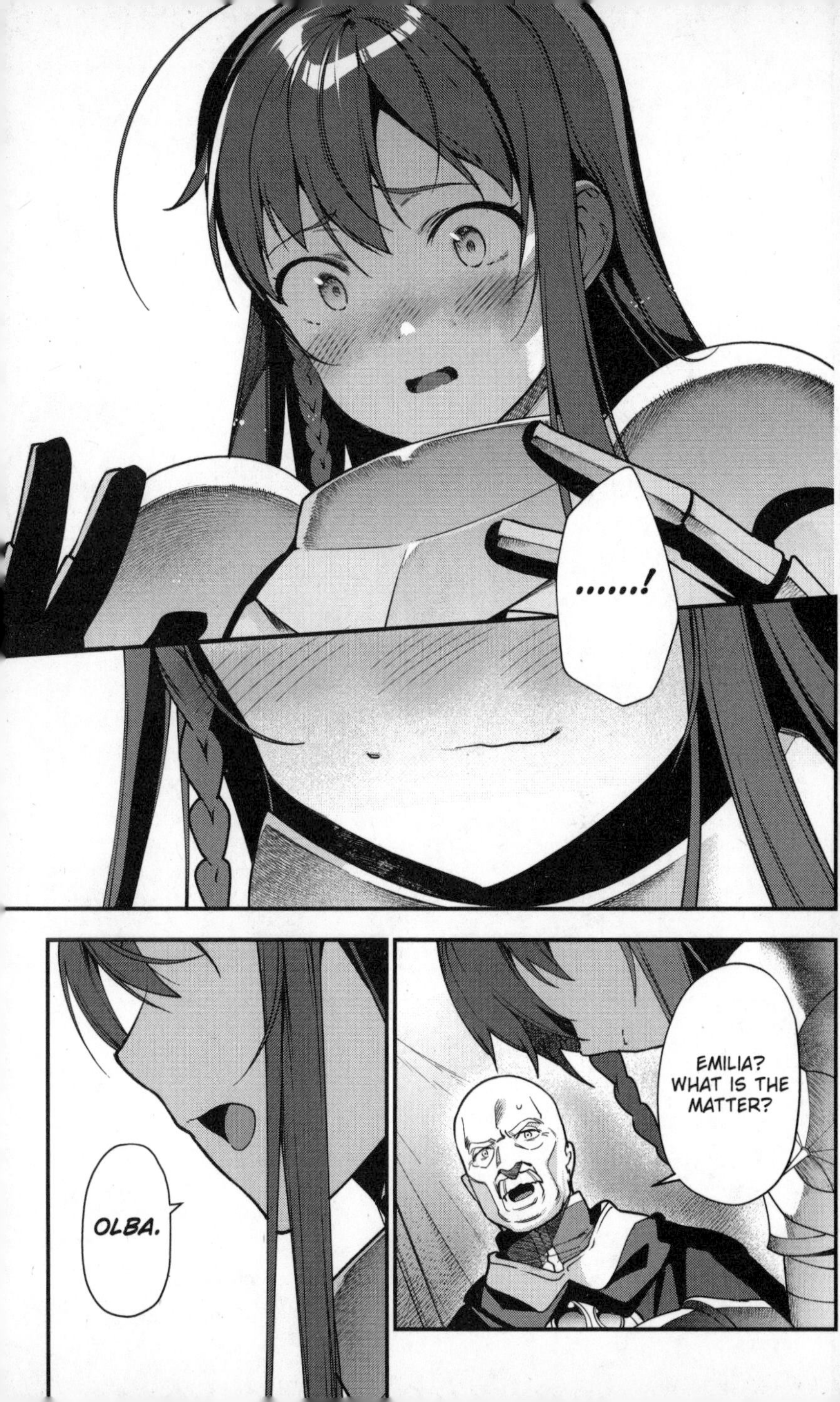
......!
EMILIA? WHAT IS THE MATTER?
OLBA.

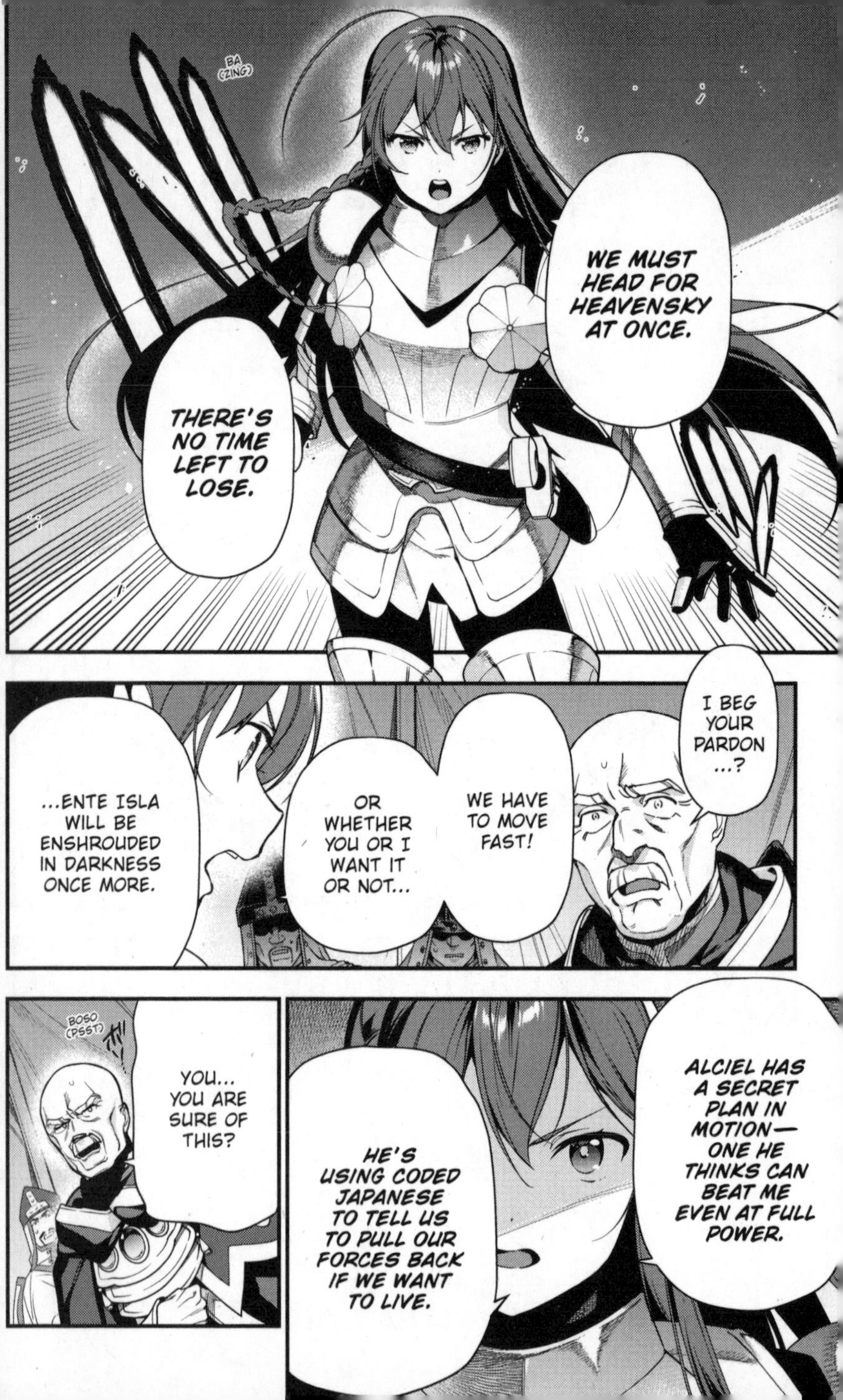
WE MUST HEAD FOR HEAVENSKY AT ONCE.
BA (ZING)
THERE'S NO TIME LEFT TO LOSE.
I BEG YOUR PARDON ...?
WE HAVE TO MOVE FAST!
OR WHETHER YOU OR I WANT IT OR NOT...
...ENTE ISLA WILL BE ENSHROUDED IN DARKNESS ONCE MORE.
ALCIEL HAS A SECRET PLAN IN MOTION— ONE HE THINKS CAN BEAT ME EVEN AT FULL POWER.
HE'S USING CODED JAPANESE TO TELL US TO PULL OUR FORCES BACK IF WE WANT TO LIVE.
BOSO (PSST)
YOU... YOU ARE SURE OF THIS?

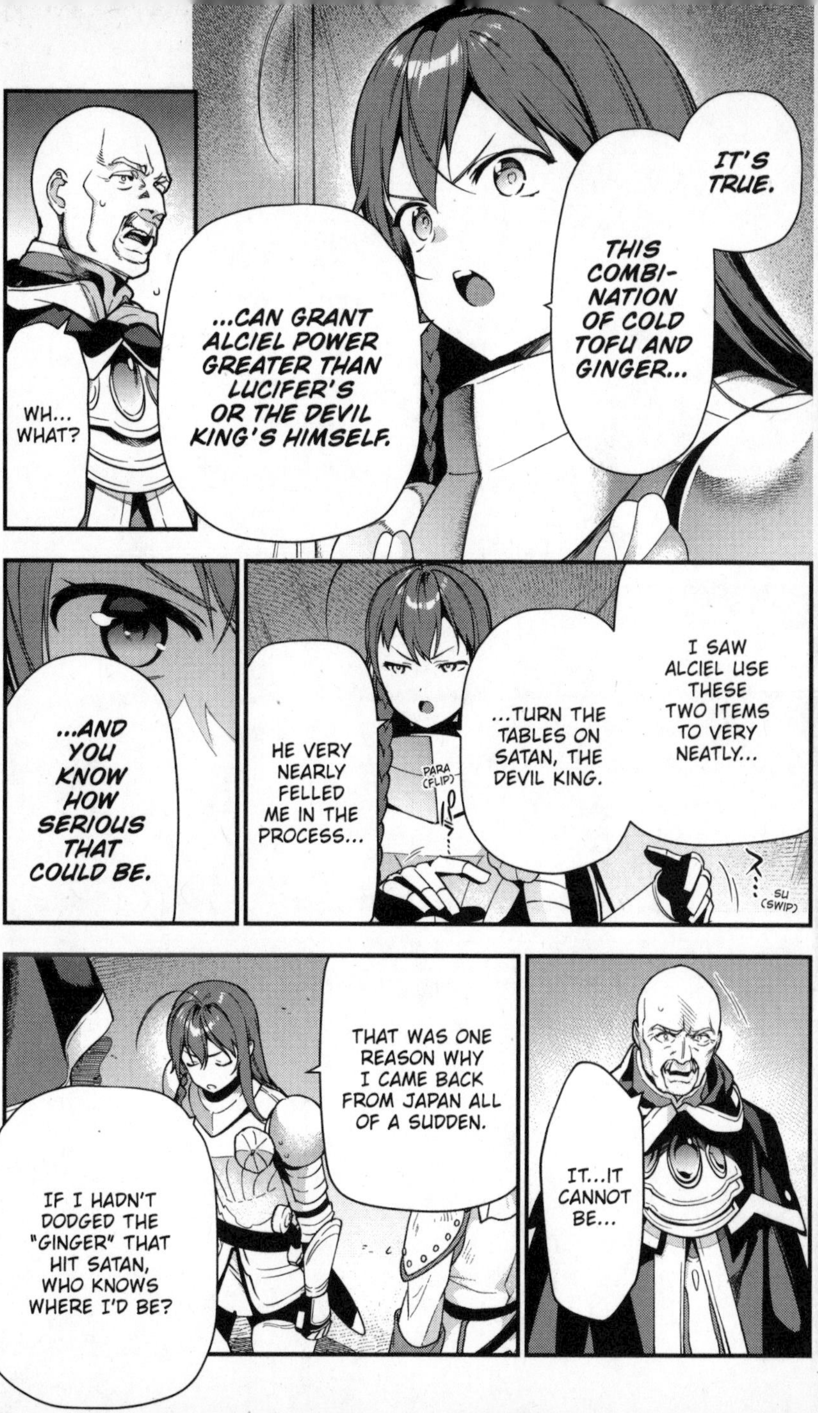
IT'S TRUE.
THIS COMBINATION OF COLD TOFU AND GINGER...
...CAN GRANT ALCIEL POWER GREATER THAN LUCIFER'S OR THE DEVIL KING'S HIMSELF.
WH... WHAT?
I SAW ALCIEL USE THESE TWO ITEMS TO VERY NEATLY...
...TURN THE TABLES ON SATAN, THE DEVIL KING.
SU (SWIP)
PARA (FLIP)
HE VERY NEARLY FELLED ME IN THE PROCESS...
...AND YOU KNOW HOW SERIOUS THAT COULD BE.
IT...IT CANNOT BE...
THAT WAS ONE REASON WHY I CAME BACK FROM JAPAN ALL OF A SUDDEN.
IF I HADN'T DODGED THE "GINGER" THAT HIT SATAN, WHO KNOWS WHERE I'D BE?

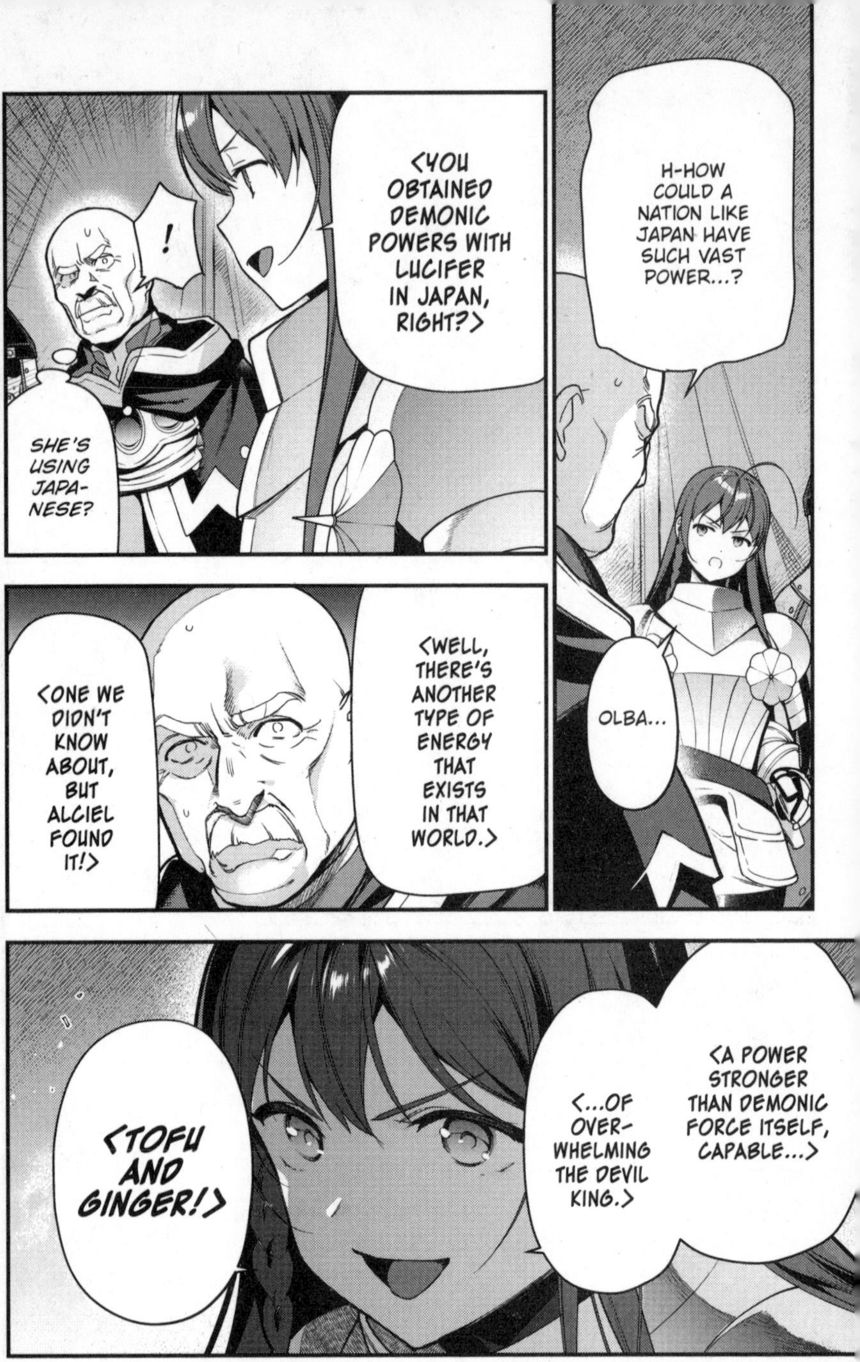
H-HOW COULD A NATION LIKE JAPAN HAVE SUCH VAST POWER...?
OLBA...
<YOU OBTAINED DEMONIC POWERS WITH LUCIFER IN JAPAN, RIGHT?>
!
SHE'S USING JAPA-NESE?
<WELL, THERE'S ANOTHER TYPE OF ENERGY THAT EXISTS IN THAT WORLD.>
<ONE WE DIDN'T KNOW ABOUT, BUT ALCIEL FOUND IT!>
<A POWER STRONGER THAN DEMONIC FORCE ITSELF, CAPABLE...>
<...OF OVER-WHELMING THE DEVIL KING.>
<TOFU AND GINGER!>

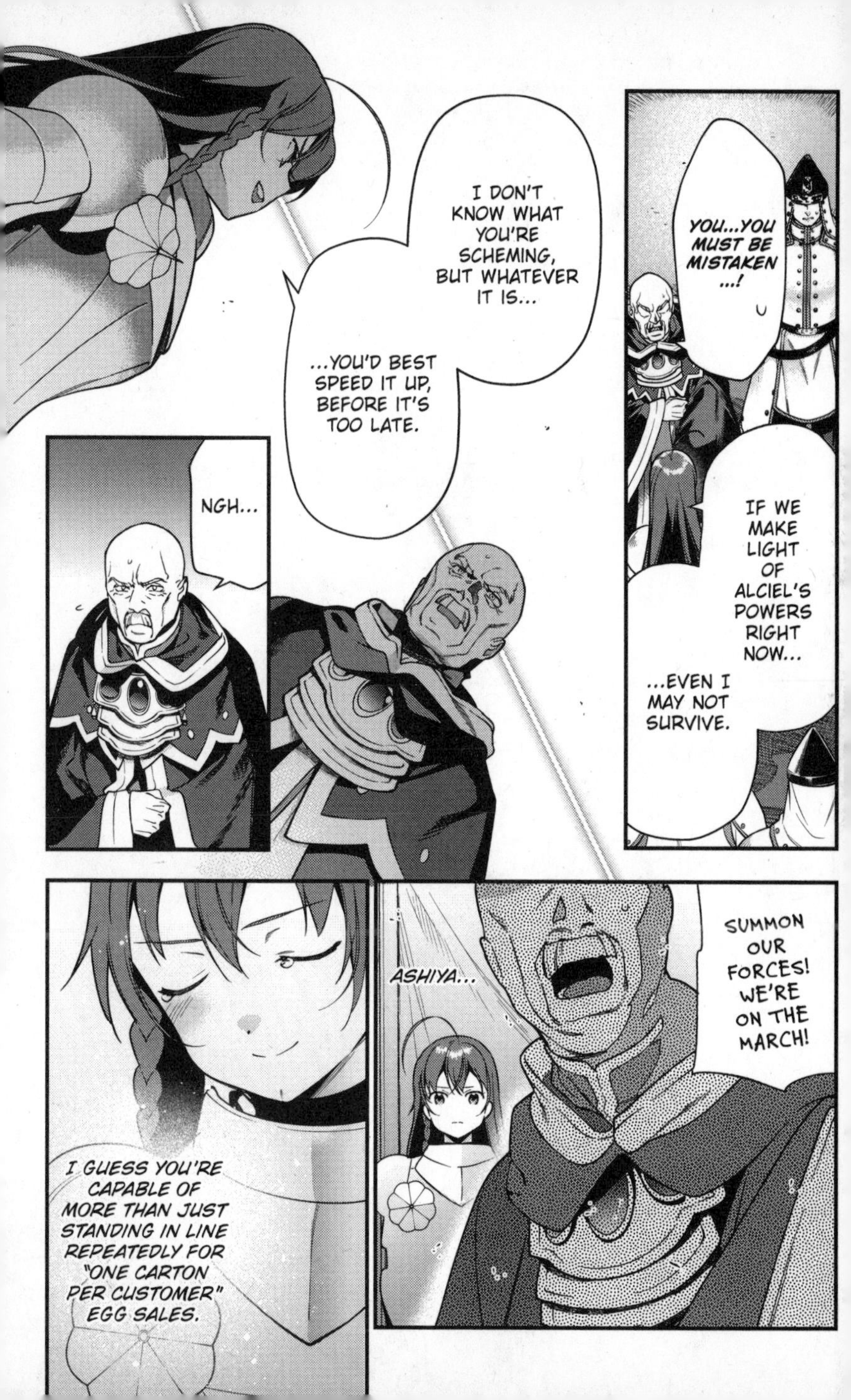
YOU...YOU MUST BE MISTAKEN ...!
IF WE MAKE LIGHT OF ALCIEL'S POWERS RIGHT NOW...
...EVEN I MAY NOT SURVIVE.
I DON'T KNOW WHAT YOU'RE SCHEMING, BUT WHATEVER IT IS...
...YOU'D BEST SPEED IT UP, BEFORE IT'S TOO LATE.
NGH...
SUMMON OUR FORCES! WE'RE ON THE MARCH!
ASHIYA...
I GUESS YOU'RE CAPABLE OF MORE THAN JUST STANDING IN LINE REPEATEDLY FOR "ONE CARTON PER CUSTOMER" EGG SALES.

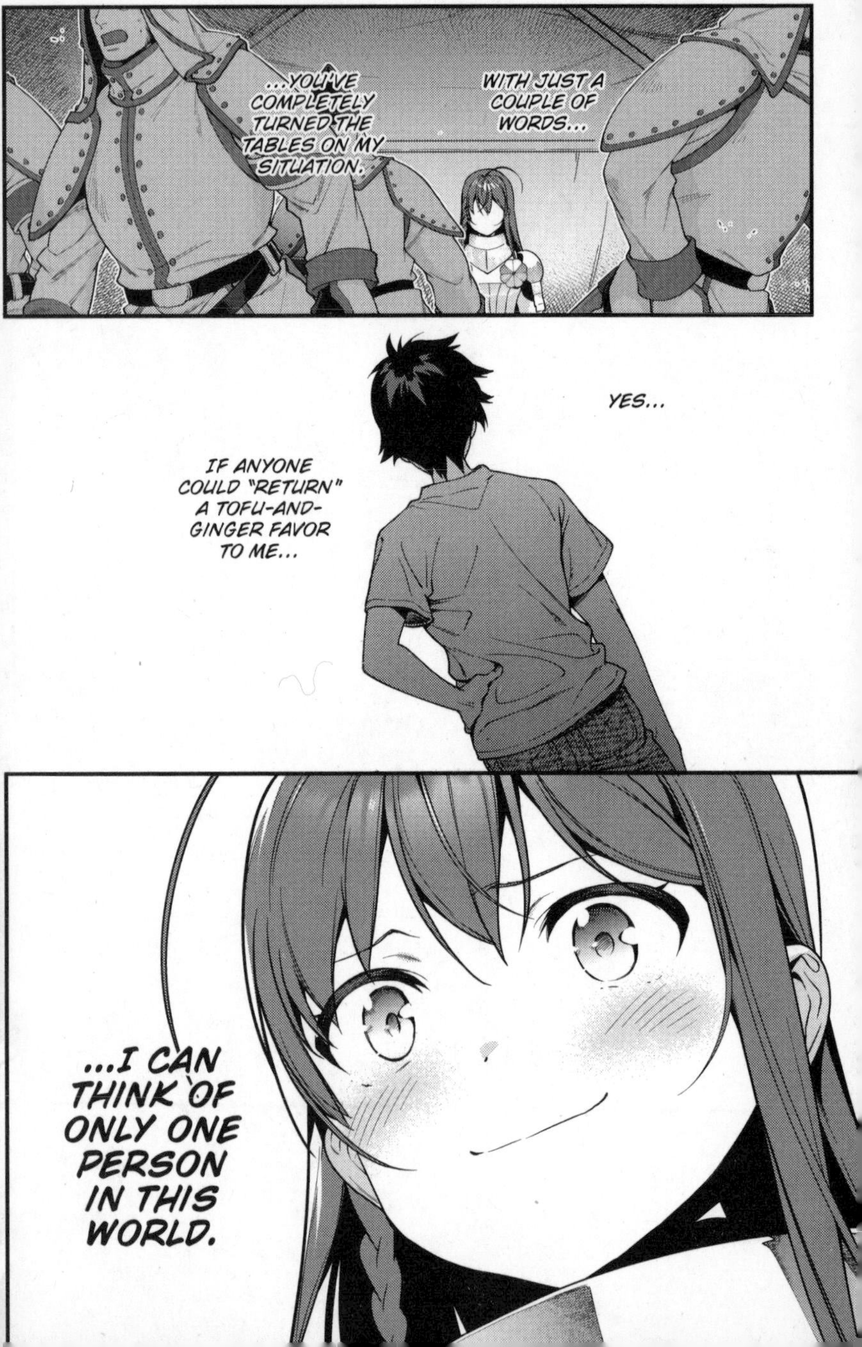
WITH JUST A COUPLE OF WORDS...
...YOU'VE COMPLETELY TURNED THE TABLES ON MY SITUATION.
YES...
IF ANYONE COULD "RETURN" A TOFU-AND-GINGER FAVOR TO ME...
...I CAN THINK OF ONLY ONE PERSON IN THIS WORLD.

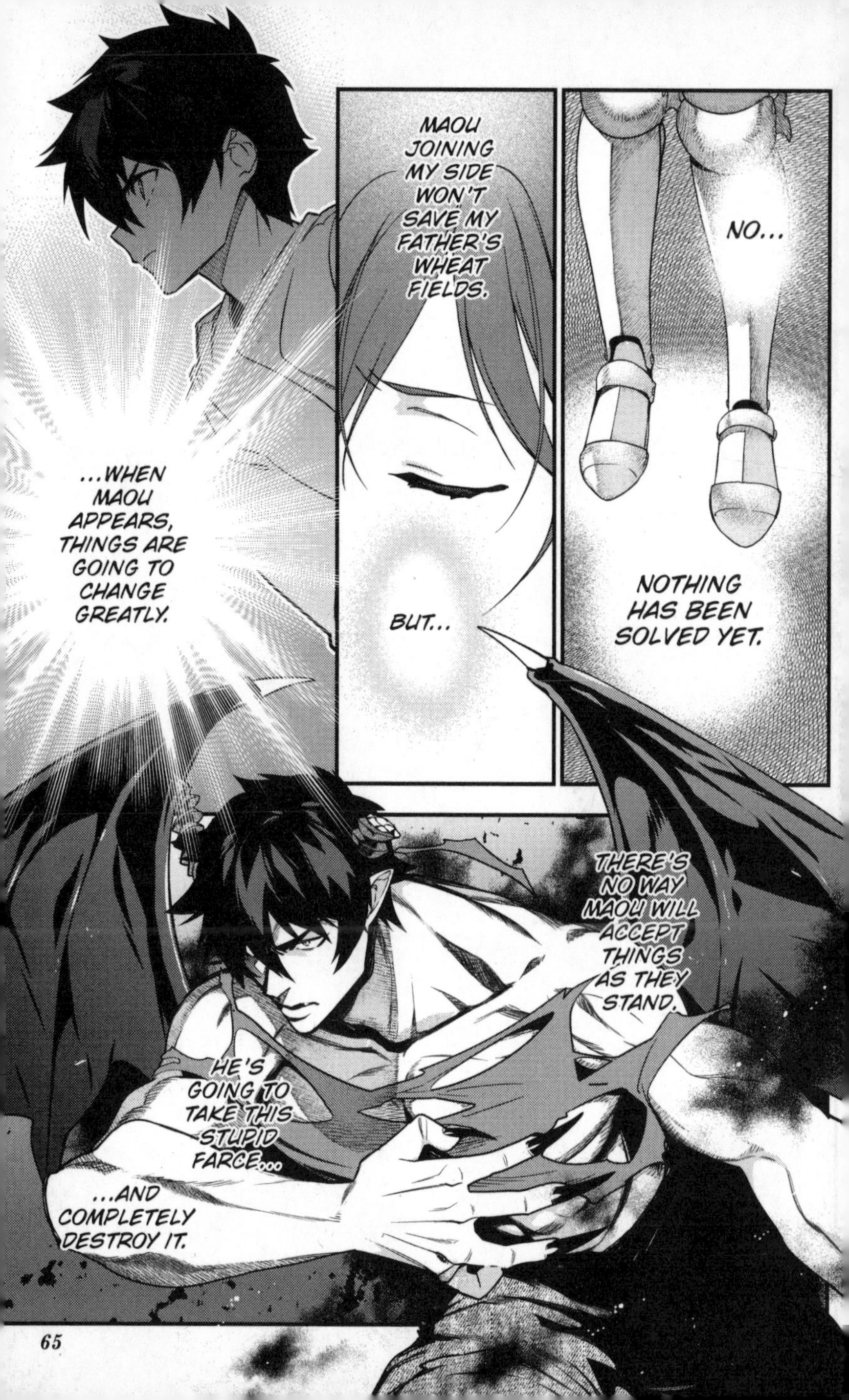
NO...
NOTHING HAS BEEN SOLVED YET.
MAOU JOINING MY SIDE WON'T SAVE MY FATHER'S WHEAT FIELDS.
BUT...
...WHEN MAOU APPEARS, THINGS ARE GOING TO CHANGE GREATLY.
THERE'S NO WAY MAOU WILL ACCEPT THINGS AS THEY STAND.
HE'S GOING TO TAKE THIS STUPID FARCE...
...AND COMPLETELY DESTROY IT.

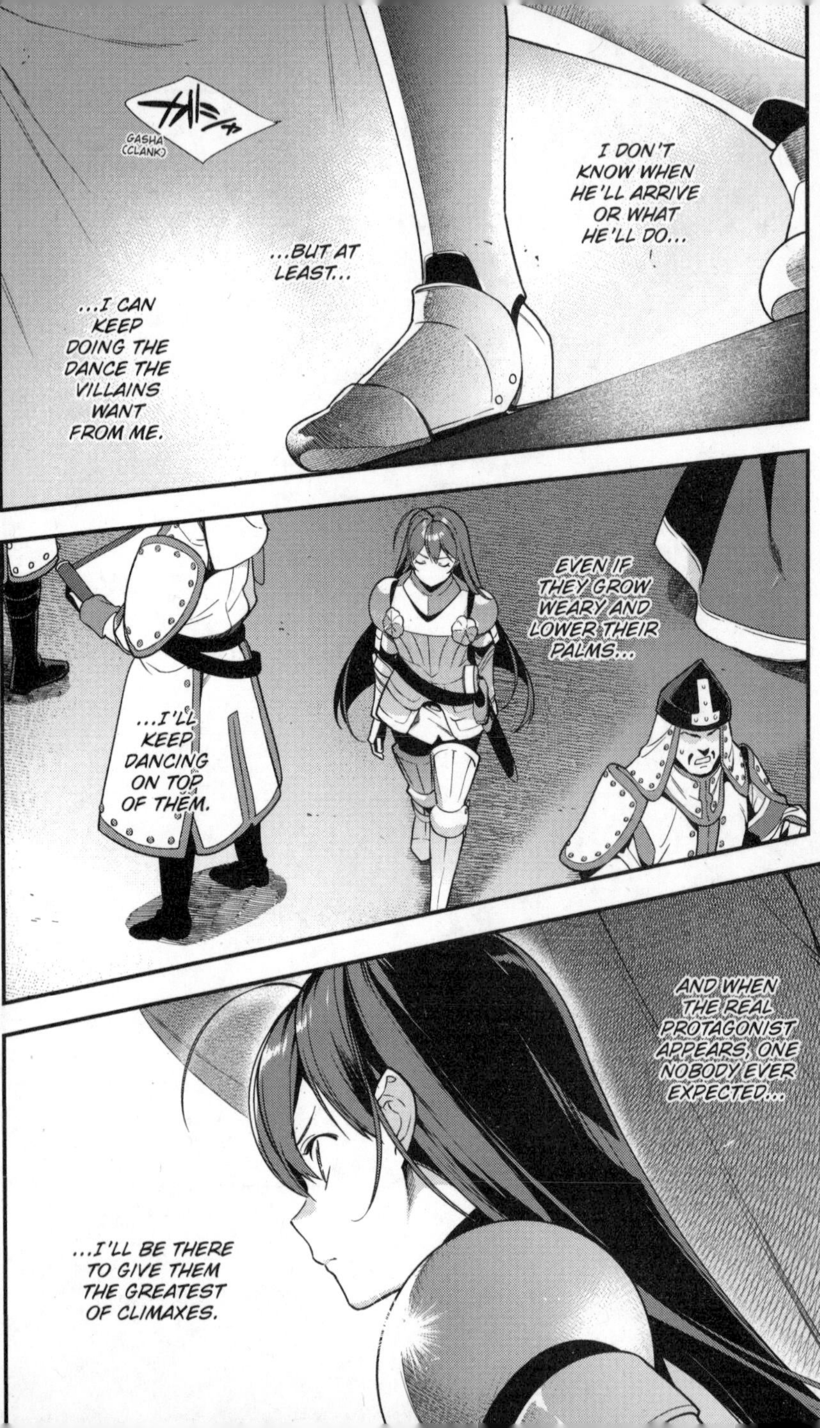
I DON'T KNOW WHEN HE'LL ARRIVE OR WHAT HE'LL DO...
GASHA (CLANK)
...BUT AT LEAST...
...I CAN KEEP DOING THE DANCE THE VILLAINS WANT FROM ME.
EVEN IF THEY GROW WEARY AND LOWER THEIR PALMS...
...I'LL KEEP DANCING ON TOP OF THEM.
AND WHEN THE REAL PROTAGONIST APPEARS, ONE NOBODY EVER EXPECTED...
...I'LL BE THERE TO GIVE THEM THE GREATEST OF CLIMAXES.

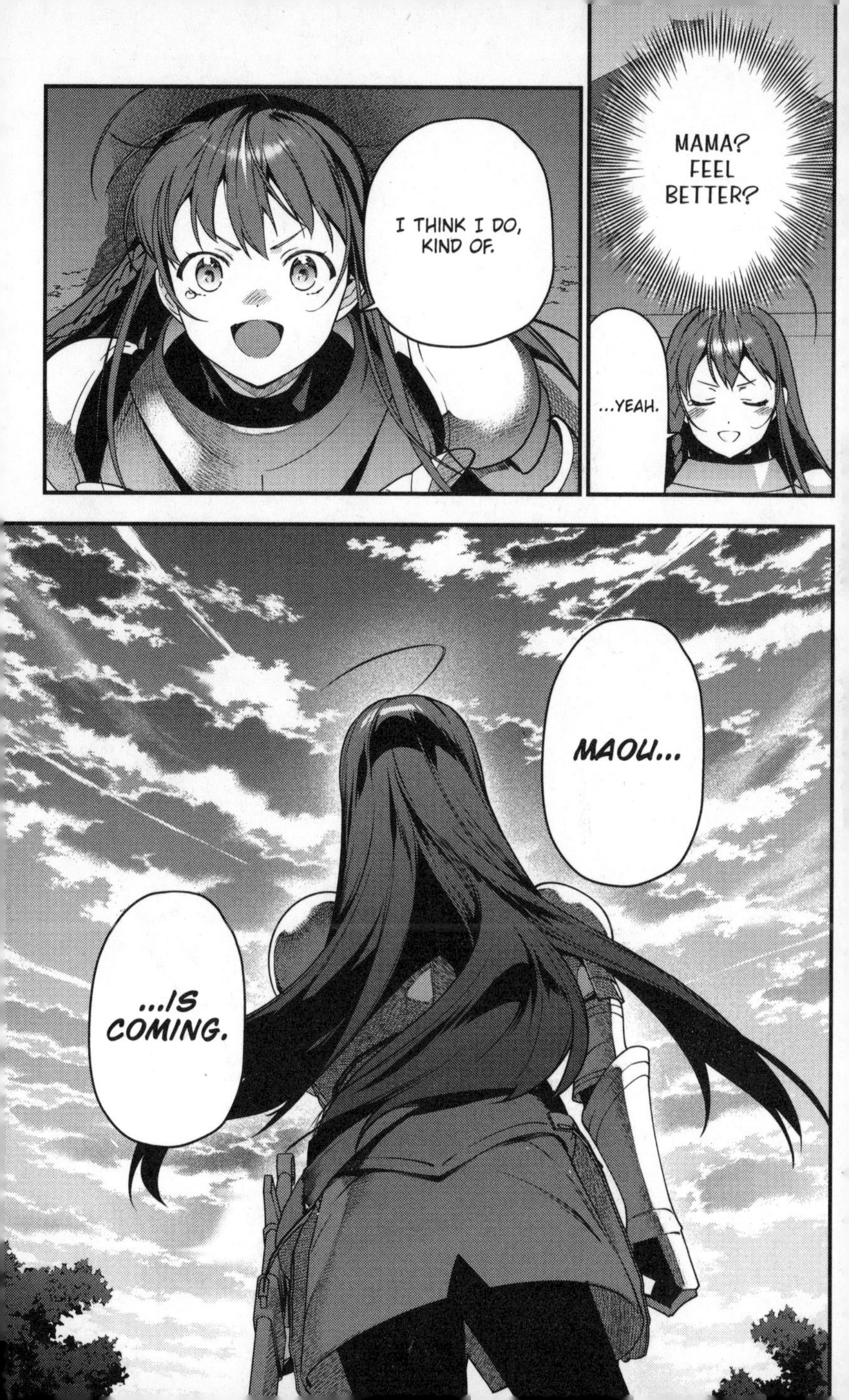
MAMA? FEEL BETTER?
...YEAH.
I THINK I DO, KIND OF.
MAOU...
...IS COMING.

THE DEVIL IS A PART-TIMER!

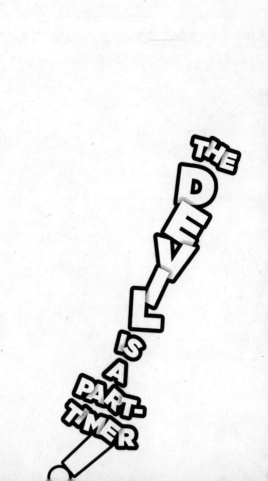

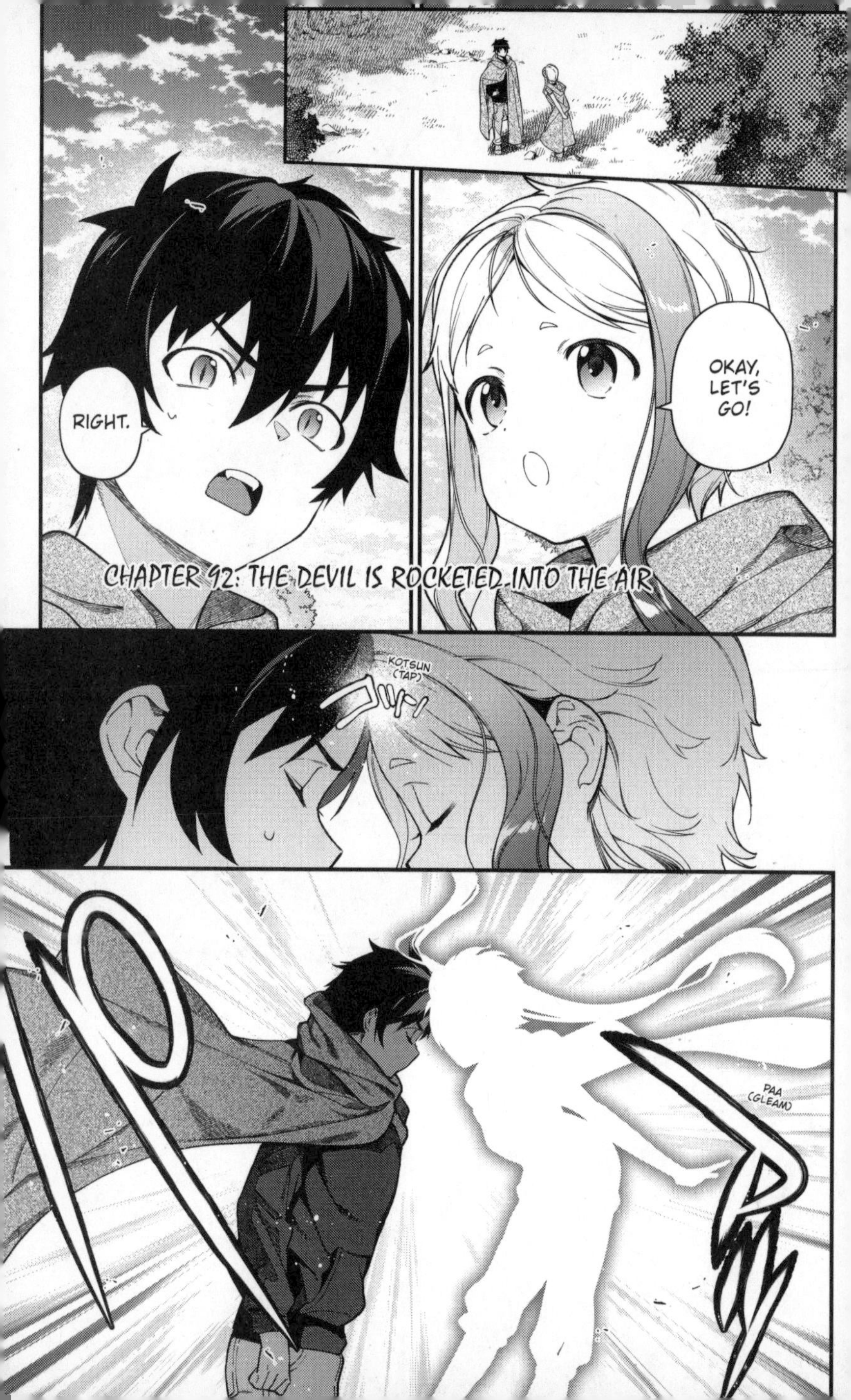
OKAY, LET'S GO!
RIGHT.
CHAPTER 92: THE DEVIL IS ROCKETED INTO THE AIR
KOTSUN (TAP)
PAA (GLEAM)

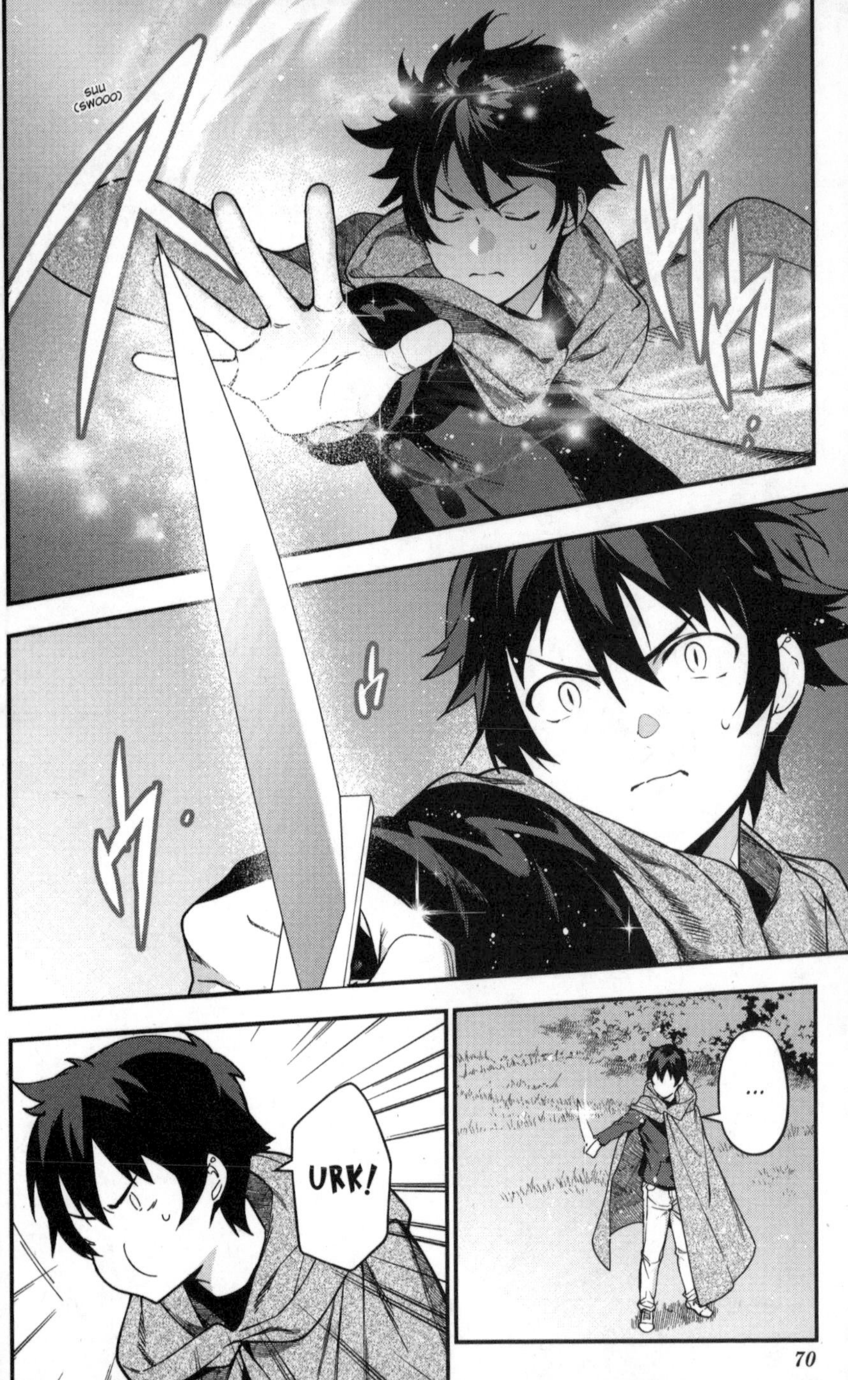
SUU (SWOOO)
...
URK!

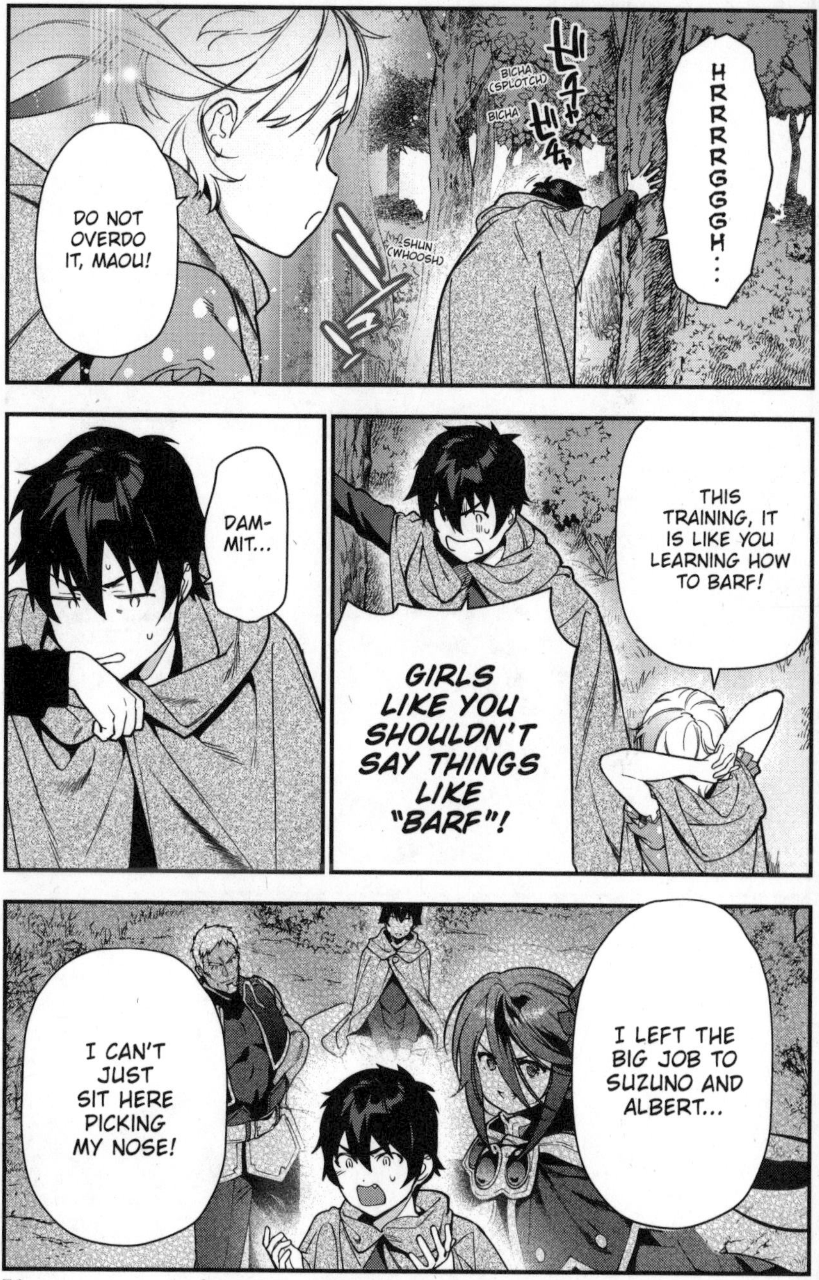
HRRRRGGGH...
BICHA (SPLOTCH)
BICHA
SHUN (WHOOSH)
DO NOT OVERDO IT, MAOU!
THIS TRAINING, IT IS LIKE YOU LEARNING HOW TO BARF!
GIRLS LIKE YOU SHOULDN'T SAY THINGS LIKE "BARF"!
DAM-MIT...
I LEFT THE BIG JOB TO SUZUNO AND ALBERT...
I CAN'T JUST SIT HERE PICKING MY NOSE!

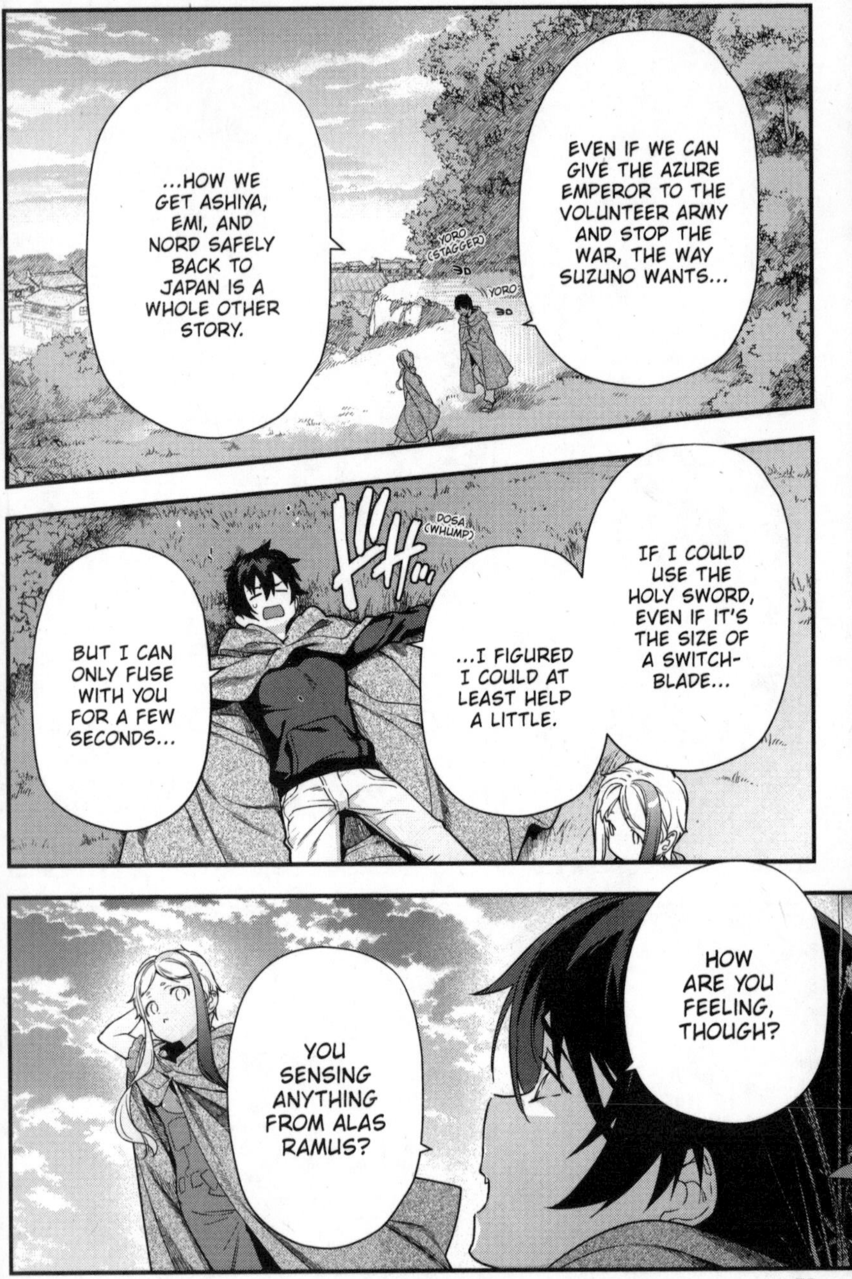
EVEN IF WE CAN GIVE THE AZURE EMPEROR TO THE VOLUNTEER ARMY AND STOP THE WAR, THE WAY SUZUNO WANTS...
YORO (STAGGER)
YORO
...HOW WE GET ASHIYA, EMI, AND NORD SAFELY BACK TO JAPAN IS A WHOLE OTHER STORY.
IF I COULD USE THE HOLY SWORD, EVEN IF IT'S THE SIZE OF A SWITCH-BLADE...
...I FIGURED I COULD AT LEAST HELP A LITTLE.
DOSA (WHUMP)
BUT I CAN ONLY FUSE WITH YOU FOR A FEW SECONDS...
HOW ARE YOU FEELING, THOUGH?
YOU SENSING ANYTHING FROM ALAS RAMUS?

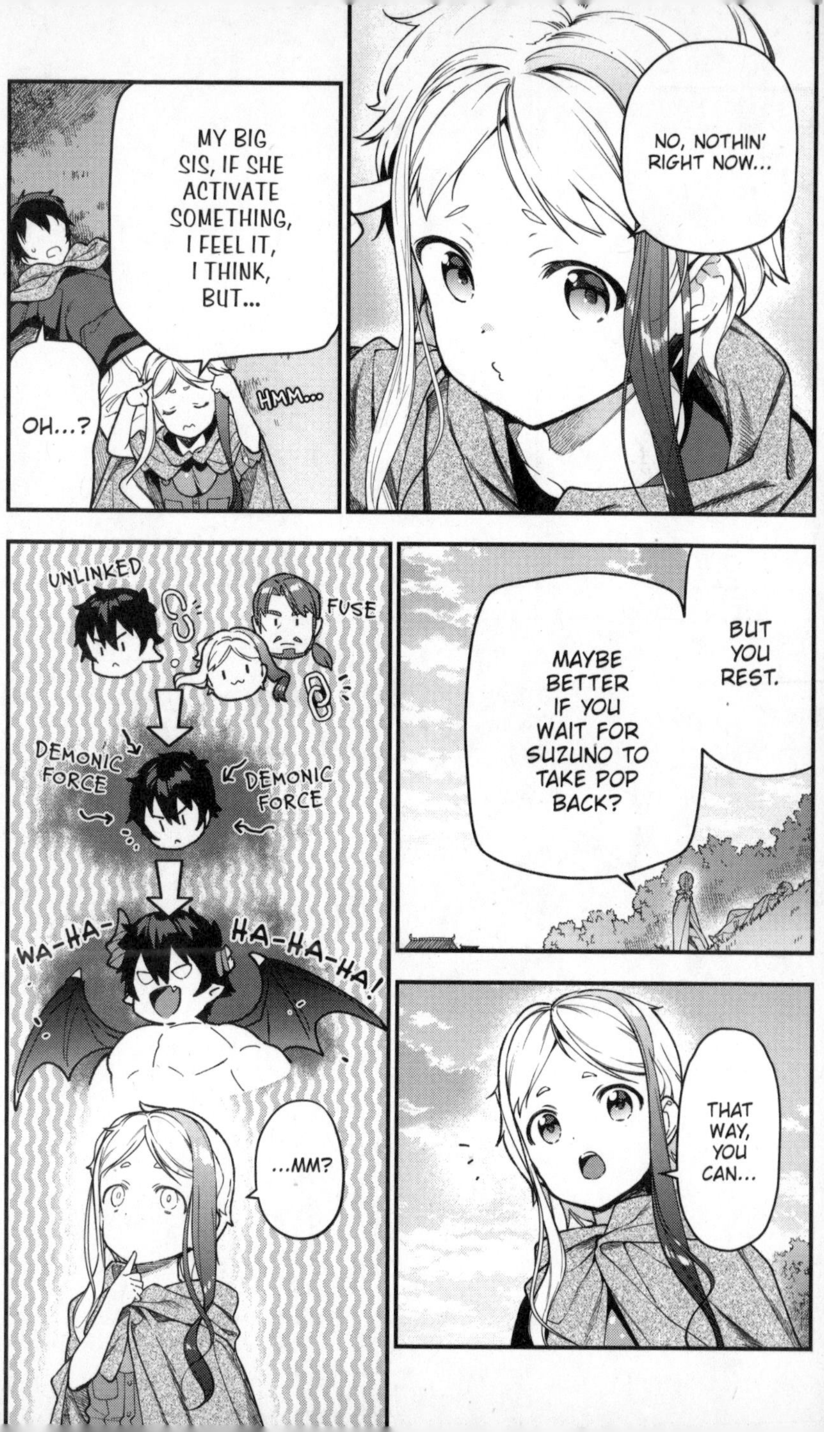
NO, NOTHIN' RIGHT NOW...
MY BIG SIS, IF SHE ACTIVATE SOMETHING, I FEEL IT, I THINK, BUT...
HMM...
OH...?
BUT YOU REST.
MAYBE BETTER IF YOU WAIT FOR SUZUNO TO TAKE POP BACK?
THAT WAY, YOU CAN...
FUSE
UNLINKED
DEMONIC FORCE
DEMONIC FORCE
WA-HA-HA-HA-HA-HA!
...MM?

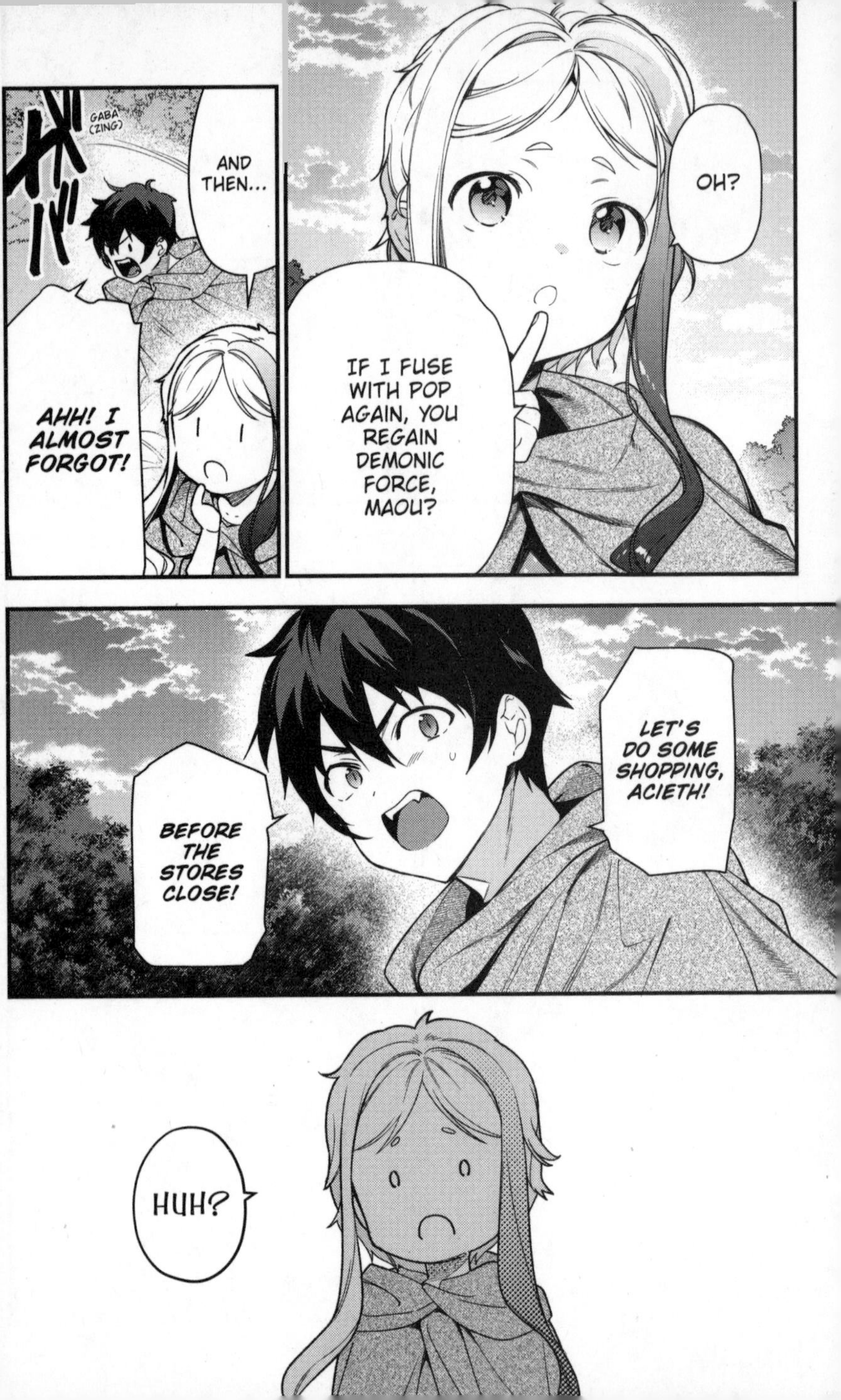
OH?
IF I FUSE WITH POP AGAIN, YOU REGAIN DEMONIC FORCE, MAOU?
GABA (ZING)
AND THEN...
AHH! I ALMOST FORGOT!
LET'S DO SOME SHOPPING, ACIETH!
BEFORE THE STORES CLOSE!
HUH?

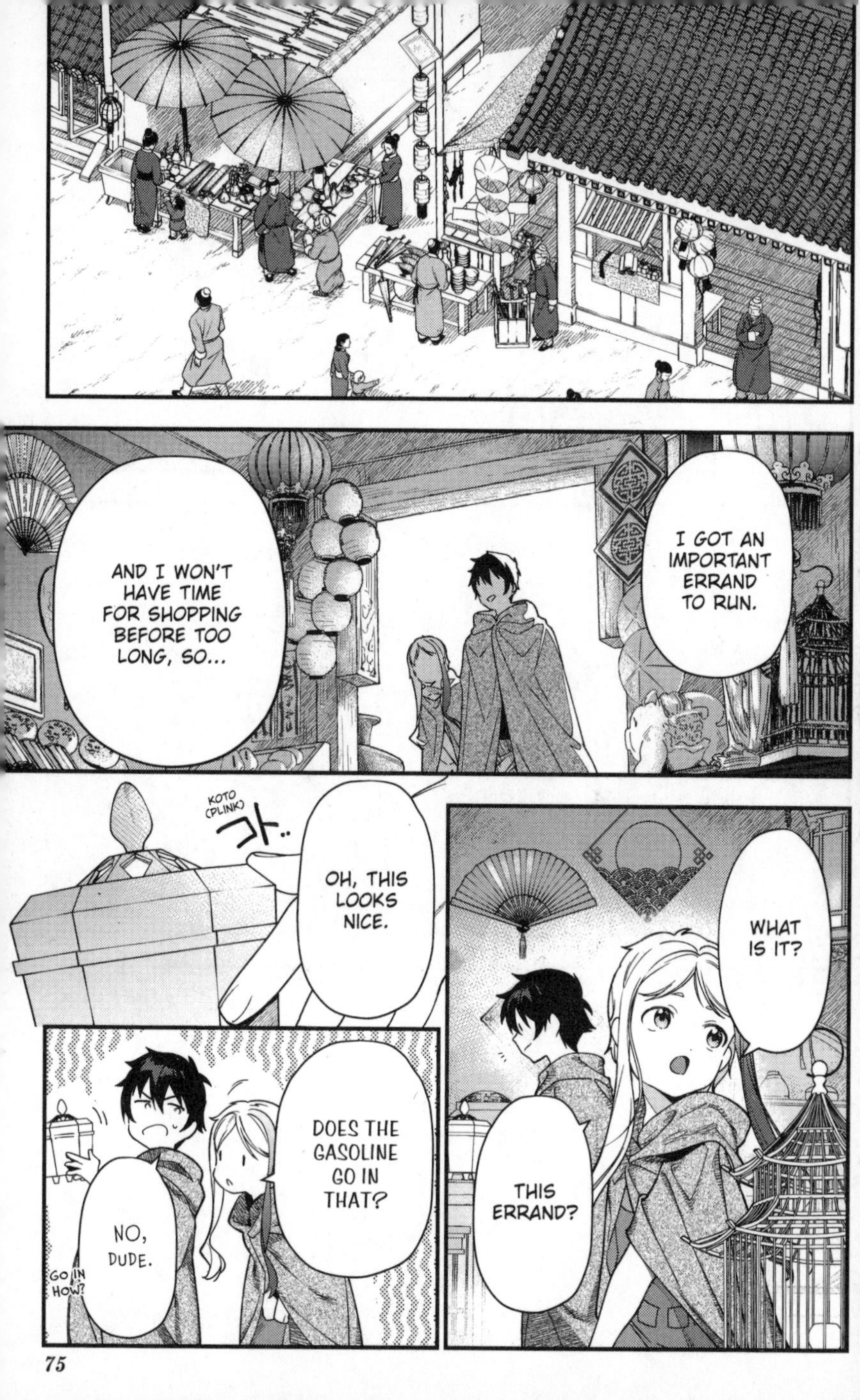
I GOT AN IMPORTANT ERRAND TO RUN.
AND I WON'T HAVE TIME FOR SHOPPING BEFORE TOO LONG, SO...
WHAT IS IT?
THIS ERRAND?
OH, THIS LOOKS NICE.
KOTO (PLINK)
DOES THE GASOLINE GO IN THAT?
NO, DUDE.
GO IN HOW?

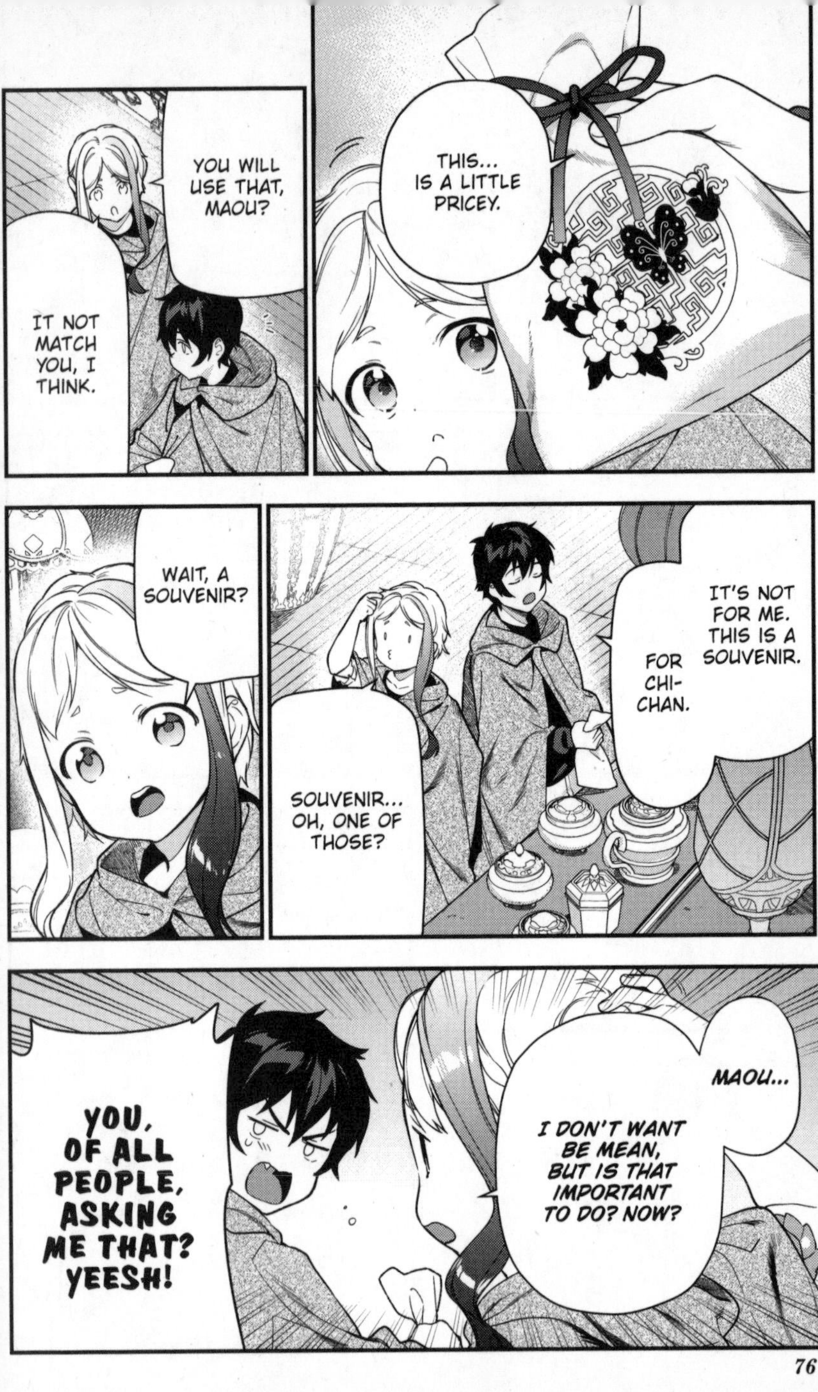
THIS... IS A LITTLE PRICEY.
YOU WILL USE THAT, MAOU?
IT NOT MATCH YOU, I THINK.
IT'S NOT FOR ME. THIS IS A SOUVENIR.
FOR CHI-CHAN.
SOUVENIR... OH, ONE OF THOSE?
WAIT, A SOUVENIR?
MAOU...
I DON'T WANT BE MEAN, BUT IS THAT IMPORTANT TO DO? NOW?
YOU, OF ALL PEOPLE, ASKING ME THAT? YEESH!

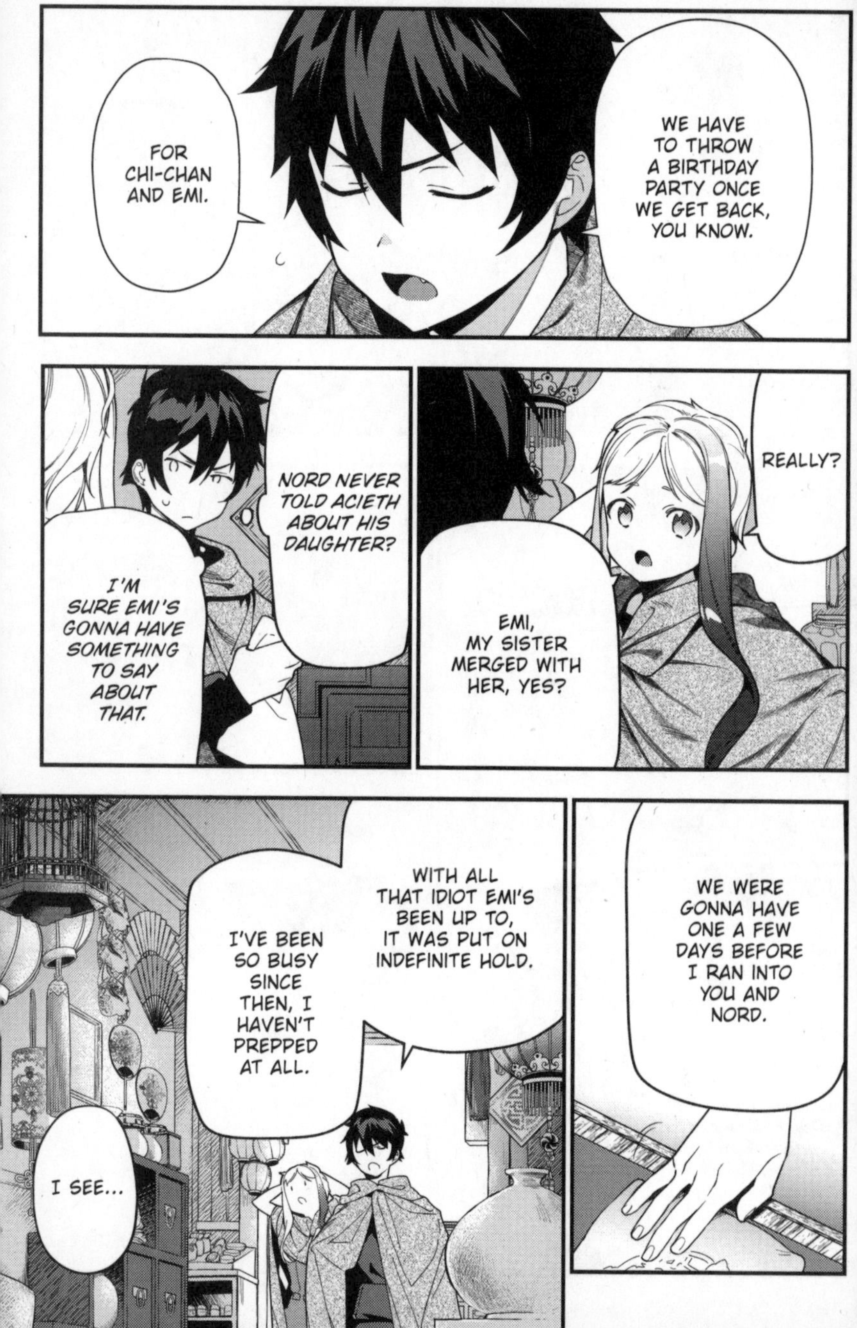
WE HAVE TO THROW A BIRTHDAY PARTY ONCE WE GET BACK, YOU KNOW.
FOR CHI-CHAN AND EMI.
REALLY?
EMI, MY SISTER MERGED WITH HER, YES?
NORD NEVER TOLD ACIETH ABOUT HIS DAUGHTER?
I'M SURE EMI'S GONNA HAVE SOMETHING TO SAY ABOUT THAT.
WE WERE GONNA HAVE ONE A FEW DAYS BEFORE I RAN INTO YOU AND NORD.
WITH ALL THAT IDIOT EMI'S BEEN UP TO, IT WAS PUT ON INDEFINITE HOLD.
I'VE BEEN SO BUSY SINCE THEN, I HAVEN'T PREPPED AT ALL.
I SEE...

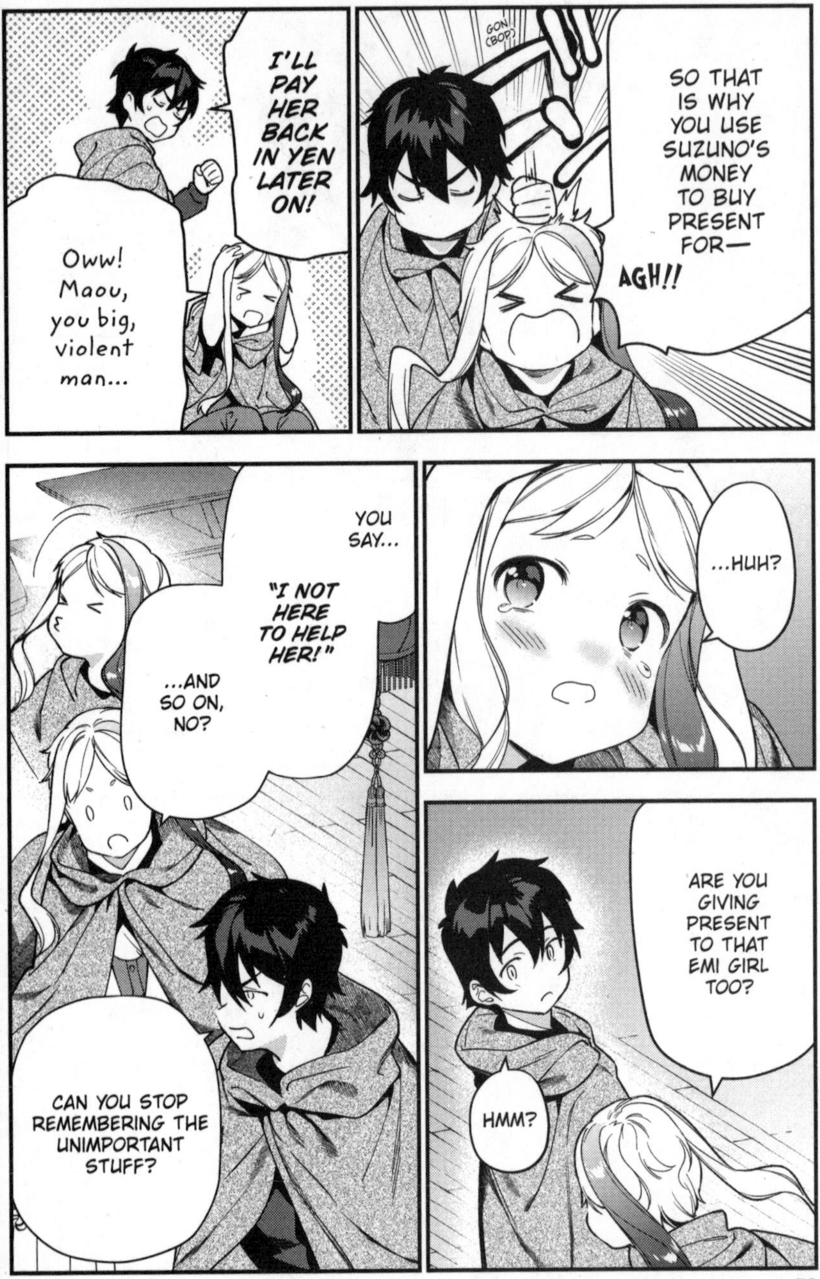
GON (BOP)
SO THAT IS WHY YOU USE SUZUNO'S MONEY TO BUY PRESENT FOR—
AGH!!
I'LL PAY HER BACK IN YEN LATER ON!
Oww! Maou, you big, violent man...
...HUH?
ARE YOU GIVING PRESENT TO THAT EMI GIRL TOO?
HMM?
YOU SAY...
"I NOT HERE TO HELP HER!"
...AND SO ON, NO?
CAN YOU STOP REMEMBERING THE UNIMPORTANT STUFF?

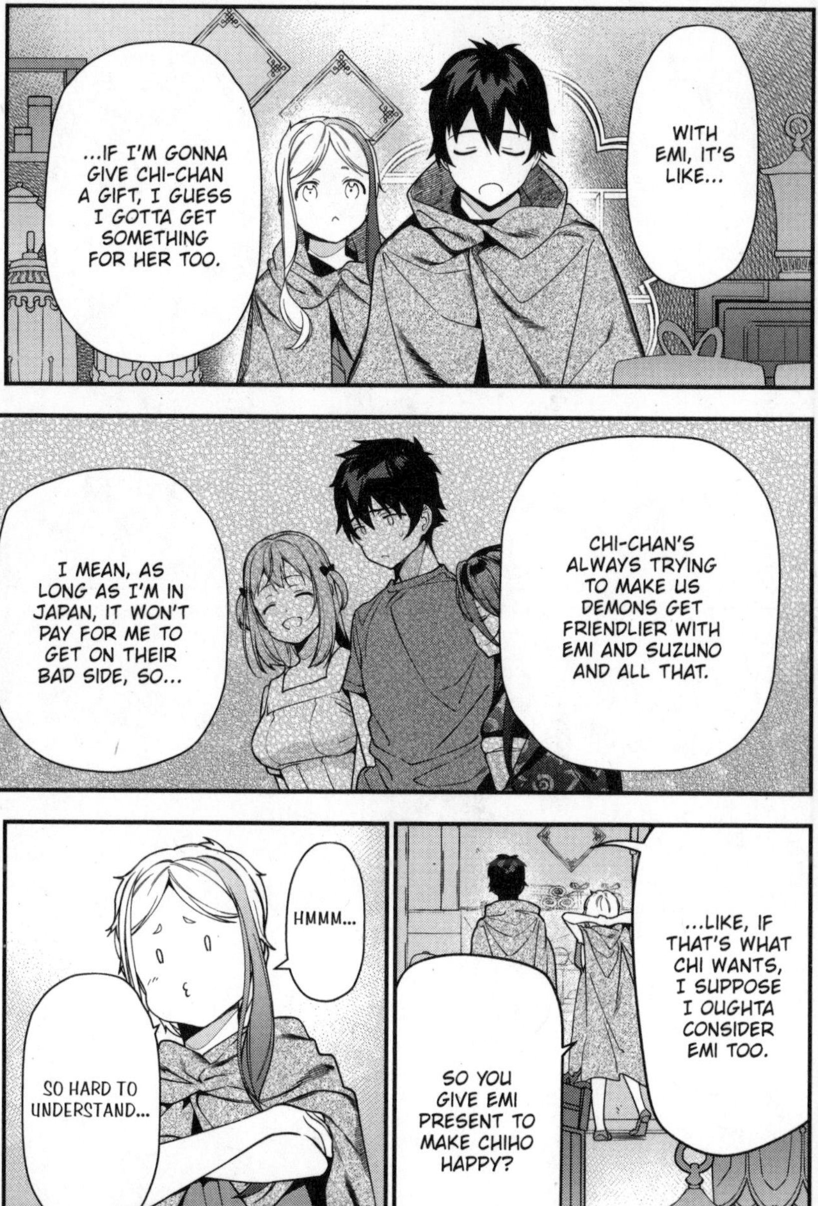
WITH EMI, IT'S LIKE...
...IF I'M GONNA GIVE CHI-CHAN A GIFT, I GUESS I GOTTA GET SOMETHING FOR HER TOO.
CHI-CHAN'S ALWAYS TRYING TO MAKE US DEMONS GET FRIENDLIER WITH EMI AND SUZUNO AND ALL THAT.
I MEAN, AS LONG AS I'M IN JAPAN, IT WON'T PAY FOR ME TO GET ON THEIR BAD SIDE, SO...
...LIKE, IF THAT'S WHAT CHI WANTS, I SUPPOSE I OUGHTA CONSIDER EMI TOO.
SO YOU GIVE EMI PRESENT TO MAKE CHIHO HAPPY?
HMMM...
SO HARD TO UNDERSTAND...

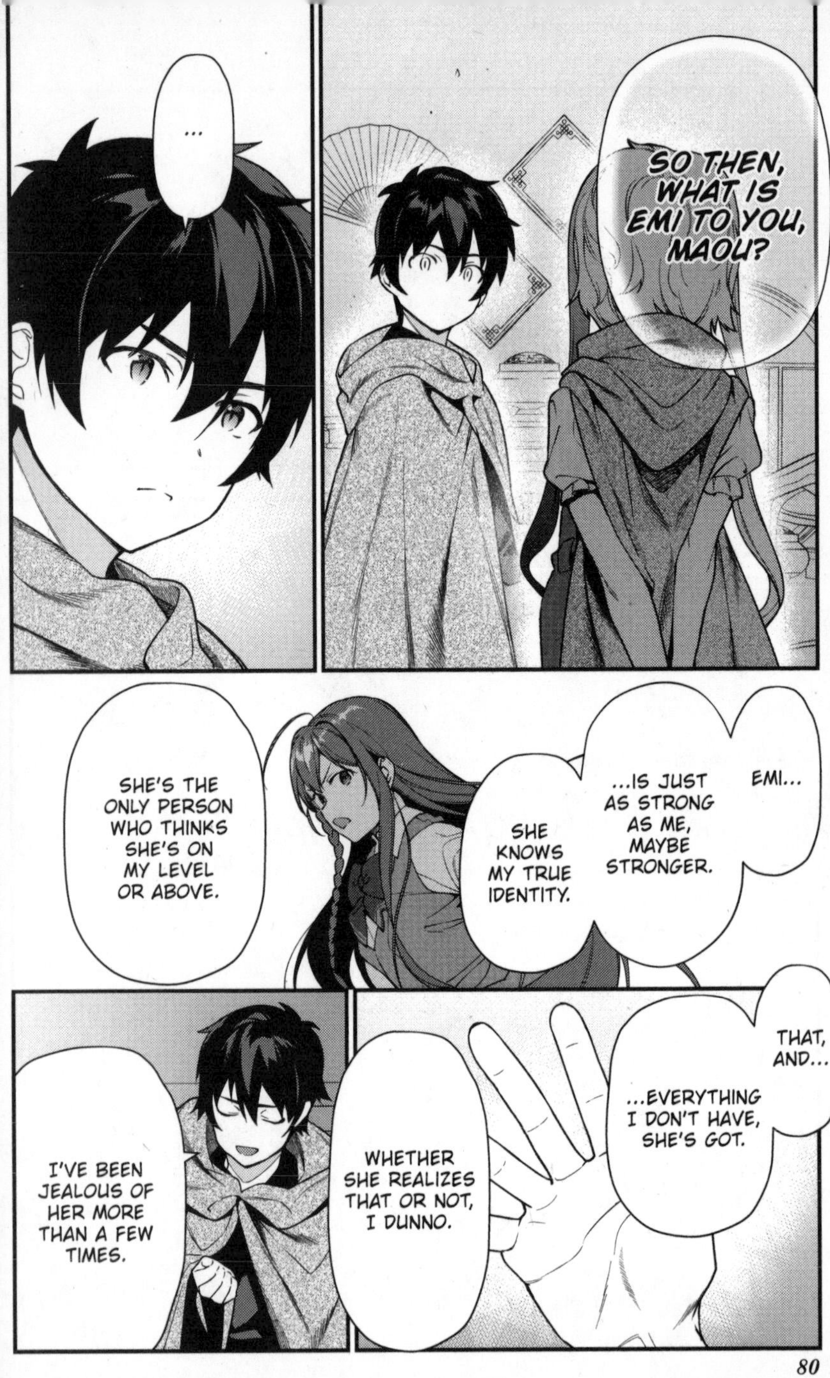
SO THEN, WHAT IS EMI TO YOU, MAOU?
...
EMI...
...IS JUST AS STRONG AS ME, MAYBE STRONGER.
SHE KNOWS MY TRUE IDENTITY.
SHE'S THE ONLY PERSON WHO THINKS SHE'S ON MY LEVEL OR ABOVE.
THAT, AND...
...EVERYTHING I DON'T HAVE, SHE'S GOT.
WHETHER SHE REALIZES THAT OR NOT, I DUNNO.
I'VE BEEN JEALOUS OF HER MORE THAN A FEW TIMES.

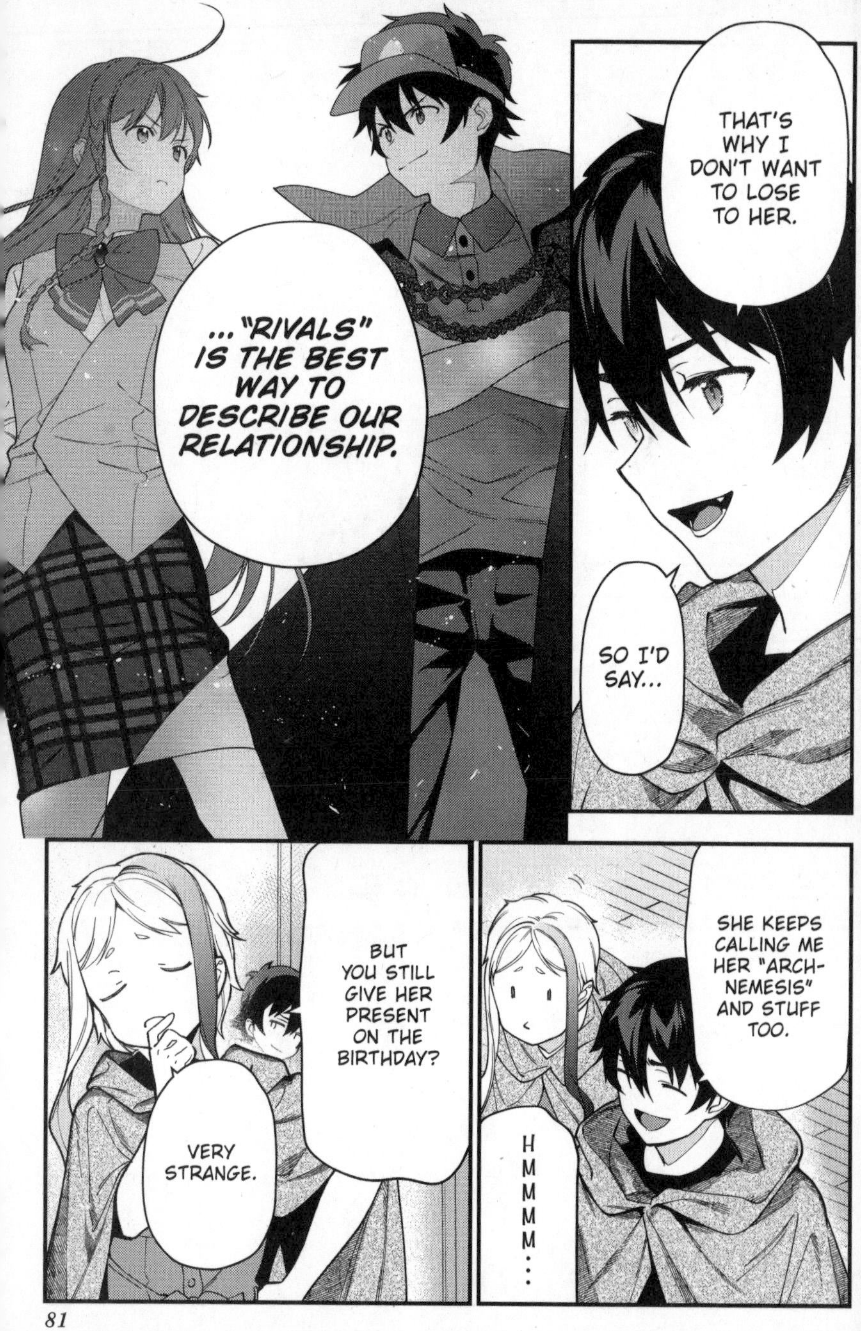
THAT'S WHY I DON'T WANT TO LOSE TO HER.
SO I'D SAY...
..."RIVALS" IS THE BEST WAY TO DESCRIBE OUR RELATIONSHIP.
SHE KEEPS CALLING ME HER "ARCH-NEMESIS" AND STUFF TOO.
HMMMM...
BUT YOU STILL GIVE HER PRESENT ON THE BIRTHDAY?
VERY STRANGE.

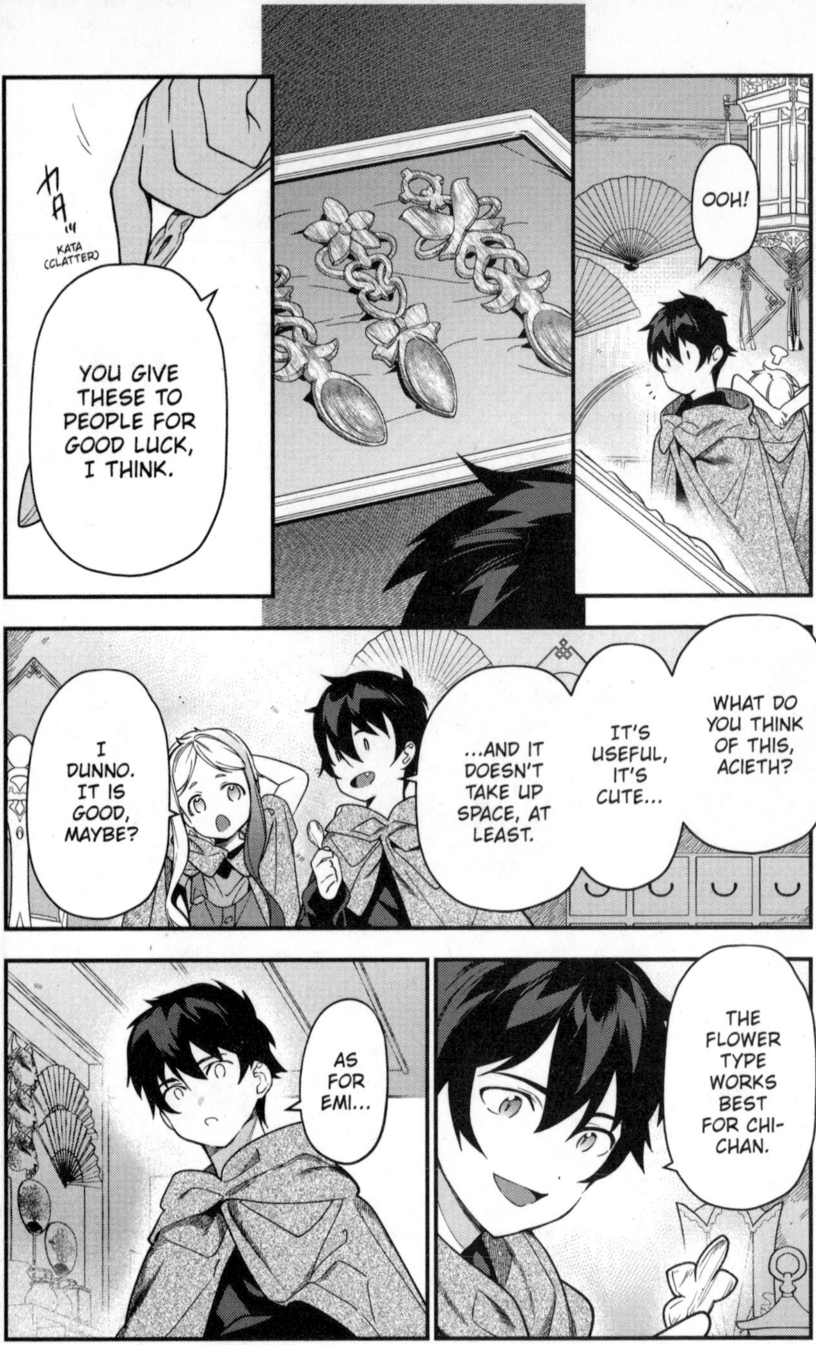
OOH!
KATA (CLATTER)
YOU GIVE THESE TO PEOPLE FOR GOOD LUCK, I THINK.
WHAT DO YOU THINK OF THIS, ACIETH?
IT'S USEFUL, IT'S CUTE...
...AND IT DOESN'T TAKE UP SPACE, AT LEAST.
I DUNNO. IT IS GOOD, MAYBE?
THE FLOWER TYPE WORKS BEST FOR CHI-CHAN.
AS FOR EMI...

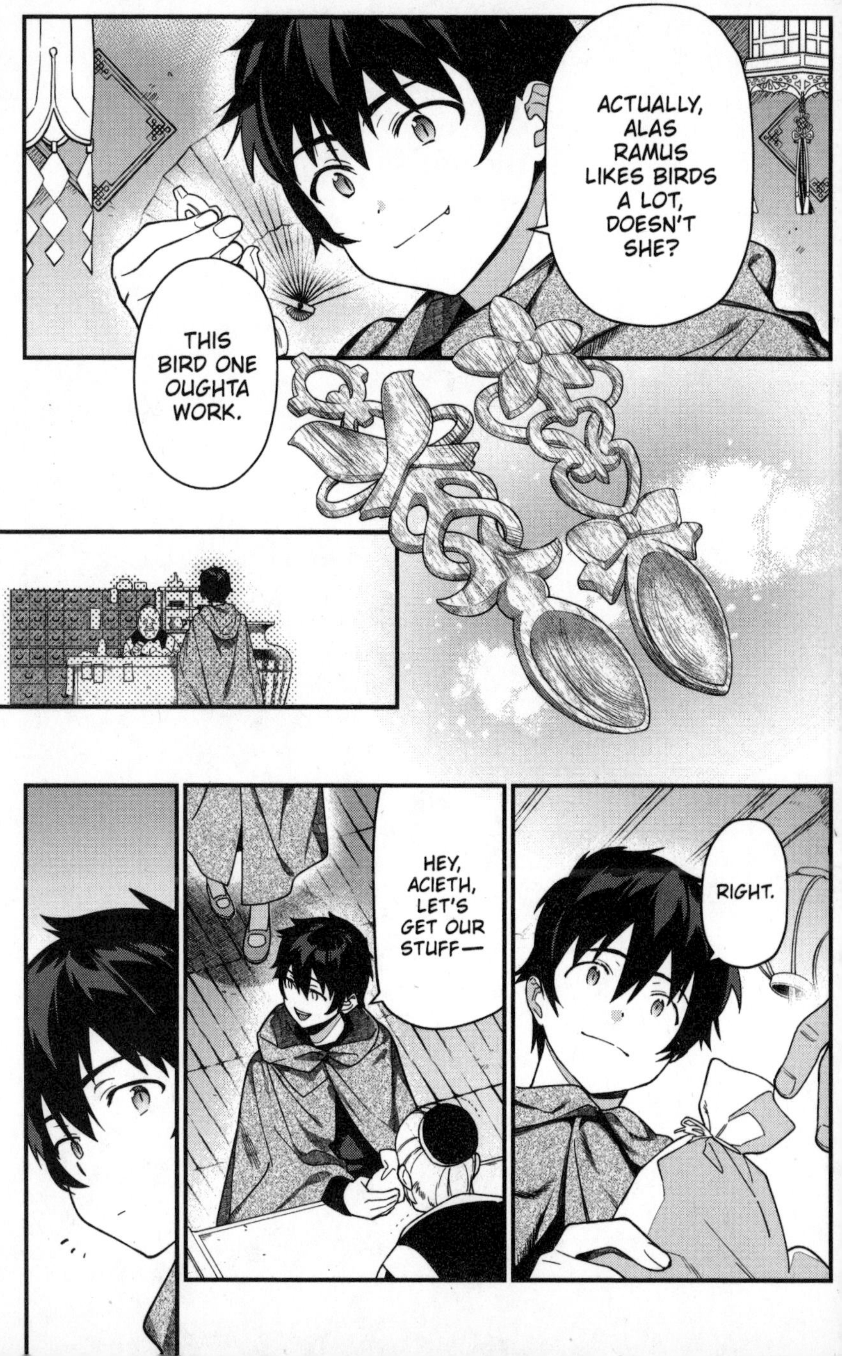
ACTUALLY, ALAS RAMUS LIKES BIRDS A LOT, DOESN'T SHE?
THIS BIRD ONE OUGHTA WORK.
RIGHT.
HEY, ACIETH, LET'S GET OUR STUFF—

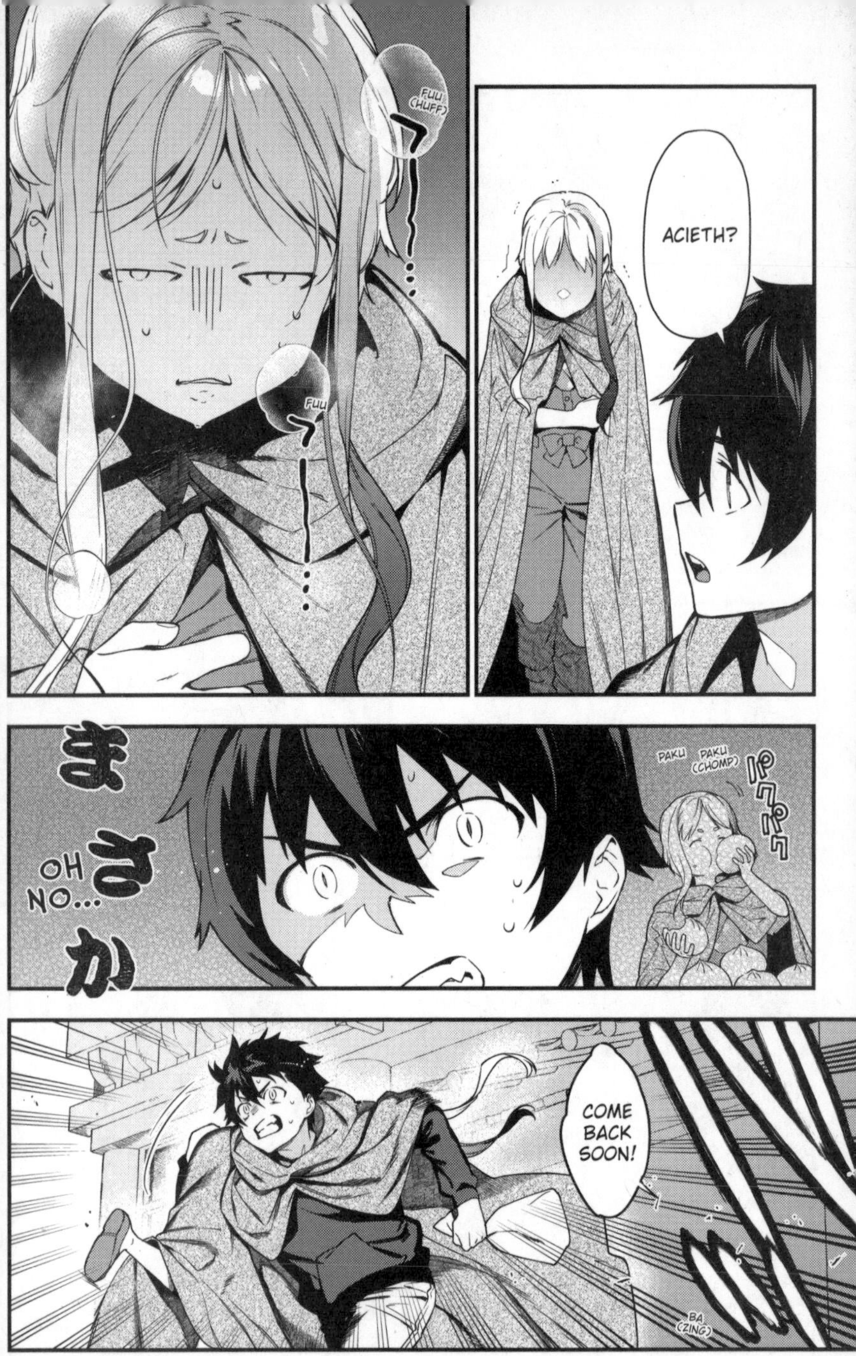
ACIETH?
FUU (HUFF)
FUU
PAKU PAKU (CHOMP)
OH NO...
COME BACK SOON!
BA (ZING)

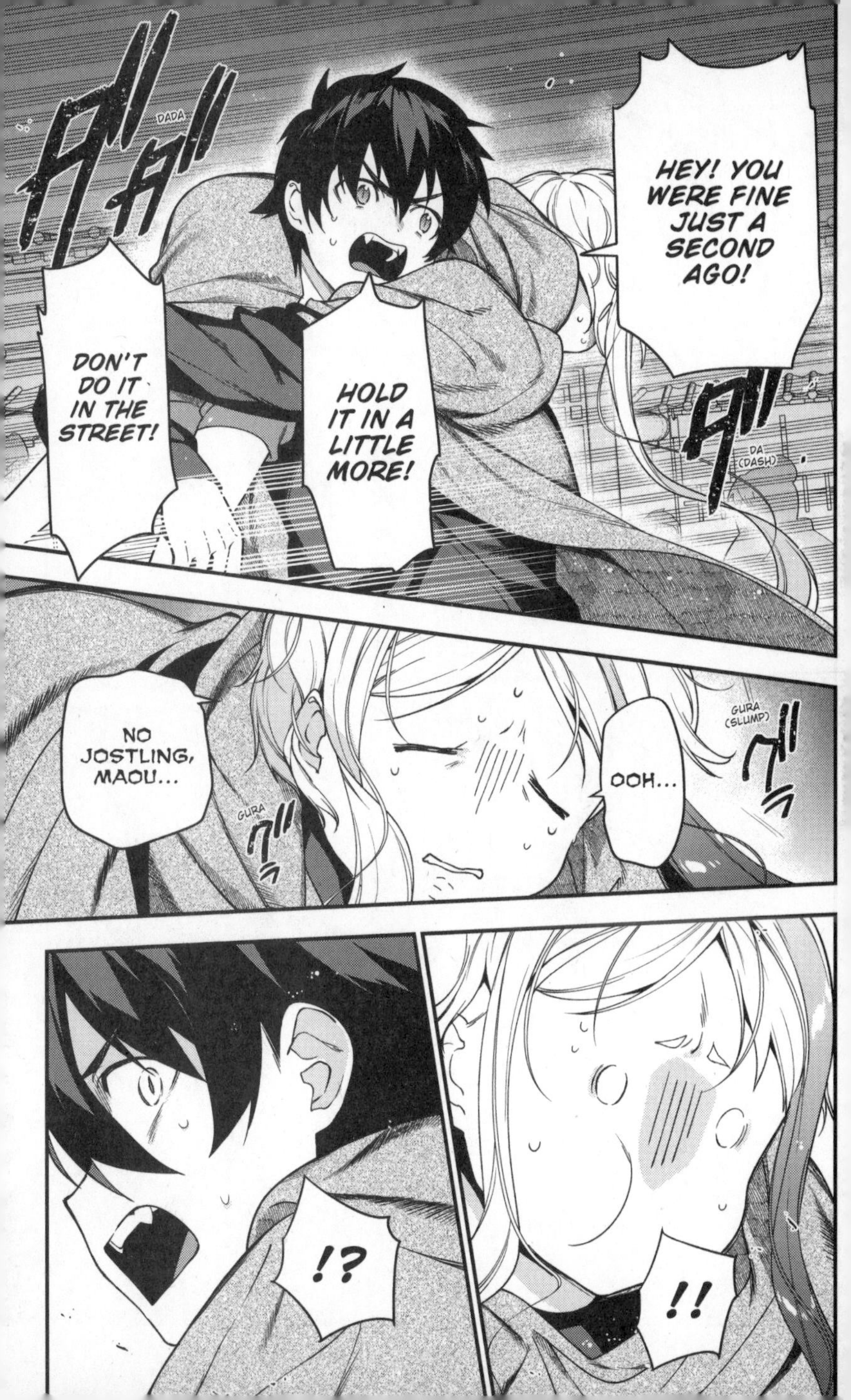
HEY! YOU WERE FINE JUST A SECOND AGO!
DA (DASH)
HOLD IT IN A LITTLE MORE!
DADA
DON'T DO IT IN THE STREET!
GURA (SLUMP)
OOH...
NO JOSTLING, MAOU...
GURA
!!
!?

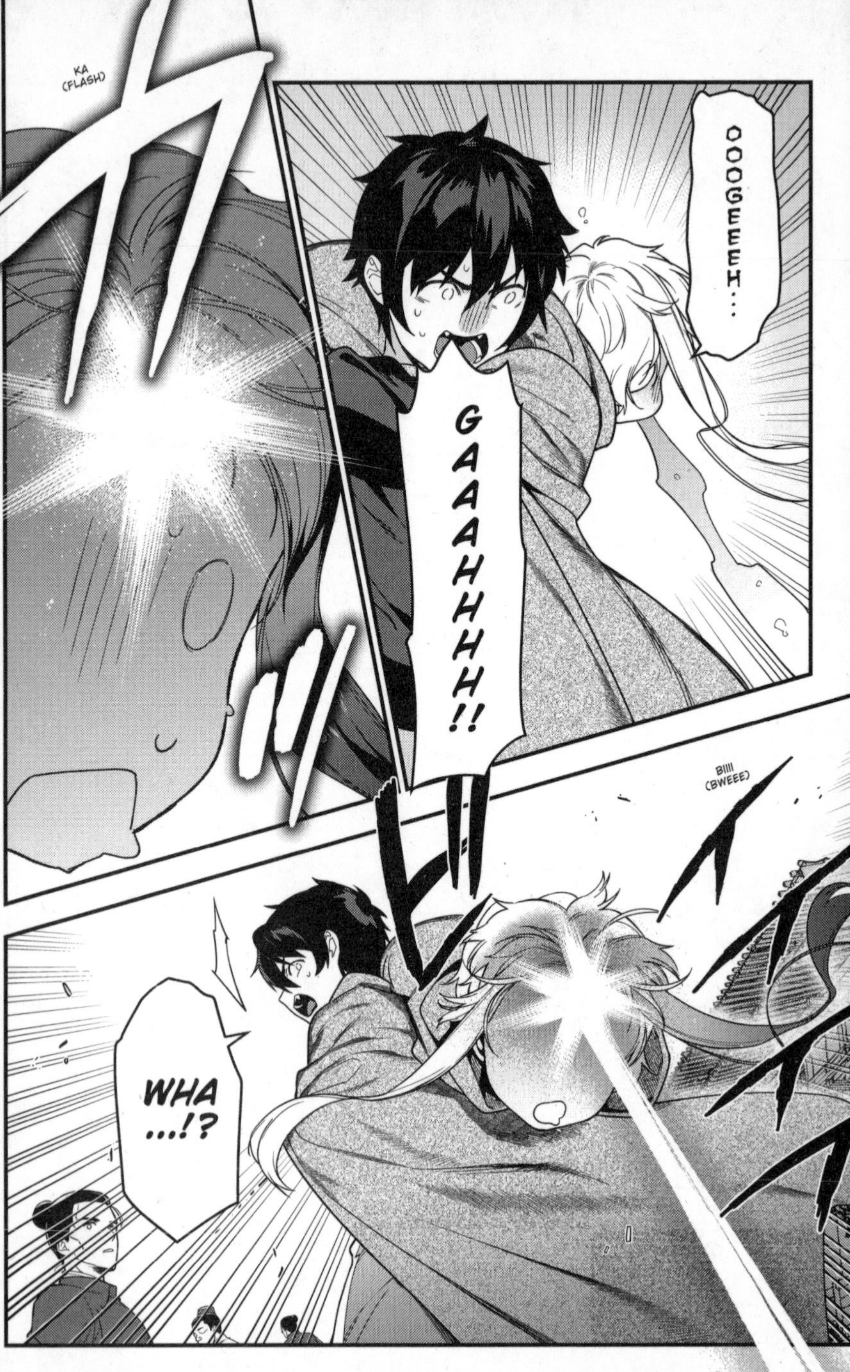
OOOGEEEH...
GAAAAHHHHHH!!
KA
(FLASH)
BIIII
(BWEEE)
WHA...!?

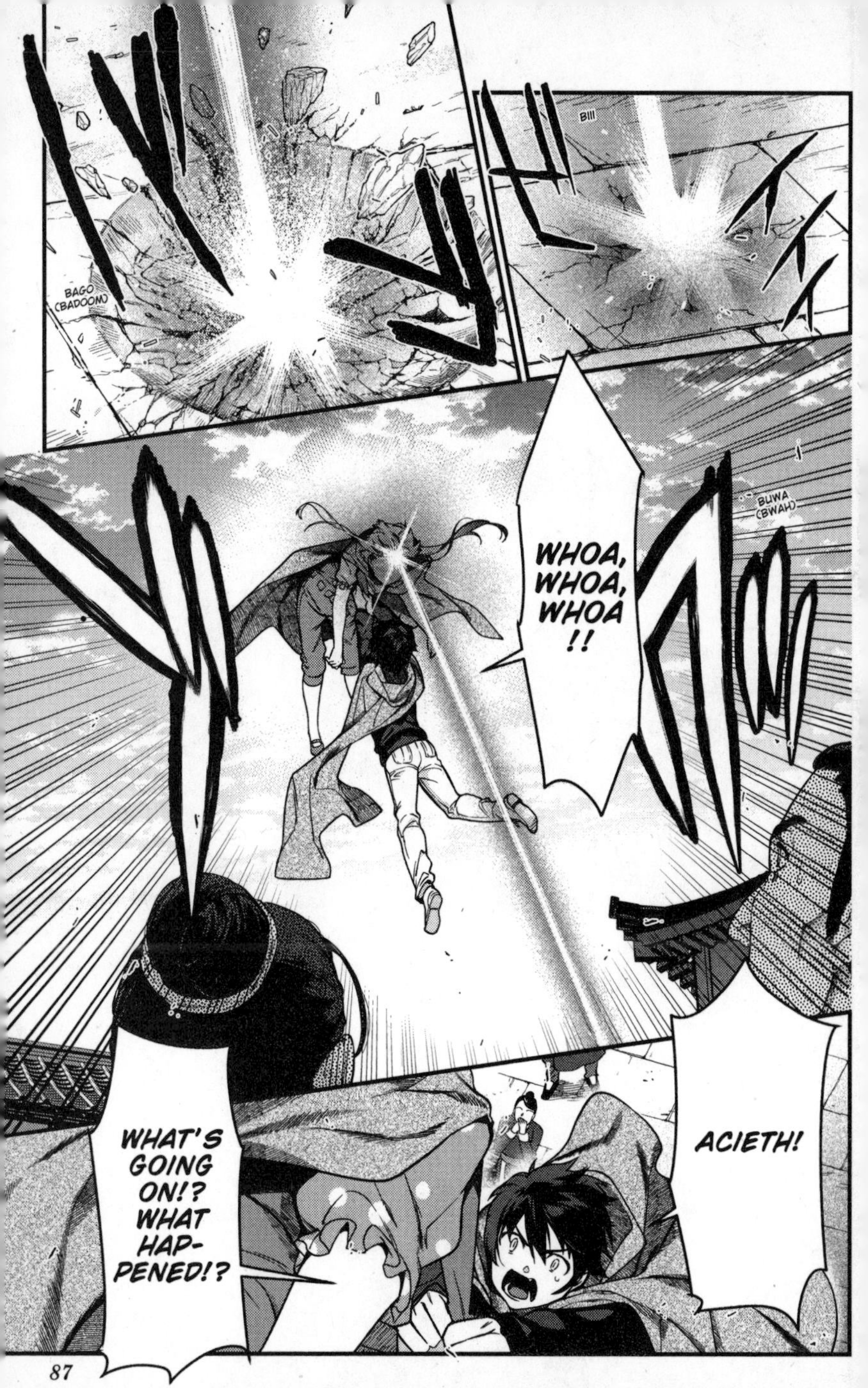
BIII
BAGO (BADOOM)
BUWA (BWAH)
WHOA, WHOA, WHOA!!
ACIETH!
WHAT'S GOING ON!? WHAT HAP-PENED!?

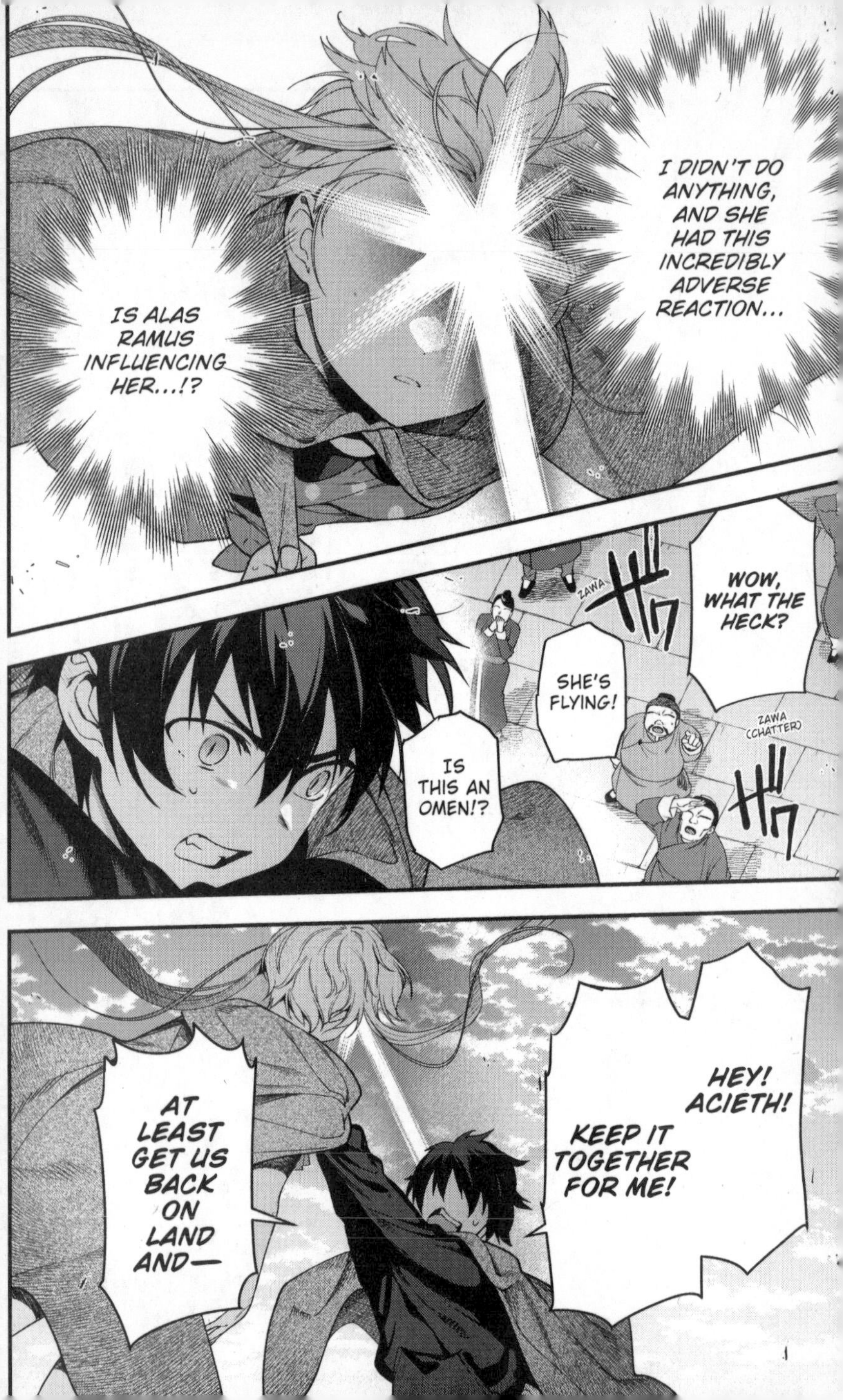
I DIDN'T DO ANYTHING, AND SHE HAD THIS INCREDIBLY ADVERSE REACTION...
IS ALAS RAMUS INFLUENCING HER...!?
WOW, WHAT THE HECK?
ZAWA
SHE'S FLYING!
ZAWA (CHATTER)
IS THIS AN OMEN!?
HEY! ACIETH!
KEEP IT TOGETHER FOR ME!
AT LEAST GET US BACK ON LAND AND—

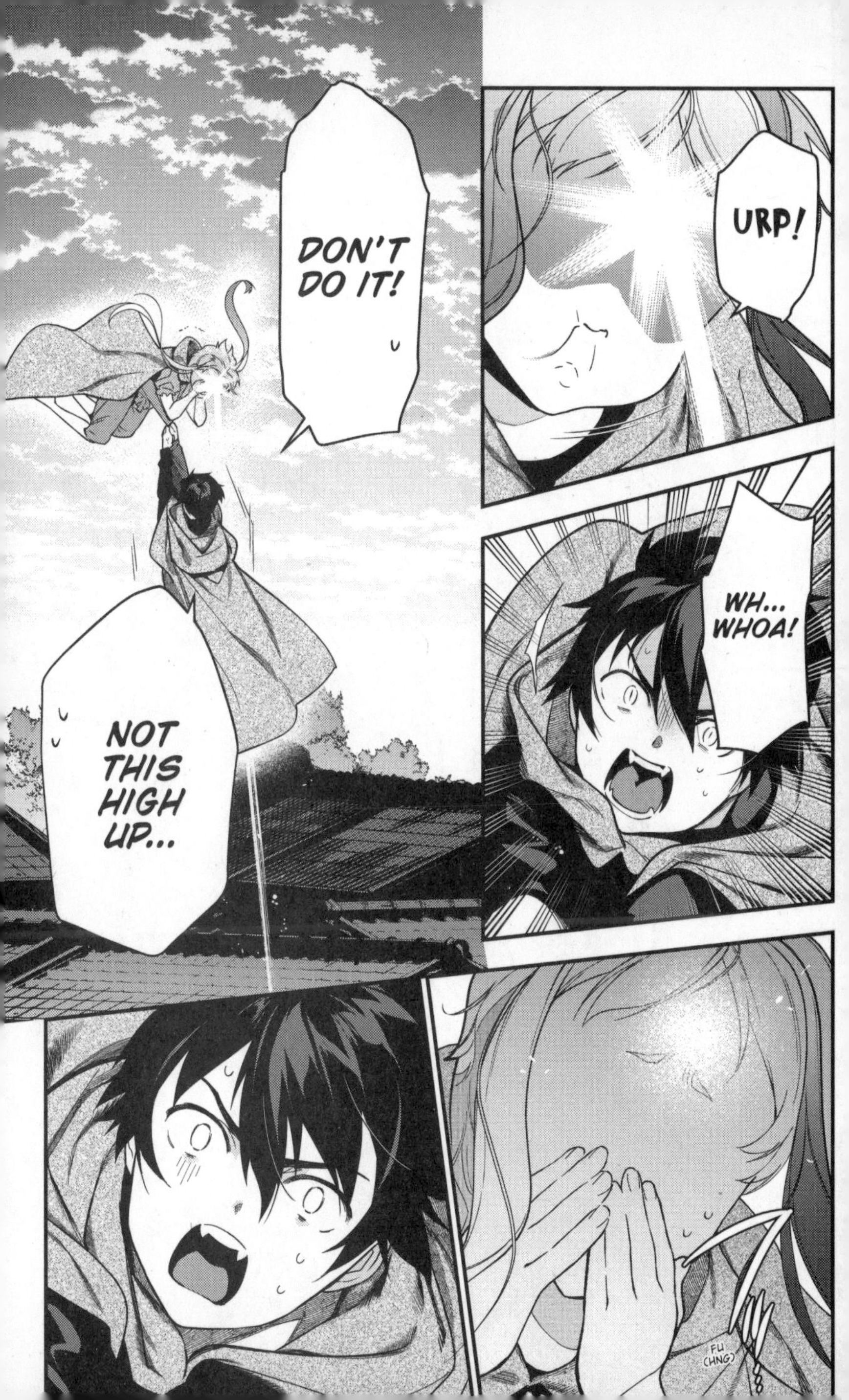
URP!
WH... WHOA!
DON'T DO IT!
NOT THIS HIGH UP...
FU (HNG)

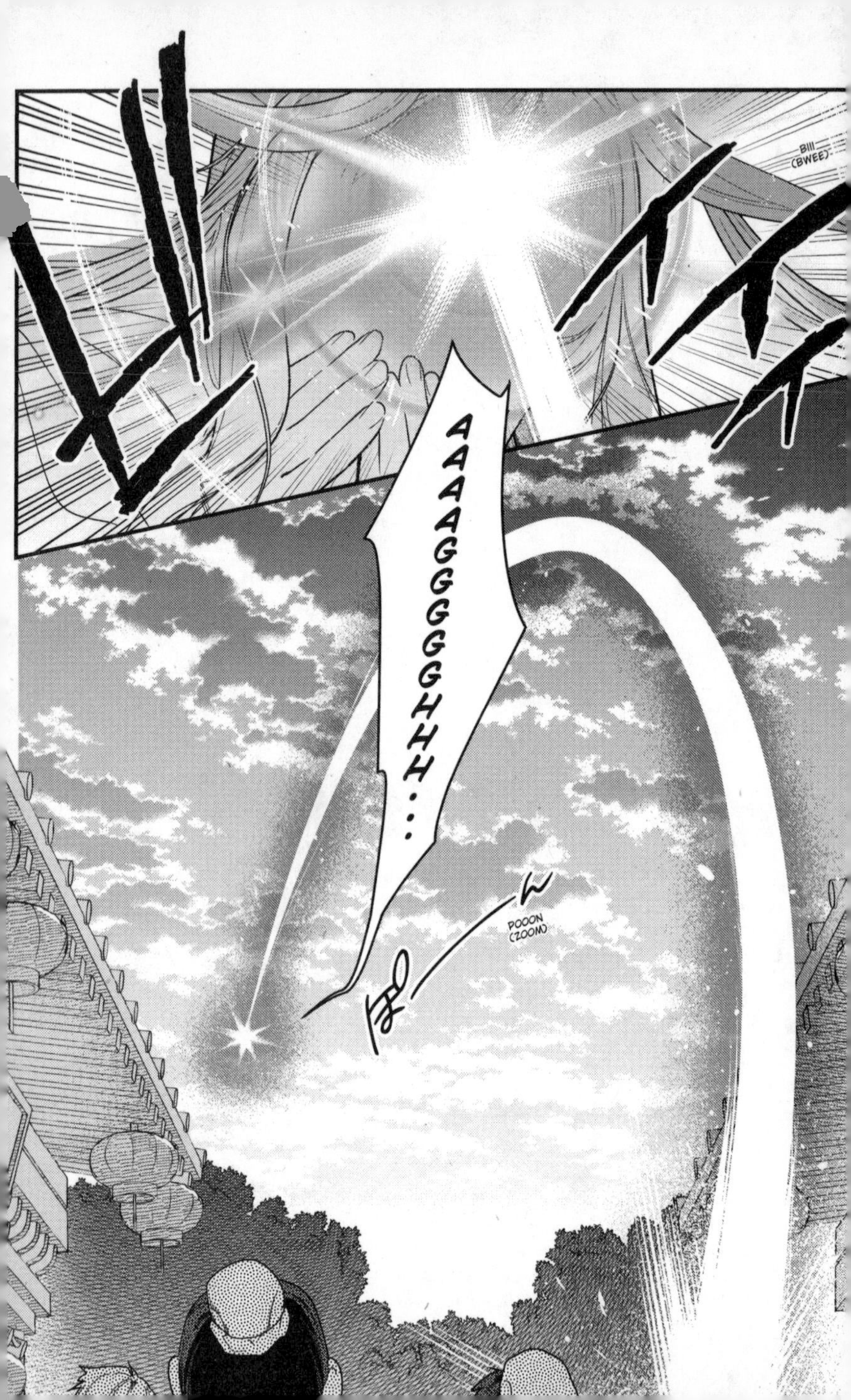
BIII
(BWEE)
AAAAGGGGGHHH...
POOON
(ZOOM)

Sadao
Maou

THE DEVIL IS A PART-TIMER!

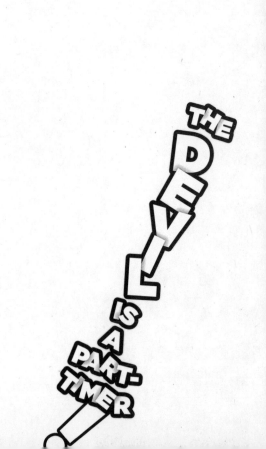

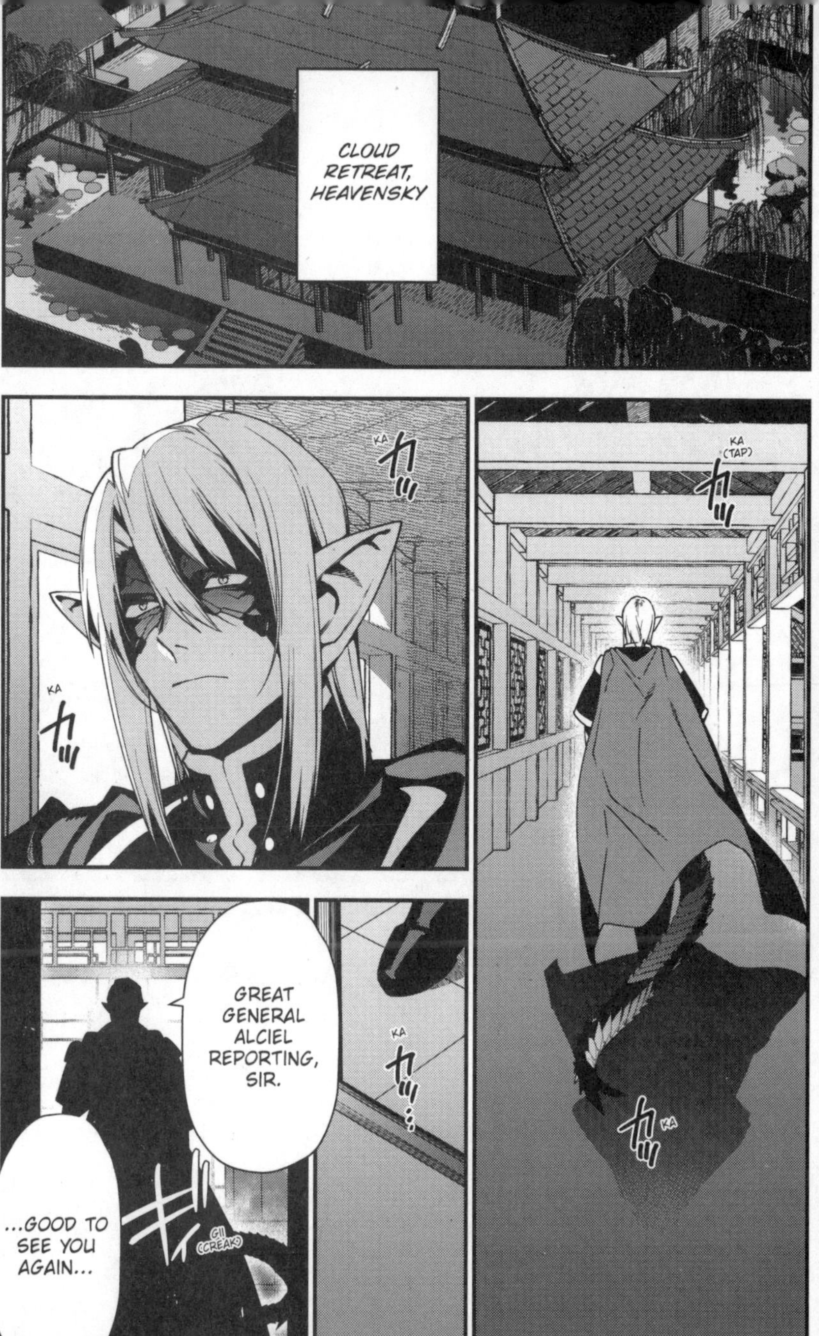
CLOUD RETREAT, HEAVENSKY
KA (TAP)
KA
KA
KA
KA
GREAT GENERAL ALCIEL REPORTING, SIR.
...GOOD TO SEE YOU AGAIN...
GII (CREAK)

CHAPTER 93: THE HERO KICKS OFF THE FINAL BATTLE

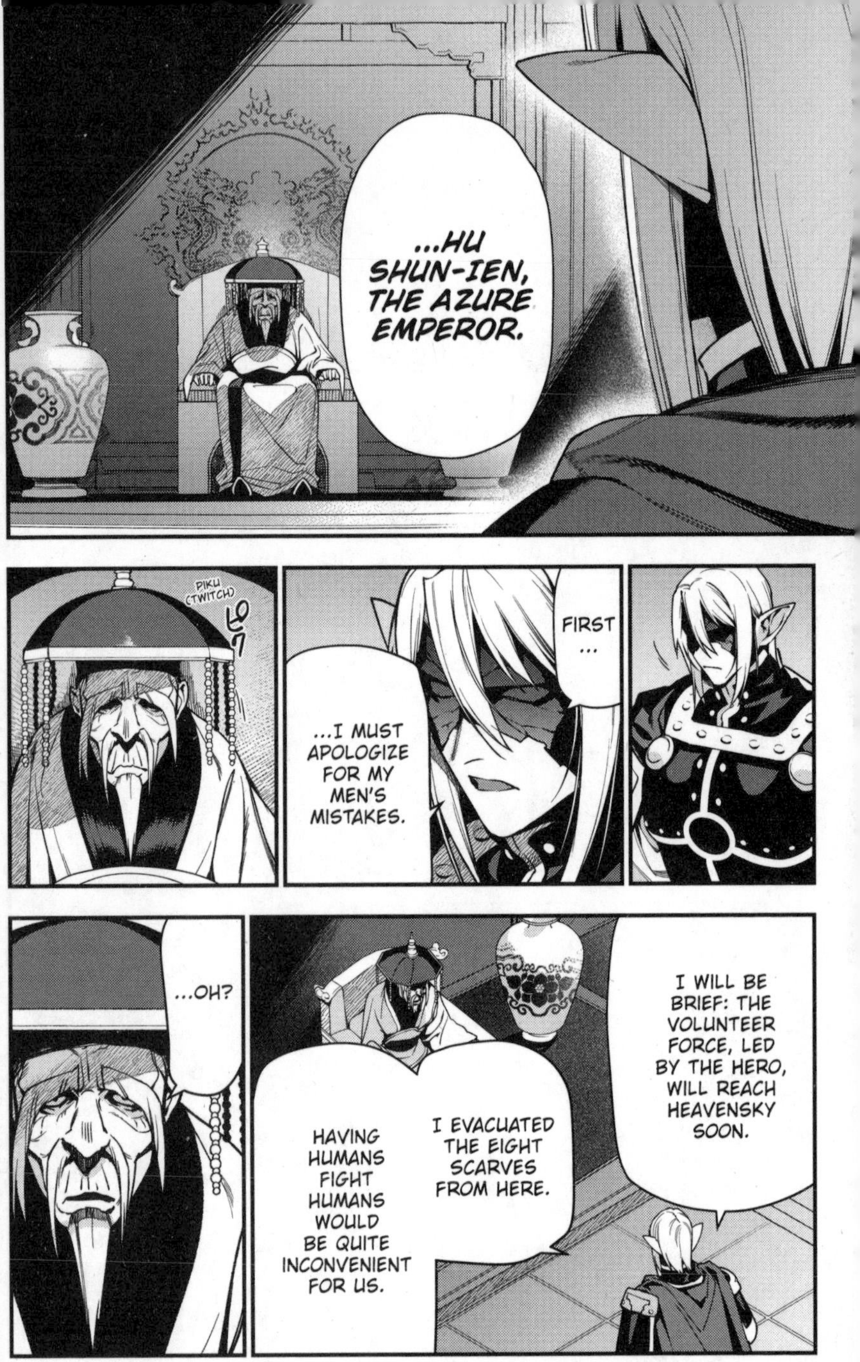
...HU SHUN-IEN, THE AZURE EMPEROR.
FIRST ...
...I MUST APOLOGIZE FOR MY MEN'S MISTAKES.
PIKU (TWITCH)
ピク
I WILL BE BRIEF: THE VOLUNTEER FORCE, LED BY THE HERO, WILL REACH HEAVENSKY SOON.
I EVACUATED THE EIGHT SCARVES FROM HERE.
HAVING HUMANS FIGHT HUMANS WOULD BE QUITE INCONVENIENT FOR US.
...OH?

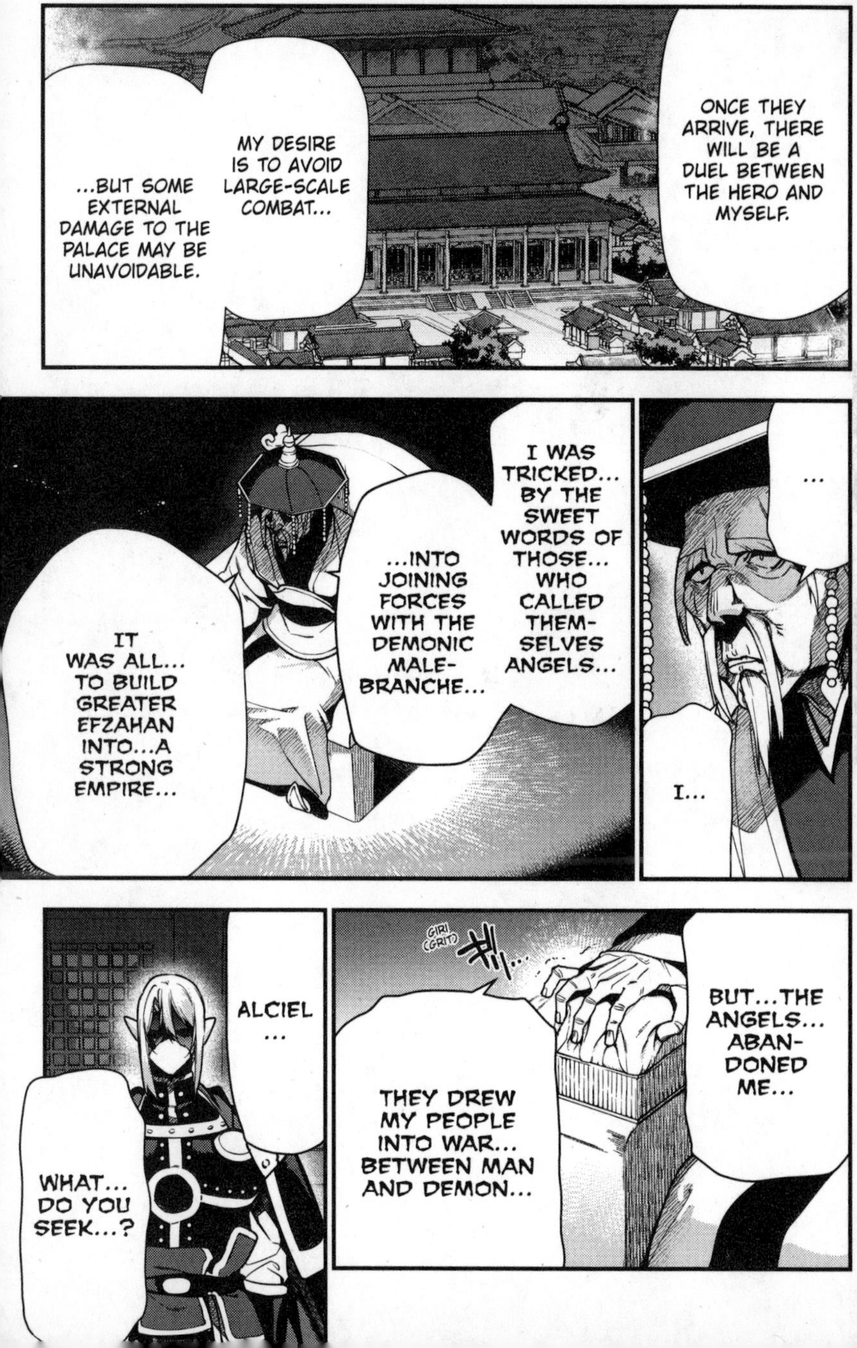
ONCE THEY ARRIVE, THERE WILL BE A DUEL BETWEEN THE HERO AND MYSELF.
MY DESIRE IS TO AVOID LARGE-SCALE COMBAT...
...BUT SOME EXTERNAL DAMAGE TO THE PALACE MAY BE UNAVOIDABLE.
...
I...
I WAS TRICKED... BY THE SWEET WORDS OF THOSE... WHO CALLED THEMSELVES ANGELS...
...INTO JOINING FORCES WITH THE DEMONIC MALEBRANCHE...
IT WAS ALL... TO BUILD GREATER EFZAHAN INTO...A STRONG EMPIRE...
BUT...THE ANGELS... ABANDONED ME...
GIRI (GRIT)
THEY DREW MY PEOPLE INTO WAR... BETWEEN MAN AND DEMON...
ALCIEL...
WHAT... DO YOU SEEK...?

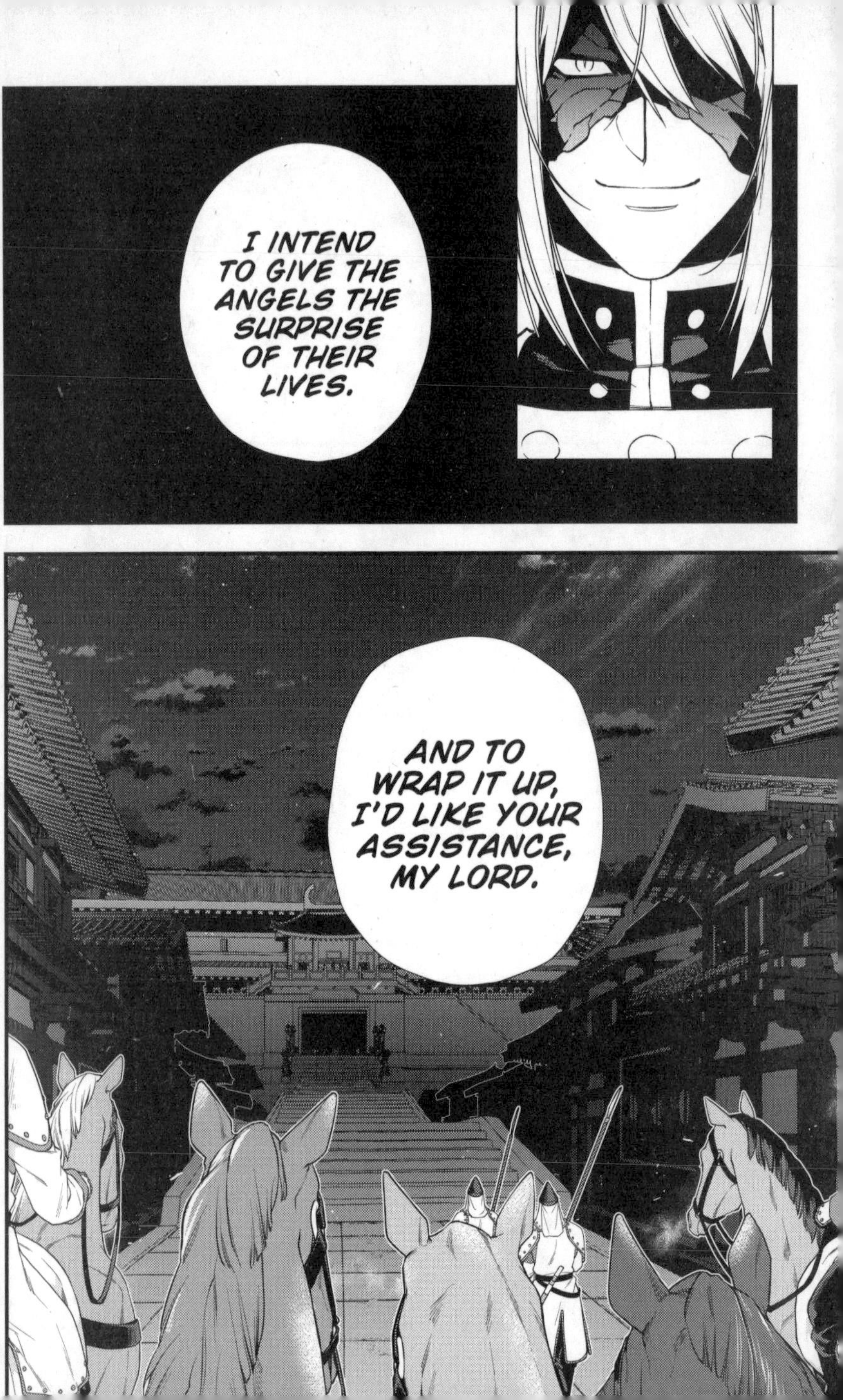
I INTEND TO GIVE THE ANGELS THE SURPRISE OF THEIR LIVES.
AND TO WRAP IT UP, I'D LIKE YOUR ASSISTANCE, MY LORD.

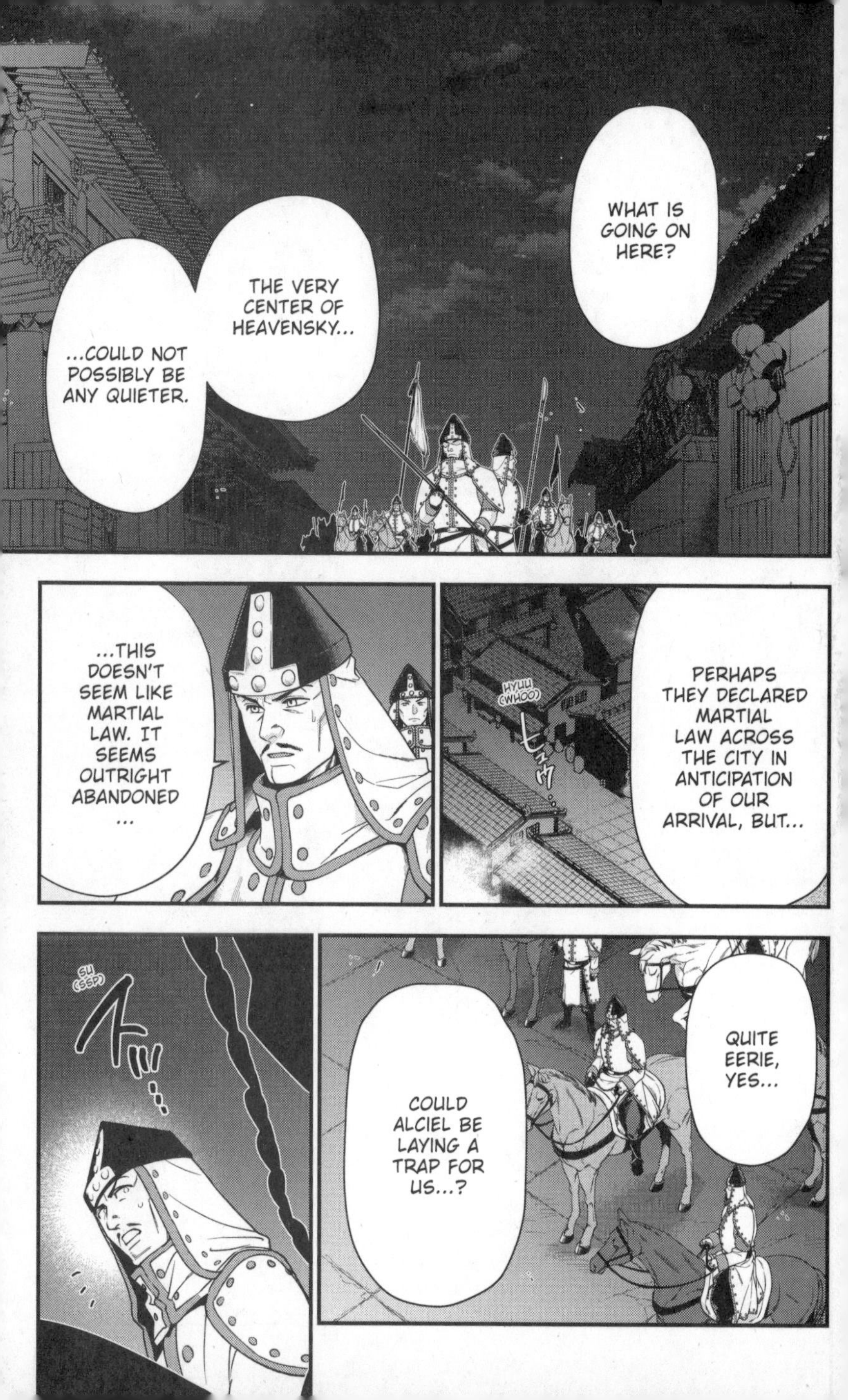
WHAT IS GOING ON HERE?
THE VERY CENTER OF HEAVENSKY...
...COULD NOT POSSIBLY BE ANY QUIETER.
HYUU (WHOO)
PERHAPS THEY DECLARED MARTIAL LAW ACROSS THE CITY IN ANTICIPATION OF OUR ARRIVAL, BUT...
...THIS DOESN'T SEEM LIKE MARTIAL LAW. IT SEEMS OUTRIGHT ABANDONED...
QUITE EERIE, YES...
COULD ALCIEL BE LAYING A TRAP FOR US...?
SU (SSP)
...

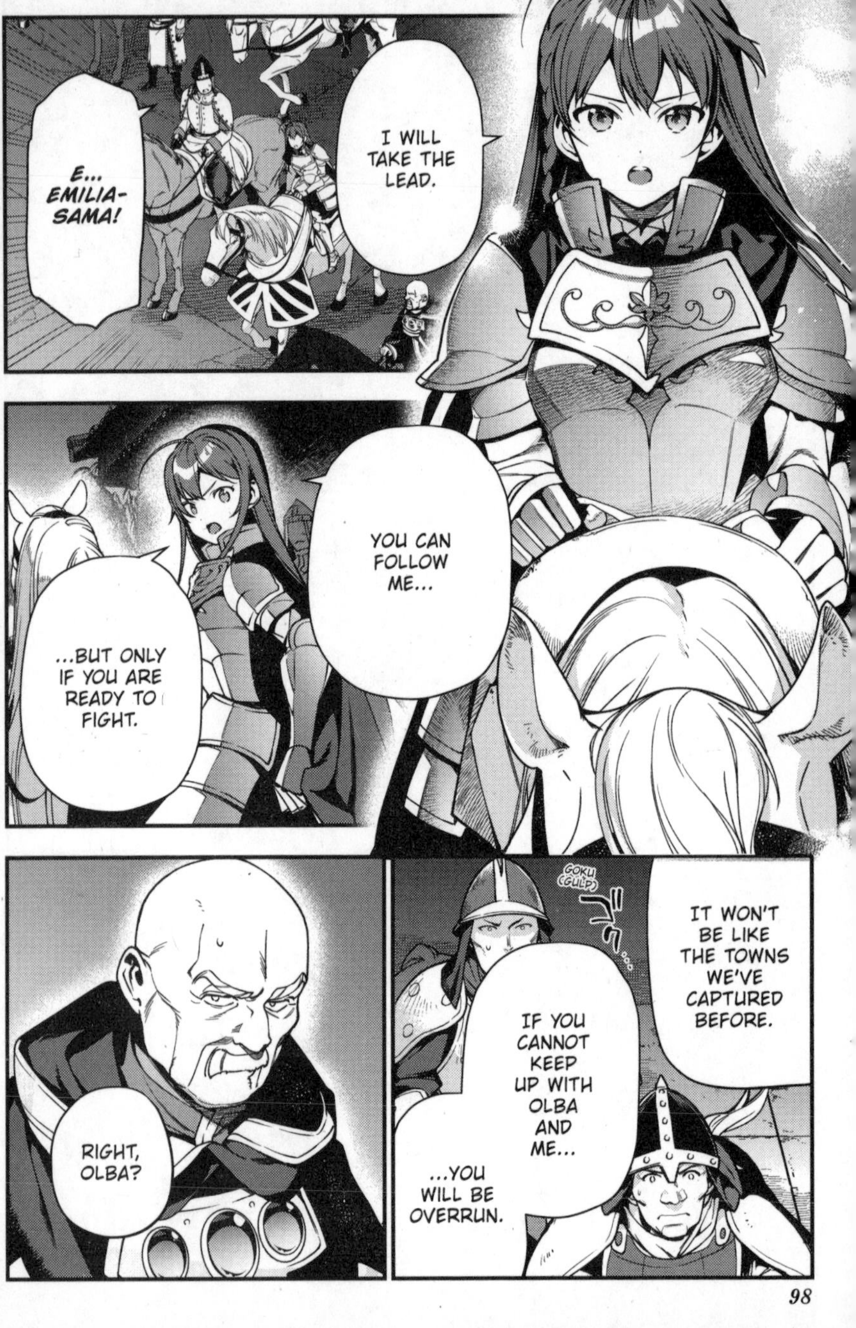
I WILL TAKE THE LEAD.
E... EMILIA-SAMA!
YOU CAN FOLLOW ME...
...BUT ONLY IF YOU ARE READY TO FIGHT.
GOKU (GULP)
IT WON'T BE LIKE THE TOWNS WE'VE CAPTURED BEFORE.
IF YOU CANNOT KEEP UP WITH OLBA AND ME...
...YOU WILL BE OVERRUN.
RIGHT, OLBA?

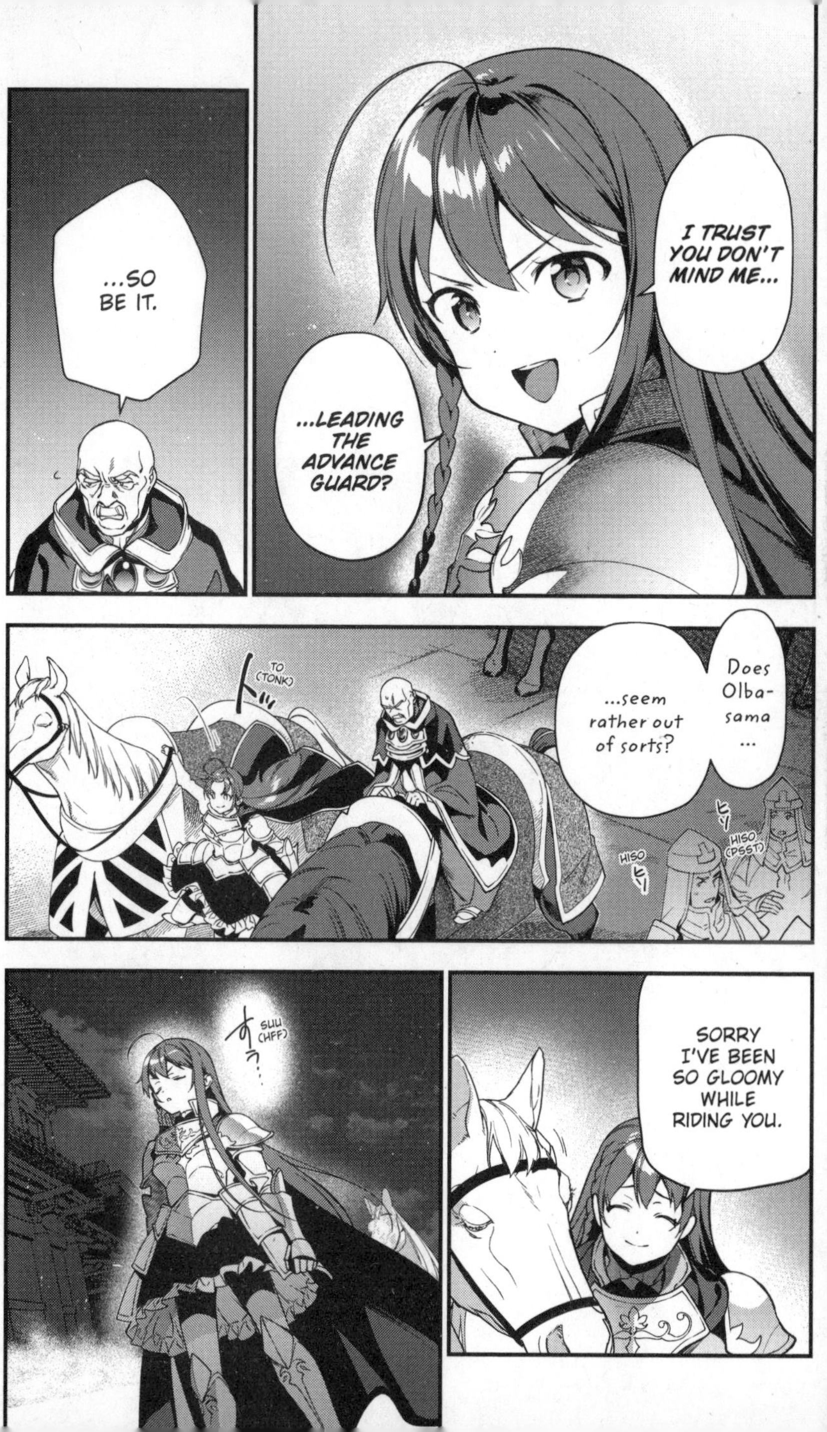
I TRUST YOU DON'T MIND ME...
...LEADING THE ADVANCE GUARD?
...SO BE IT.
Does Olba-sama ...
...seem rather out of sorts?
HISO (PSSST)
HISO
TO (TONK)
SORRY I'VE BEEN SO GLOOMY WHILE RIDING YOU.
SUU (HFF)

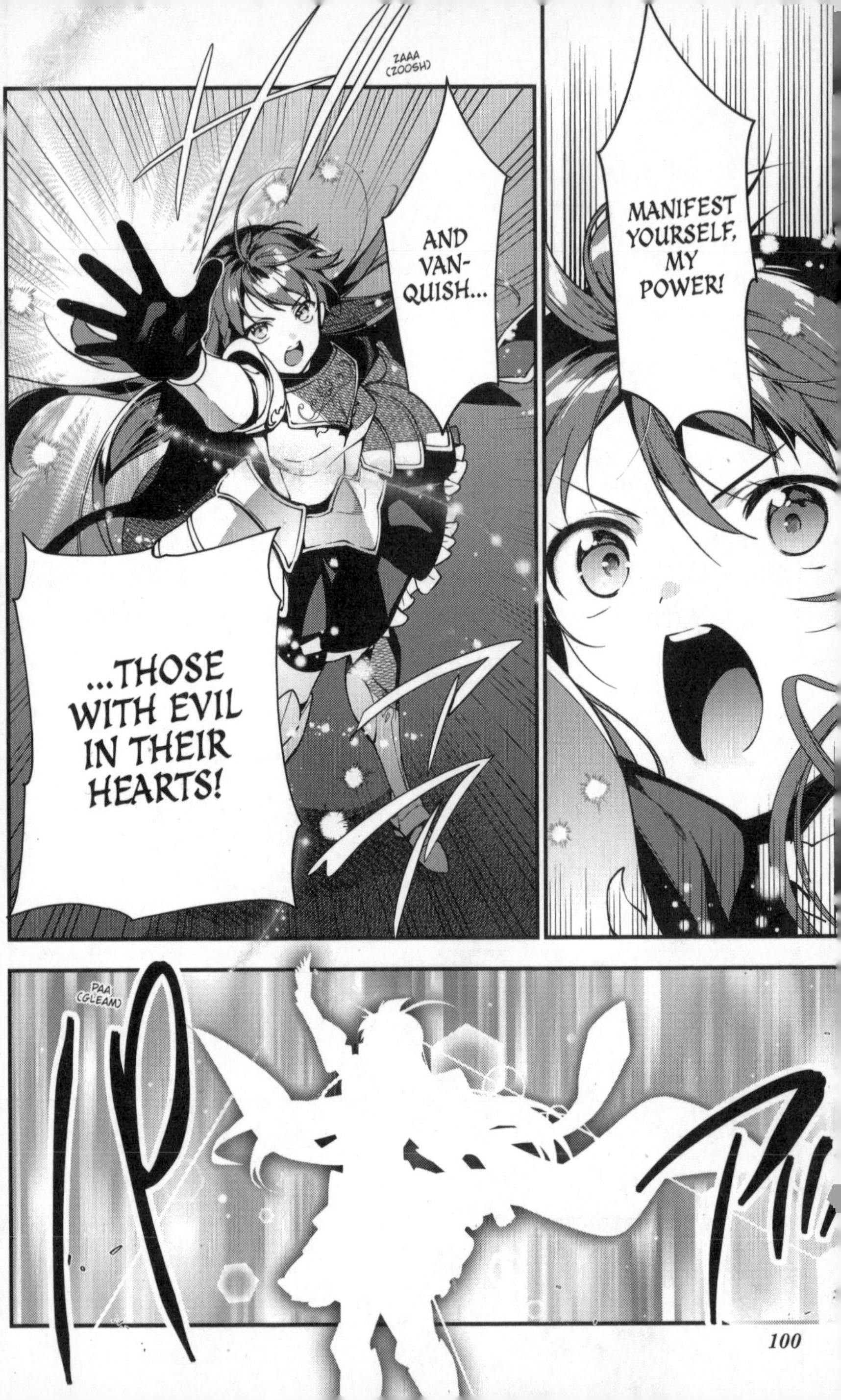
MANIFEST YOURSELF, MY POWER!
ZAAA (ZOOSH)
AND VAN-QUISH...
...THOSE WITH EVIL IN THEIR HEARTS!
PAA (GLEAM)

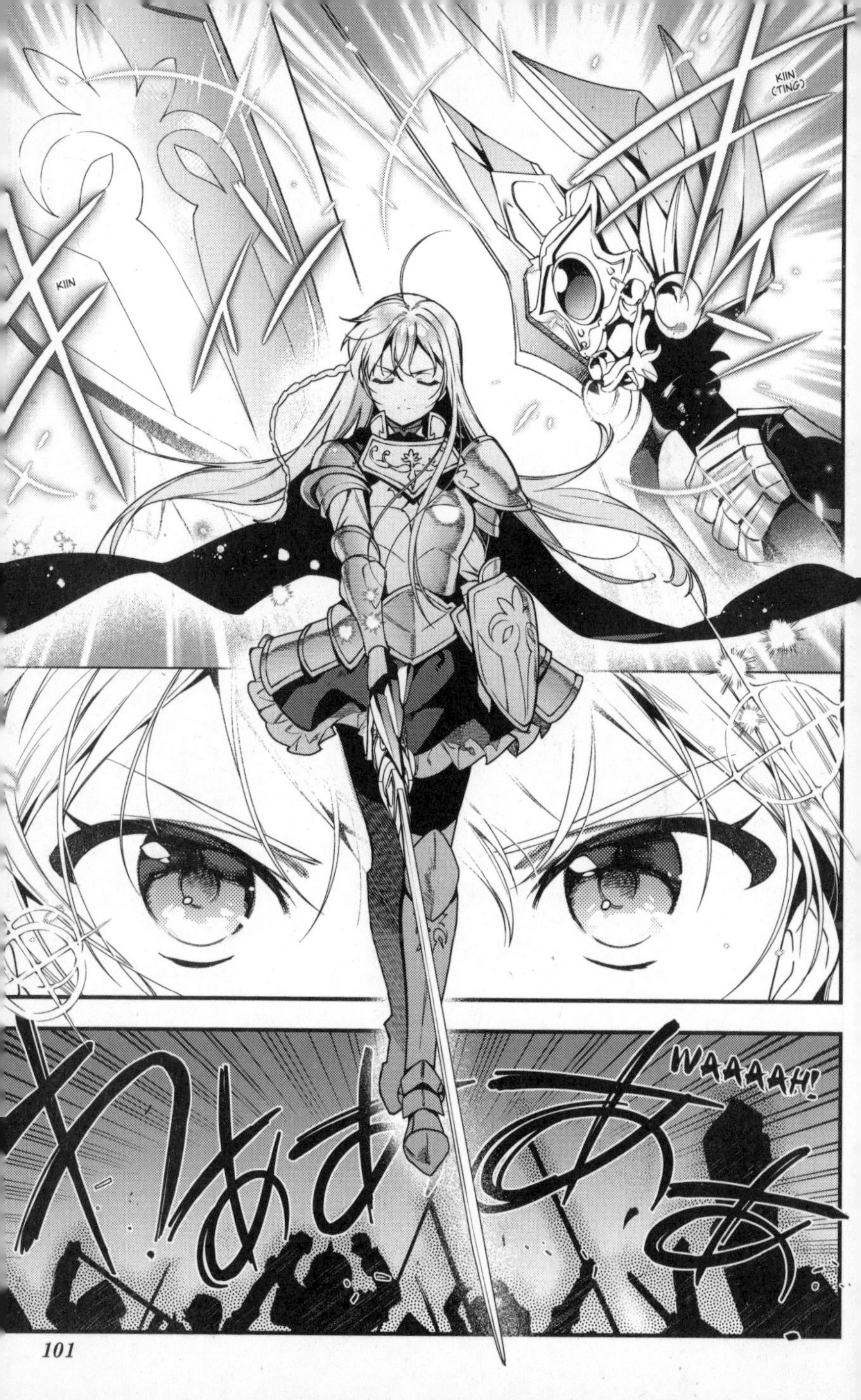
KIIN
(TING)
KIIN
WAAAAH!

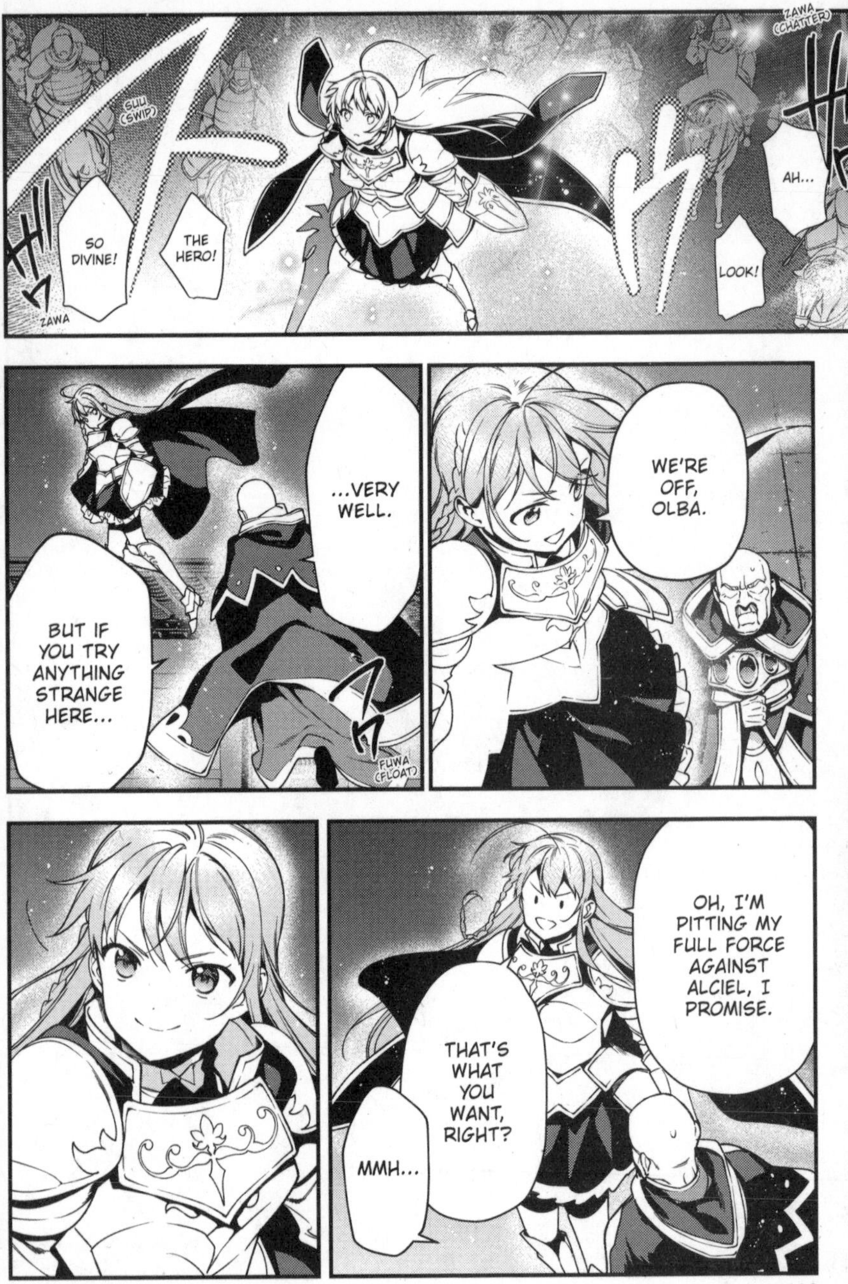
ZAWA (CHATTER)
AH...
LOOK!
THE HERO!
SULI (SWIP)
SO DIVINE!
ZAWA
WE'RE OFF, OLBA.
...VERY WELL.
BUT IF YOU TRY ANYTHING STRANGE HERE...
FUWA (FLOAT)
OH, I'M PITTING MY FULL FORCE AGAINST ALCIEL, I PROMISE.
THAT'S WHAT YOU WANT, RIGHT?
MMH...

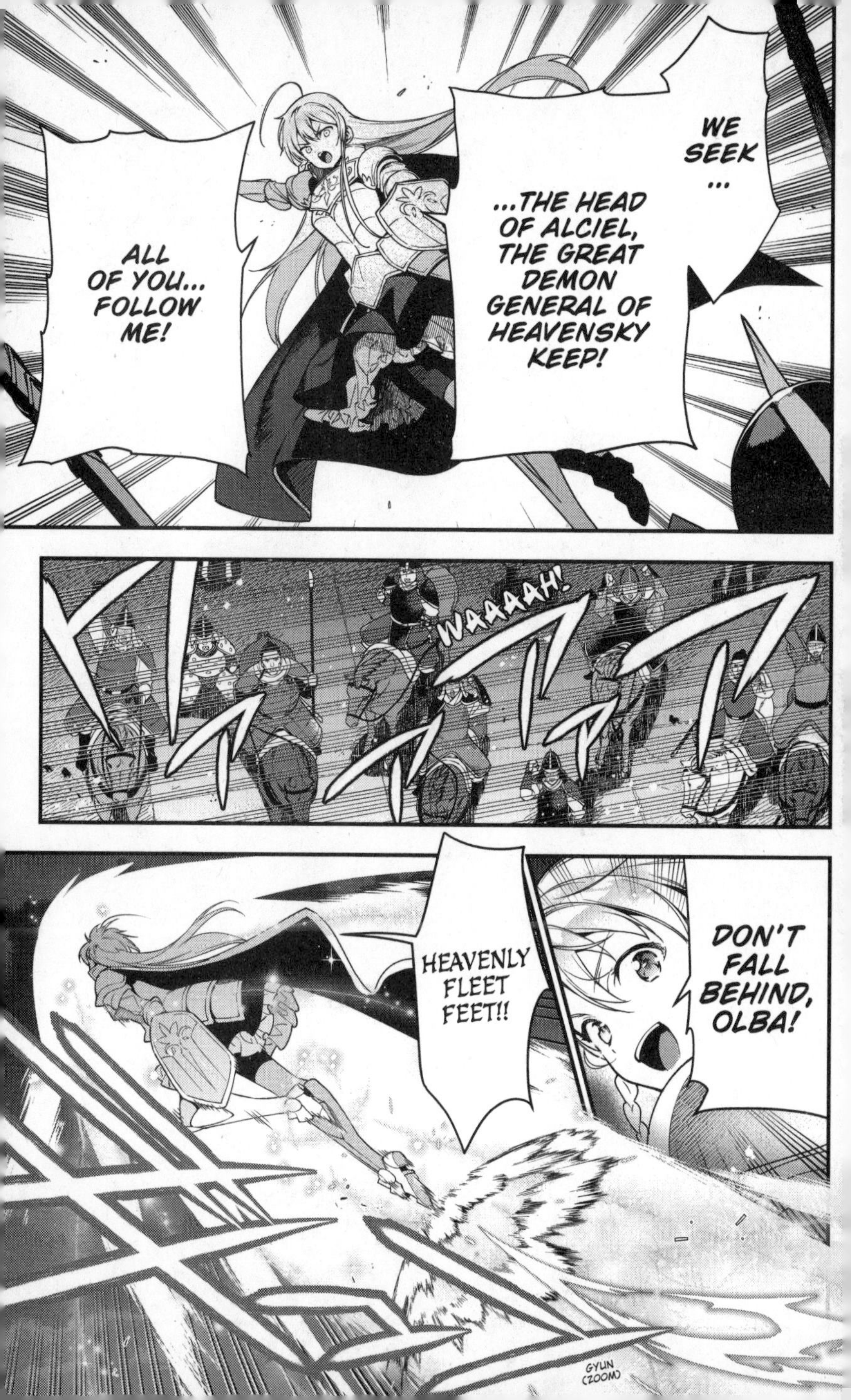
WE SEEK...
...THE HEAD OF ALCIEL, THE GREAT DEMON GENERAL OF HEAVENSKY KEEP!
ALL OF YOU... FOLLOW ME!
WAAAAAH!
DON'T FALL BEHIND, OLBA!
HEAVENLY FLEET FEET!!
GYUN (ZOOM)

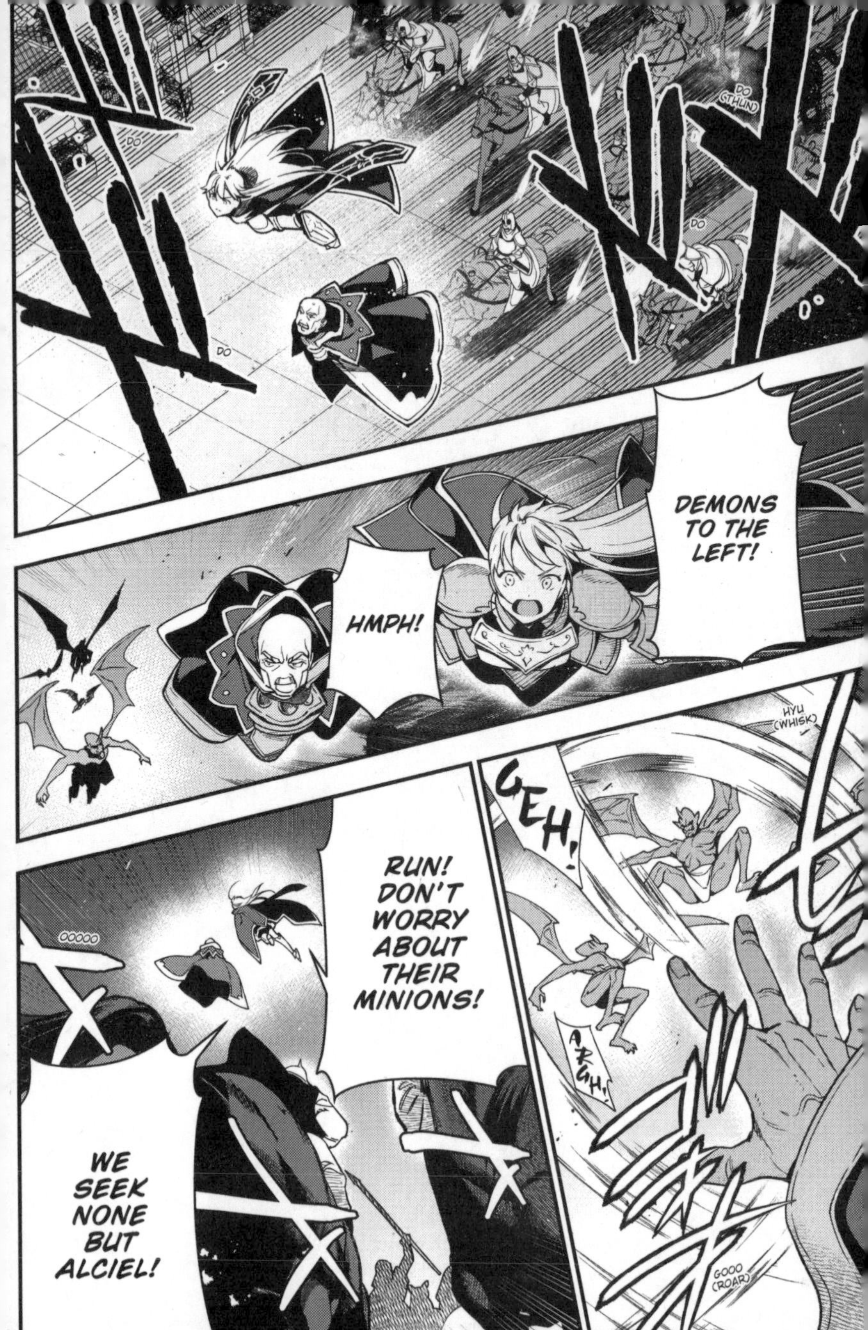
DO (THUD)
DO
DO
DO
DO
DEMONS TO THE LEFT!
HMPH!
HYU (WHISK)
GEH!
ARGH!
GOOO (ROAR)
RUN! DON'T WORRY ABOUT THEIR MINIONS!
OOOOO
WE SEEK NONE BUT ALCIEL!

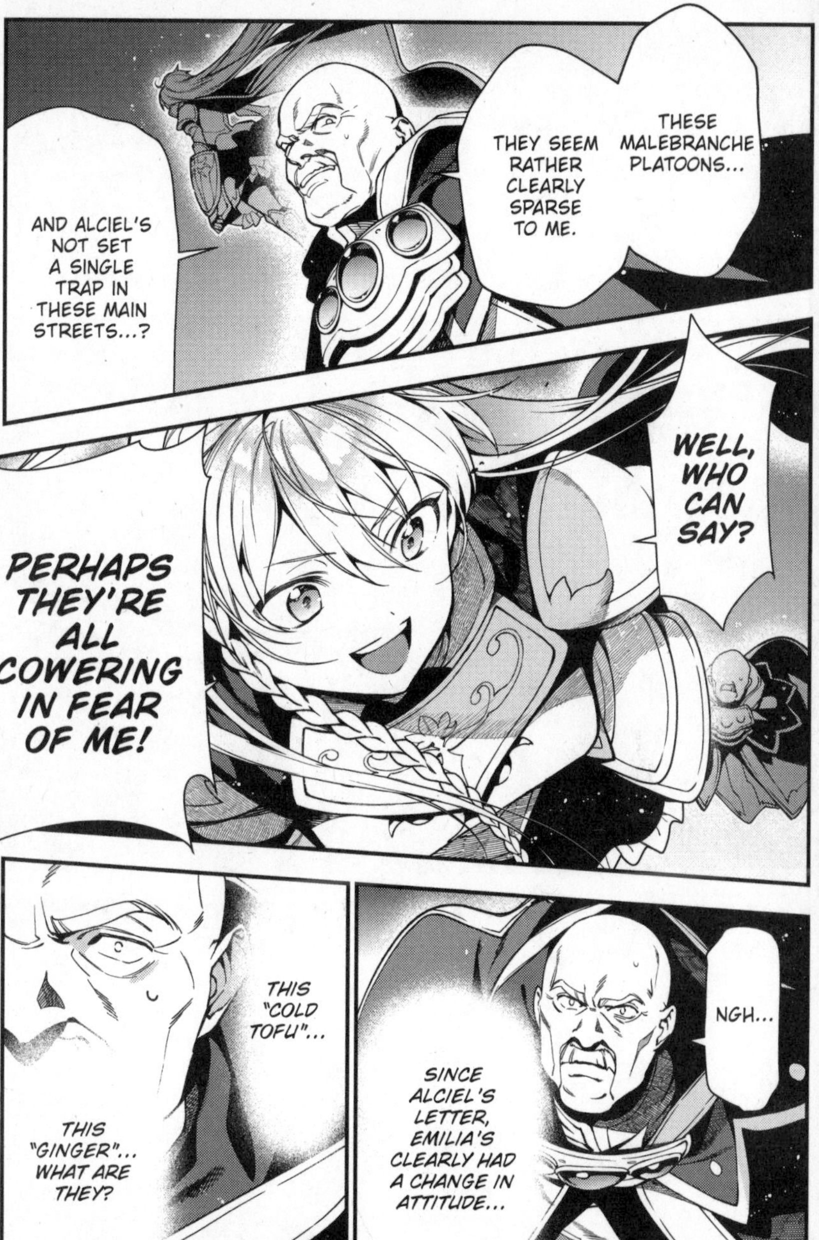
THESE MALEBRANCHE PLATOONS...
THEY SEEM RATHER CLEARLY SPARSE TO ME.
AND ALCIEL'S NOT SET A SINGLE TRAP IN THESE MAIN STREETS...?
WELL, WHO CAN SAY?
PERHAPS THEY'RE ALL COWERING IN FEAR OF ME!
NGH...
SINCE ALCIEL'S LETTER, EMILIA'S CLEARLY HAD A CHANGE IN ATTITUDE...
THIS "COLD TOFU"...
THIS "GINGER"... WHAT ARE THEY?

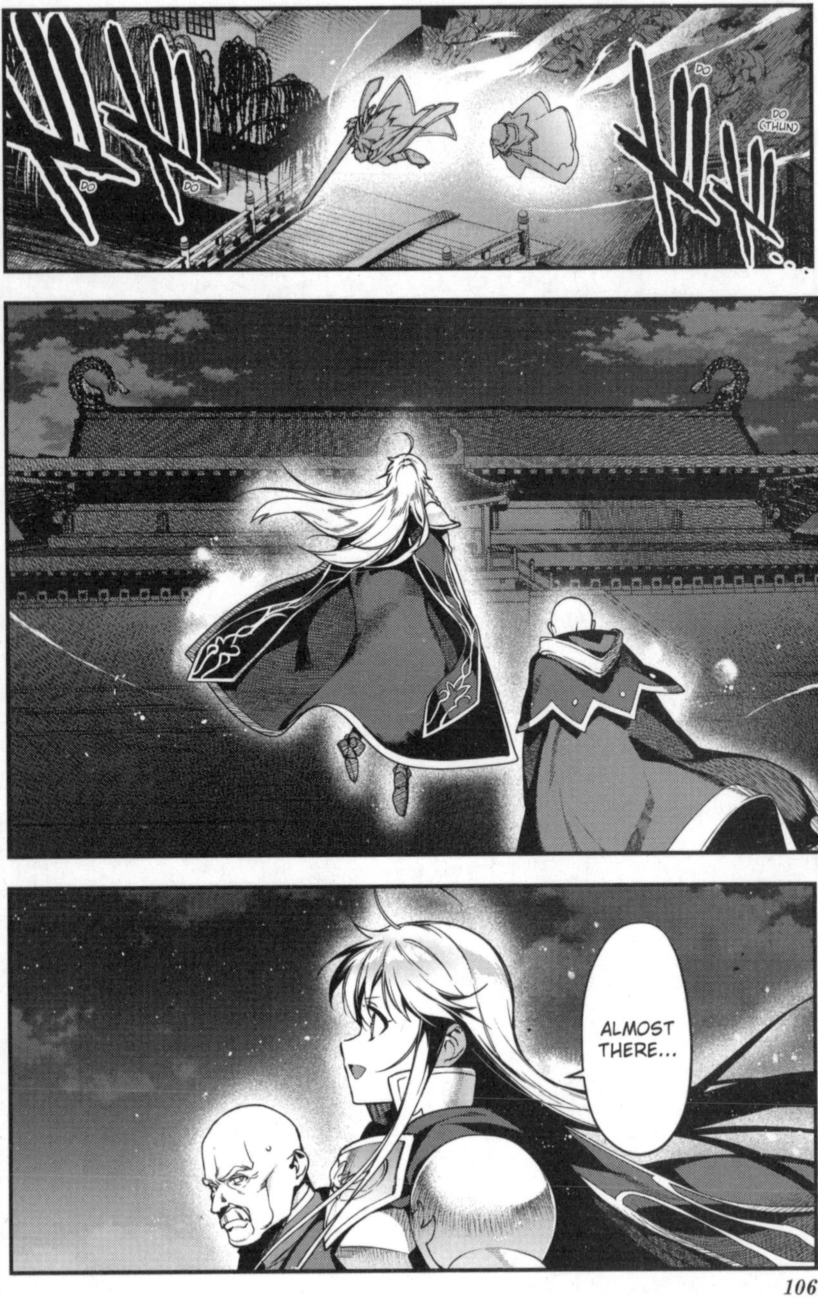
DO
DO (THUN)
DO
DO
ALMOST THERE...

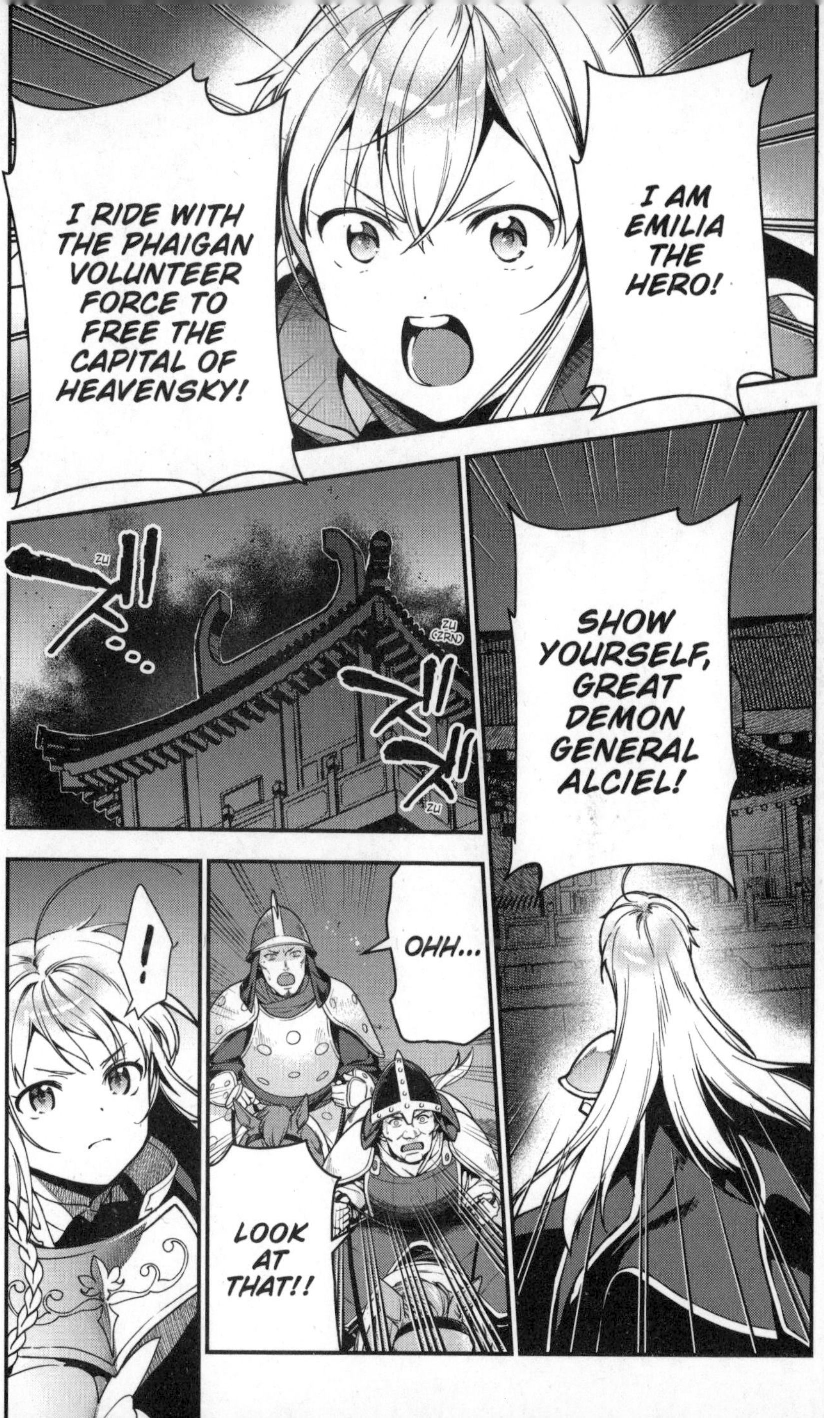
I AM EMILIA THE HERO!
I RIDE WITH THE PHAIGAN VOLUNTEER FORCE TO FREE THE CAPITAL OF HEAVENSKY!
SHOW YOURSELF, GREAT DEMON GENERAL ALCIEL!
ZU (ZRN)
ZU
ZU
OHH...
LOOK AT THAT!!
!

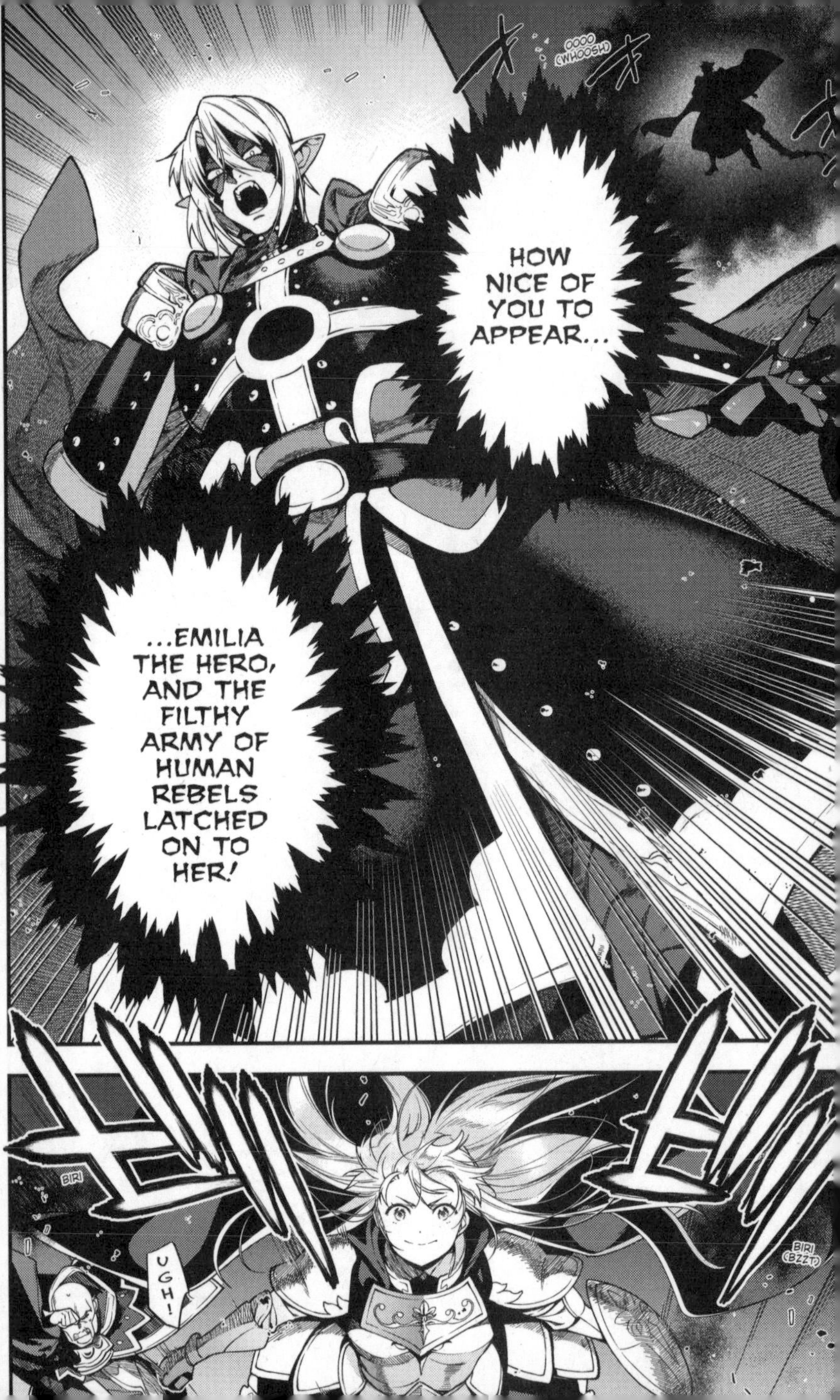
OOOO (WHOOSH)
HOW NICE OF YOU TO APPEAR...
...EMILIA THE HERO, AND THE FILTHY ARMY OF HUMAN REBELS LATCHED ON TO HER!
BIRI (BZZT)
BIRI
UGH!

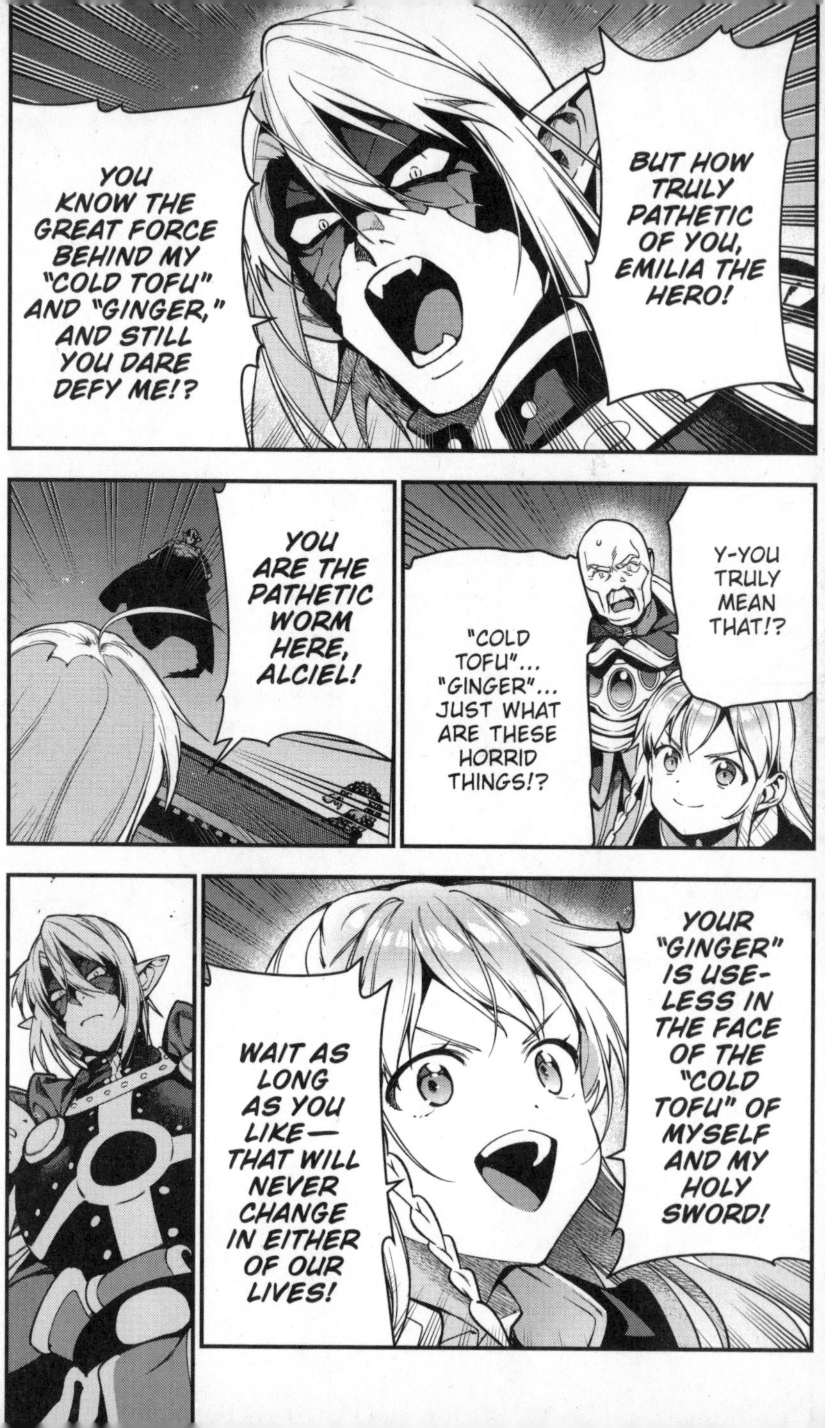
BUT HOW TRULY PATHETIC OF YOU, EMILIA THE HERO!
YOU KNOW THE GREAT FORCE BEHIND MY "COLD TOFU" AND "GINGER," AND STILL YOU DARE DEFY ME!?
Y-YOU TRULY MEAN THAT!?
"COLD TOFU"... "GINGER"... JUST WHAT ARE THESE HORRID THINGS!?
YOU ARE THE PATHETIC WORM HERE, ALCIEL!
YOUR "GINGER" IS USE-LESS IN THE FACE OF THE "COLD TOFU" OF MYSELF AND MY HOLY SWORD!
WAIT AS LONG AS YOU LIKE—THAT WILL NEVER CHANGE IN EITHER OF OUR LIVES!

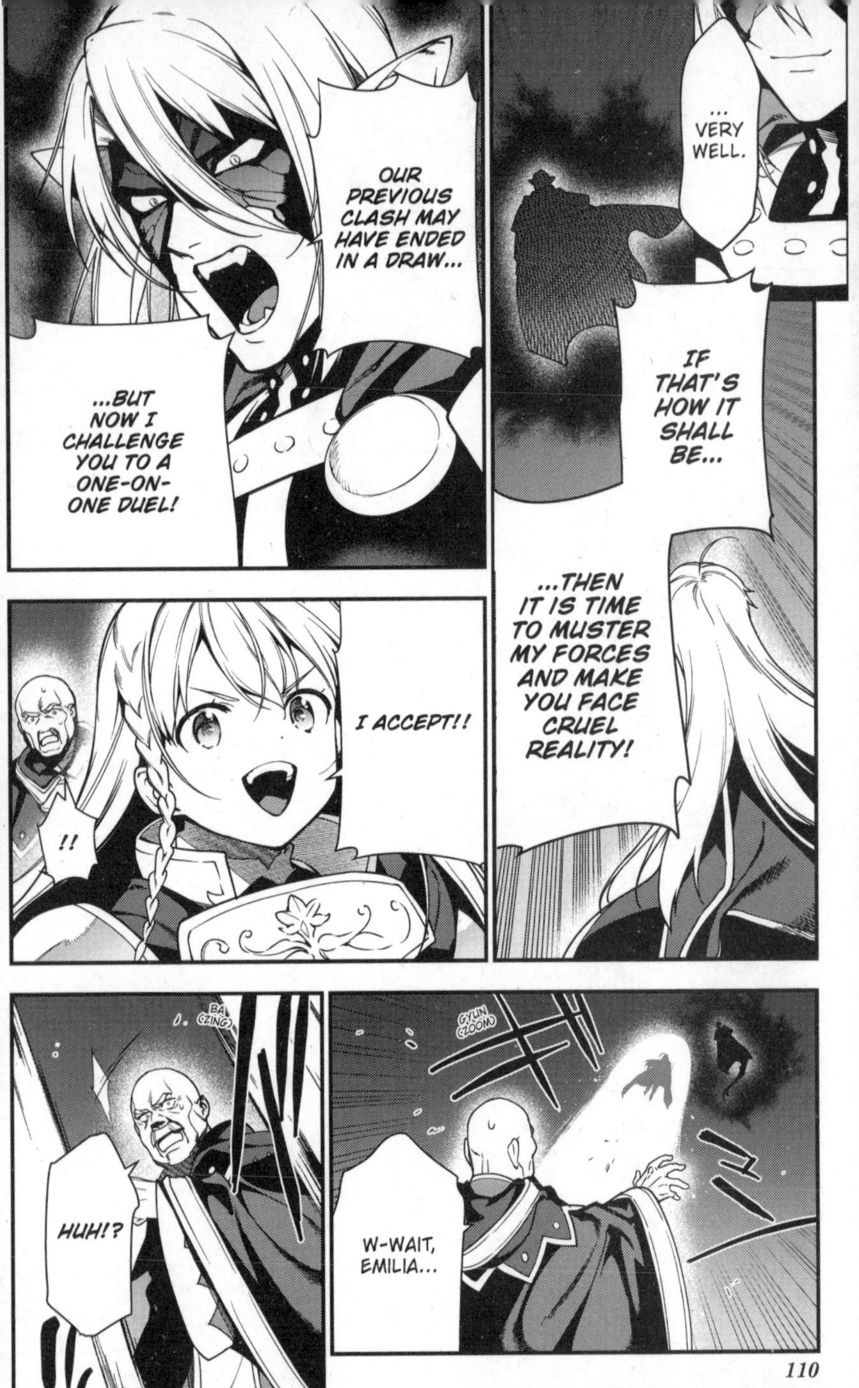
...
VERY WELL.
IF THAT'S HOW IT SHALL BE...
...THEN IT IS TIME TO MUSTER MY FORCES AND MAKE YOU FACE CRUEL REALITY!
OUR PREVIOUS CLASH MAY HAVE ENDED IN A DRAW...
...BUT NOW I CHALLENGE YOU TO A ONE-ON-ONE DUEL!
I ACCEPT!!
!!
GYUN (ZOOM)
W-WAIT, EMILIA...
BA (ZING)
HUH!?

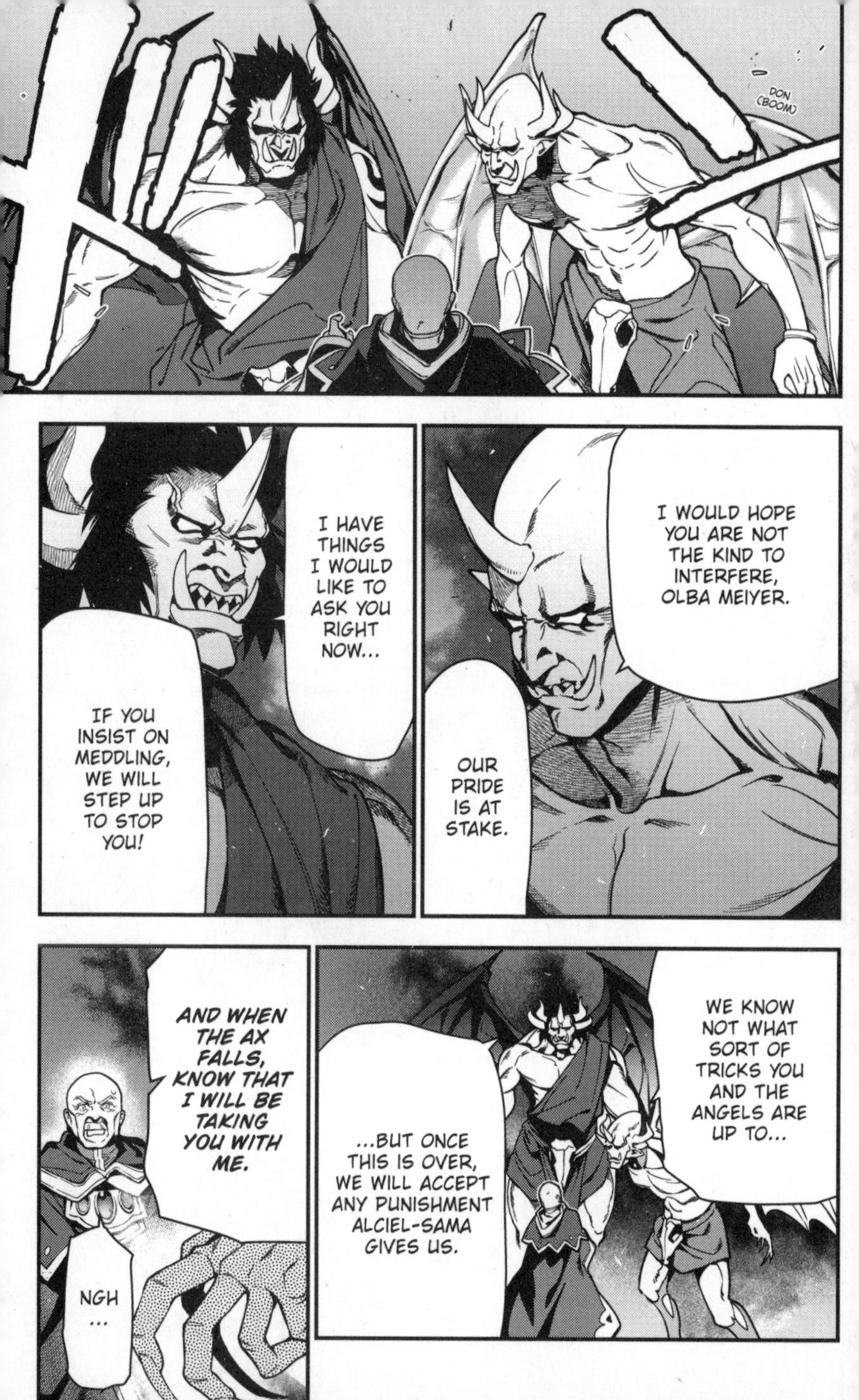
DON (BOOM)
I WOULD HOPE YOU ARE NOT THE KIND TO INTERFERE, OLBA MEIYER.
OUR PRIDE IS AT STAKE.
I HAVE THINGS I WOULD LIKE TO ASK YOU RIGHT NOW...
IF YOU INSIST ON MEDDLING, WE WILL STEP UP TO STOP YOU!
WE KNOW NOT WHAT SORT OF TRICKS YOU AND THE ANGELS ARE UP TO...
...BUT ONCE THIS IS OVER, WE WILL ACCEPT ANY PUNISHMENT ALCIEL-SAMA GIVES US.
AND WHEN THE AX FALLS, KNOW THAT I WILL BE TAKING YOU WITH ME.
NGH ...

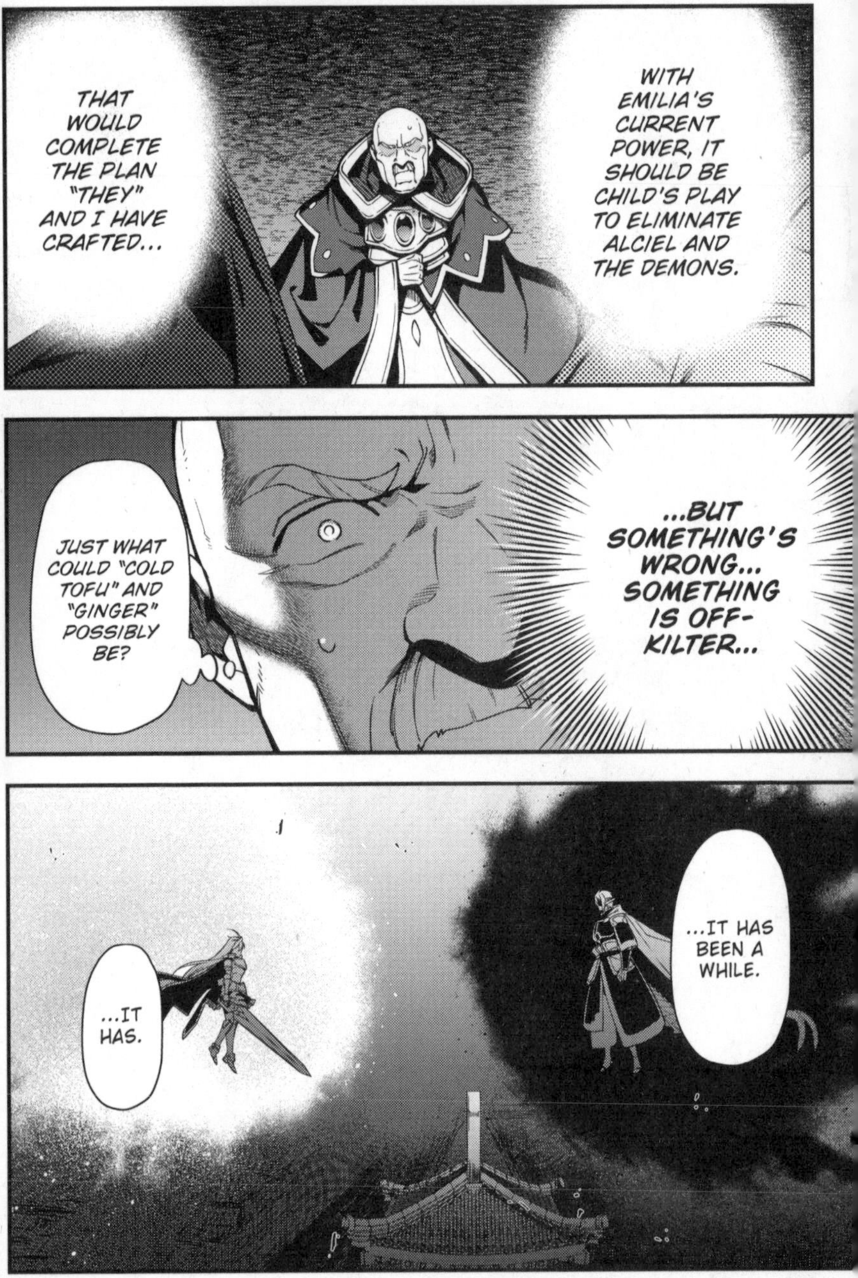
WITH EMILIA'S CURRENT POWER, IT SHOULD BE CHILD'S PLAY TO ELIMINATE ALCIEL AND THE DEMONS.
THAT WOULD COMPLETE THE PLAN "THEY" AND I HAVE CRAFTED...
...BUT SOMETHING'S WRONG... SOMETHING IS OFF-KILTER...
JUST WHAT COULD "COLD TOFU" AND "GINGER" POSSIBLY BE?
...IT HAS BEEN A WHILE.
...IT HAS.

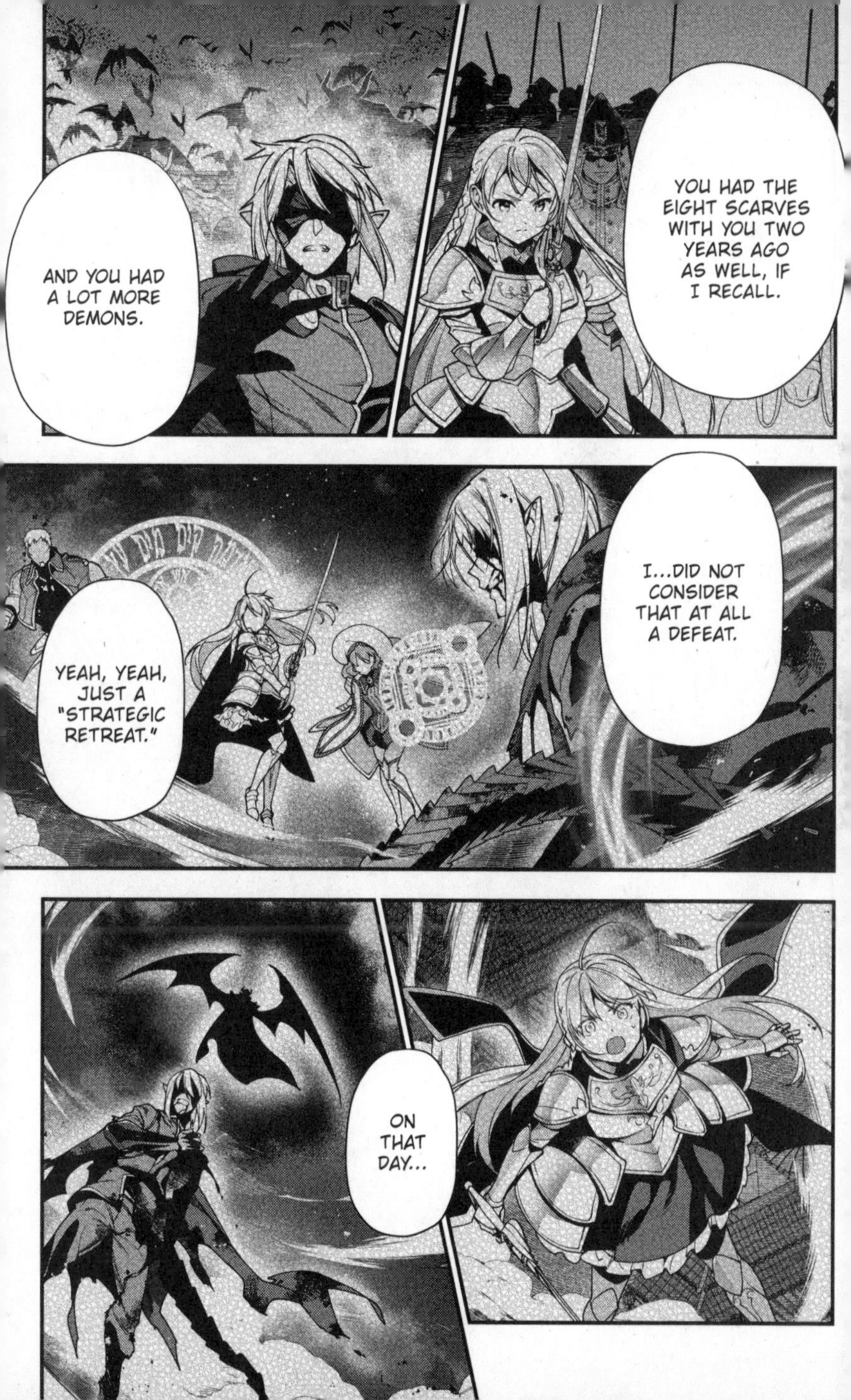
YOU HAD THE EIGHT SCARVES WITH YOU TWO YEARS AGO AS WELL, IF I RECALL.
AND YOU HAD A LOT MORE DEMONS.
I...DID NOT CONSIDER THAT AT ALL A DEFEAT.
YEAH, YEAH, JUST A "STRATEGIC RETREAT."
ON THAT DAY...

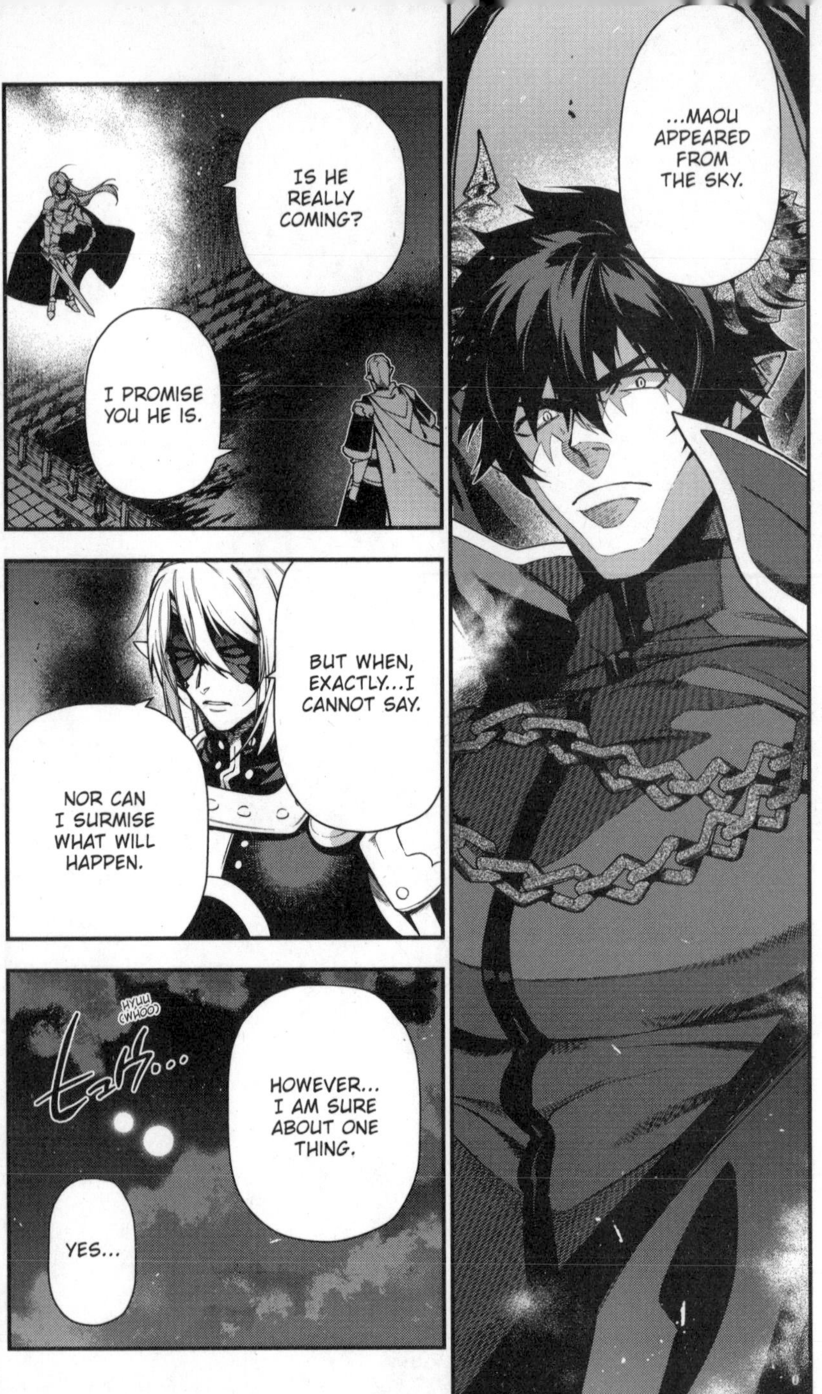
...MAOU APPEARED FROM THE SKY.
IS HE REALLY COMING?
I PROMISE YOU HE IS.
BUT WHEN, EXACTLY...I CANNOT SAY.
NOR CAN I SURMISE WHAT WILL HAPPEN.
HYUU (WHOO)
HOWEVER... I AM SURE ABOUT ONE THING.
YES...

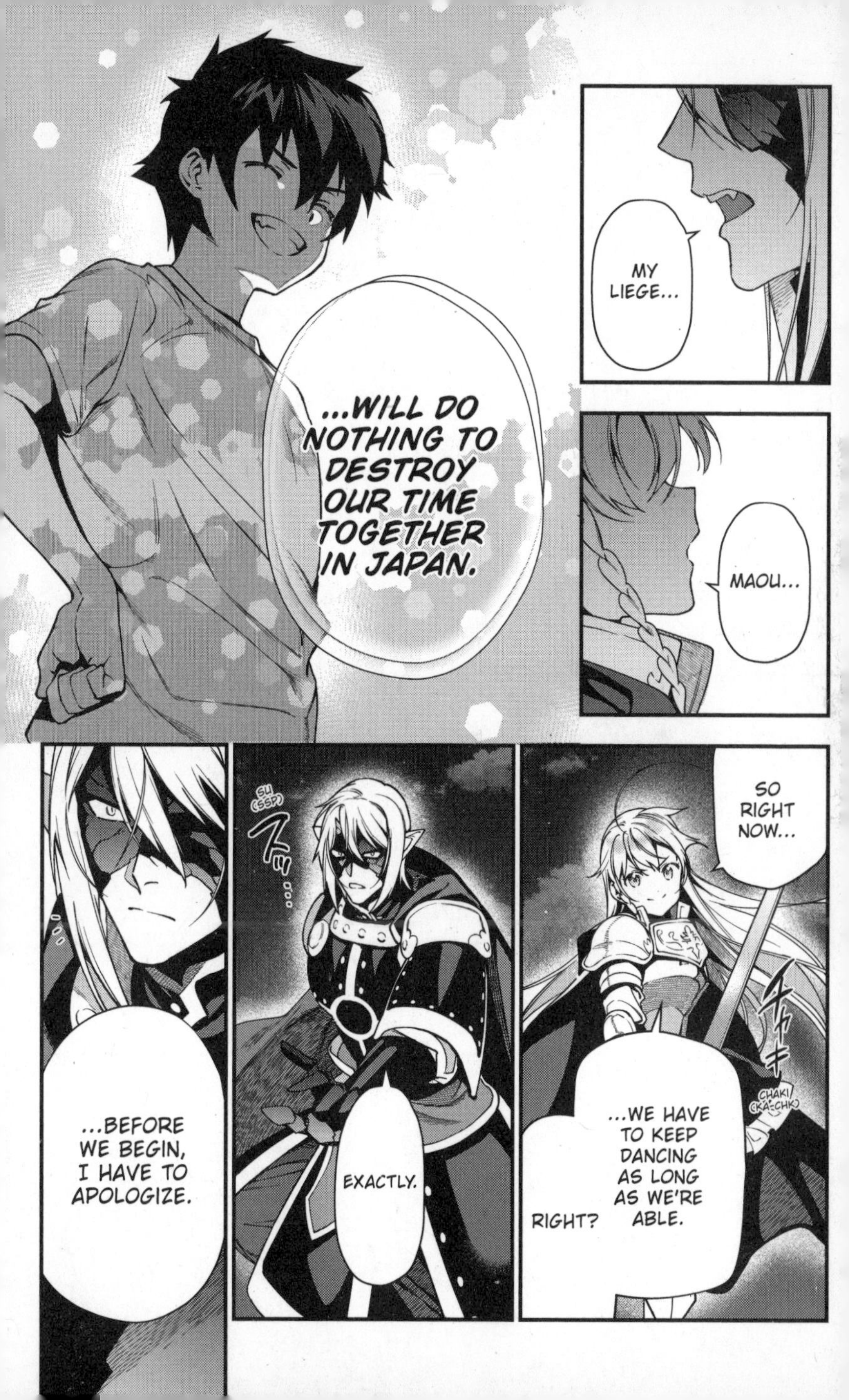
MY LIEGE...
MAOU...
...WILL DO NOTHING TO DESTROY OUR TIME TOGETHER IN JAPAN.
SO RIGHT NOW...
CHAKI (KA-CHK)
...WE HAVE TO KEEP DANCING AS LONG AS WE'RE ABLE.
RIGHT?
SU (SSP)
EXACTLY.
...BEFORE WE BEGIN, I HAVE TO APOLOGIZE.

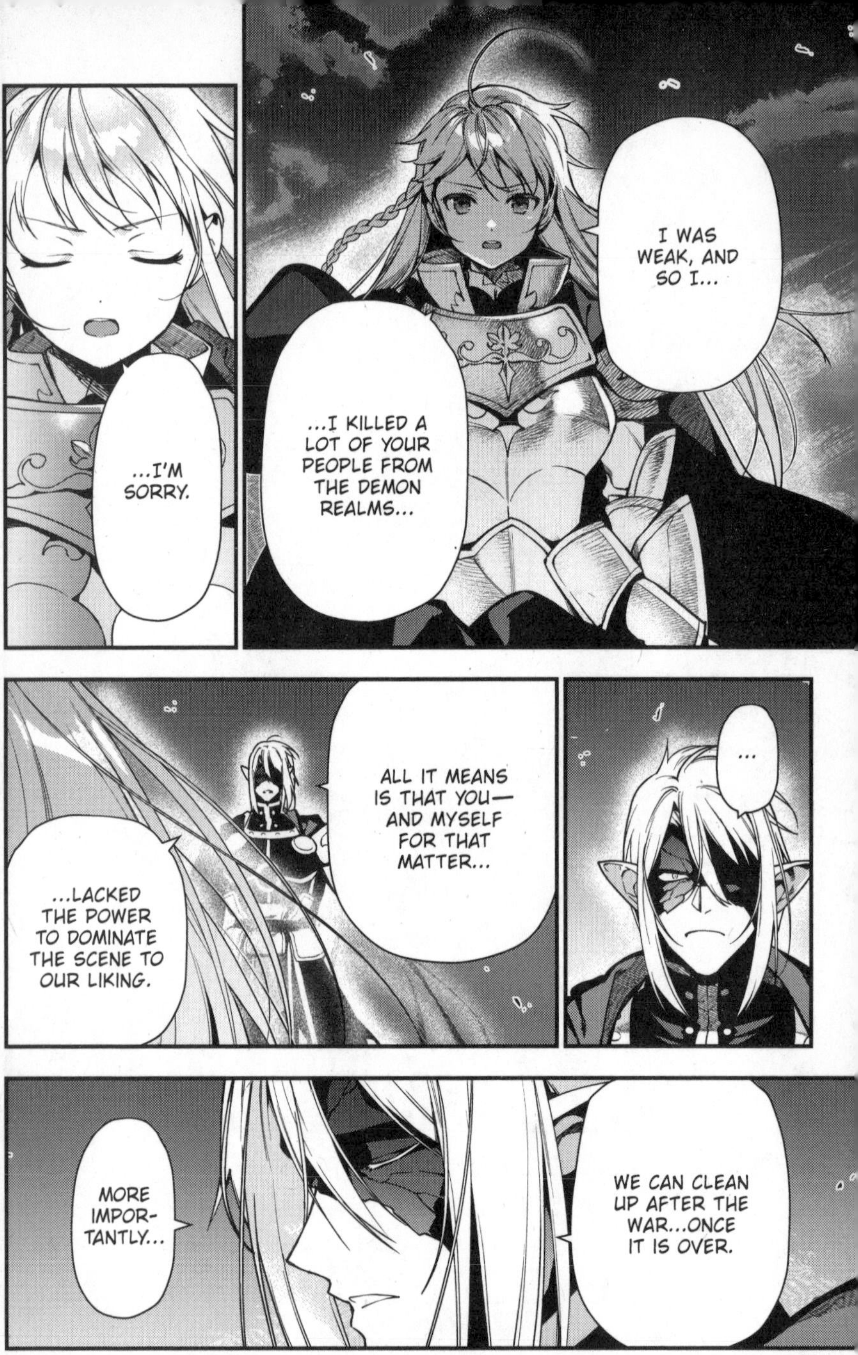
I WAS WEAK, AND SO I...
...I KILLED A LOT OF YOUR PEOPLE FROM THE DEMON REALMS...
...I'M SORRY.
...
ALL IT MEANS IS THAT YOU— AND MYSELF FOR THAT MATTER...
...LACKED THE POWER TO DOMINATE THE SCENE TO OUR LIKING.
WE CAN CLEAN UP AFTER THE WAR...ONCE IT IS OVER.
MORE IMPOR-TANTLY...

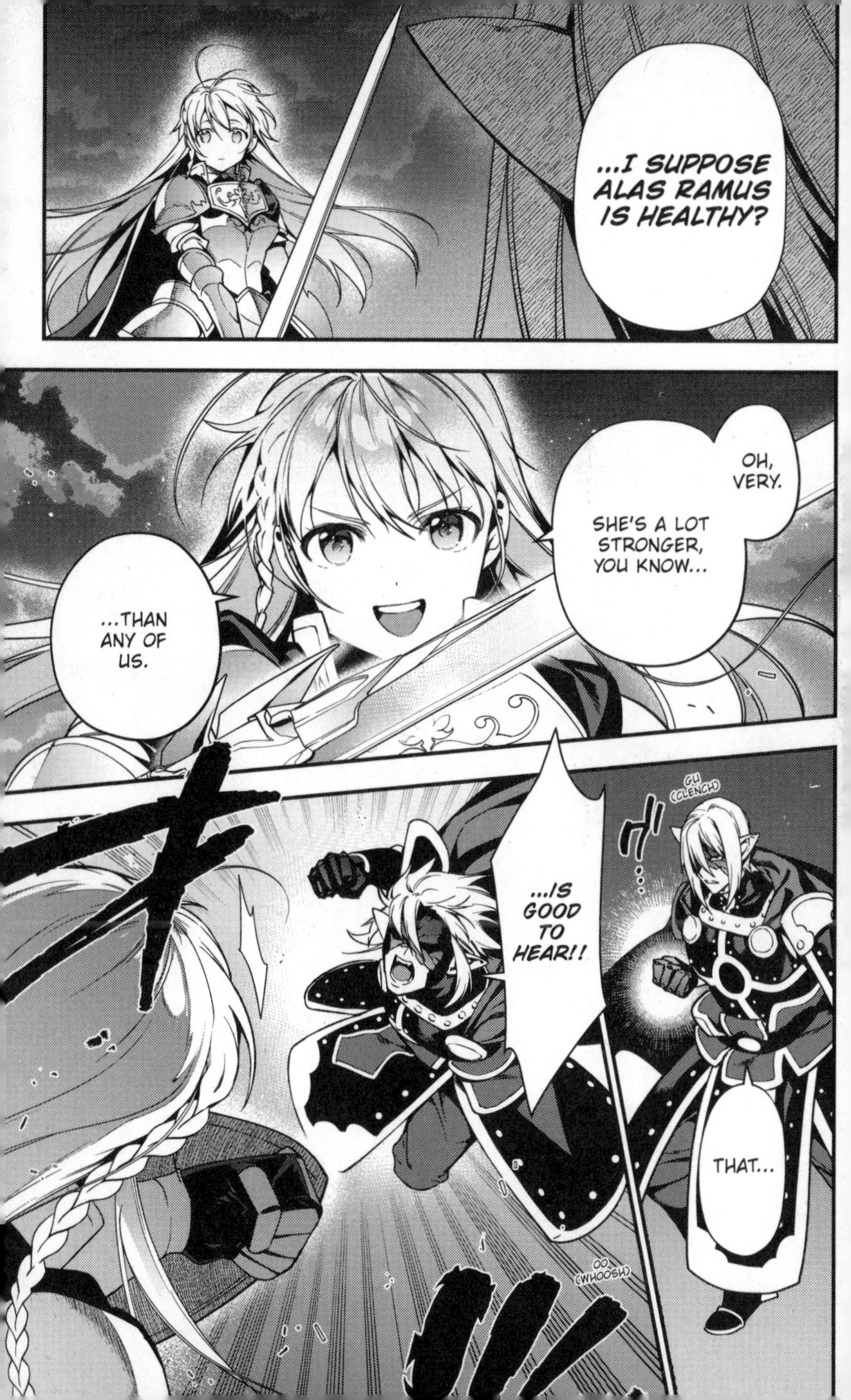
...I SUPPOSE ALAS RAMUS IS HEALTHY?
OH, VERY.
SHE'S A LOT STRONGER, YOU KNOW...
...THAN ANY OF US.
GU (CLENCH)
THAT...
...IS GOOD TO HEAR!!
OO (WHOOSH)

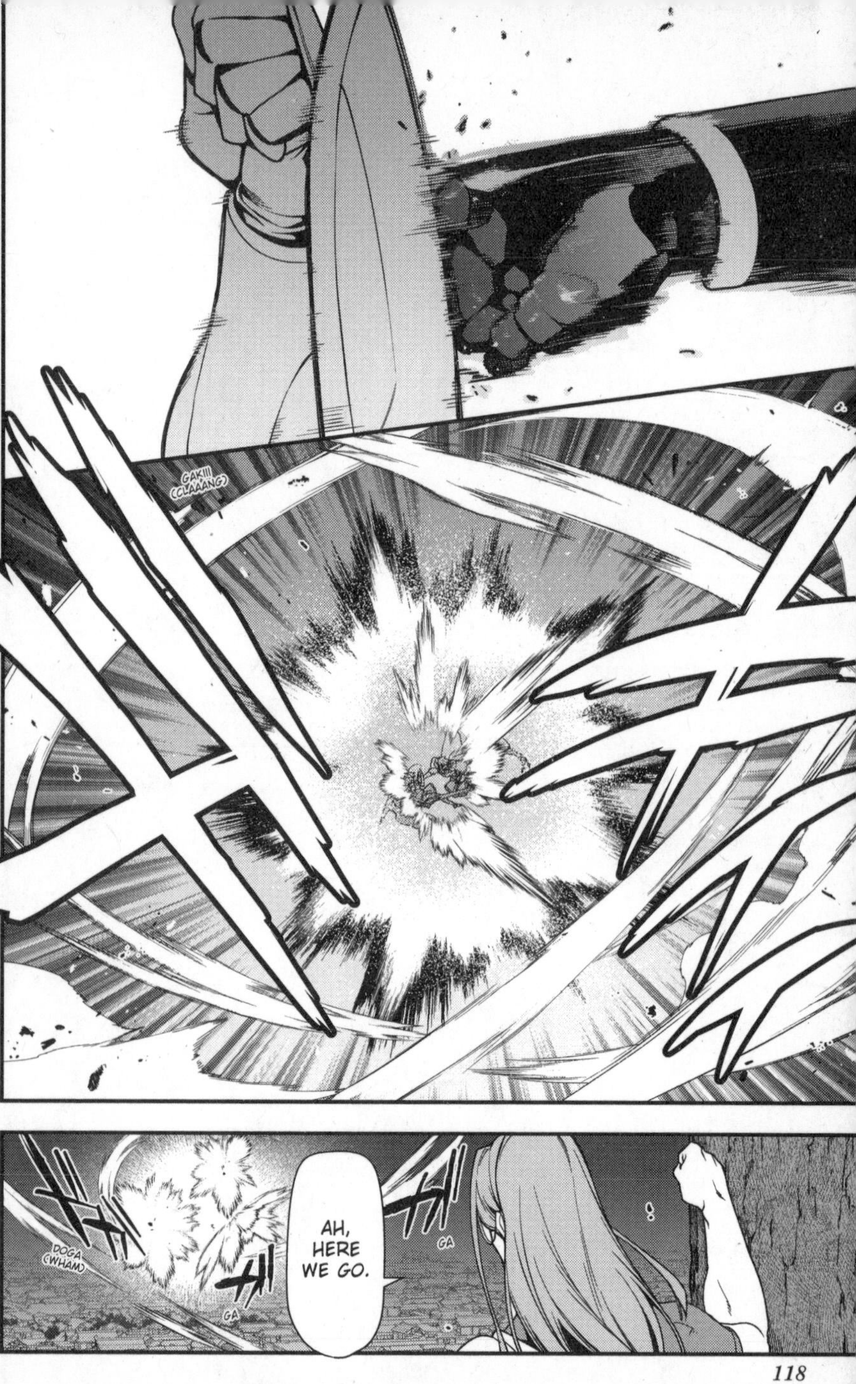
GAKIII
(CLAAANG)
AH, HERE WE GO.
GA
DOGA
(WHAM)
GA

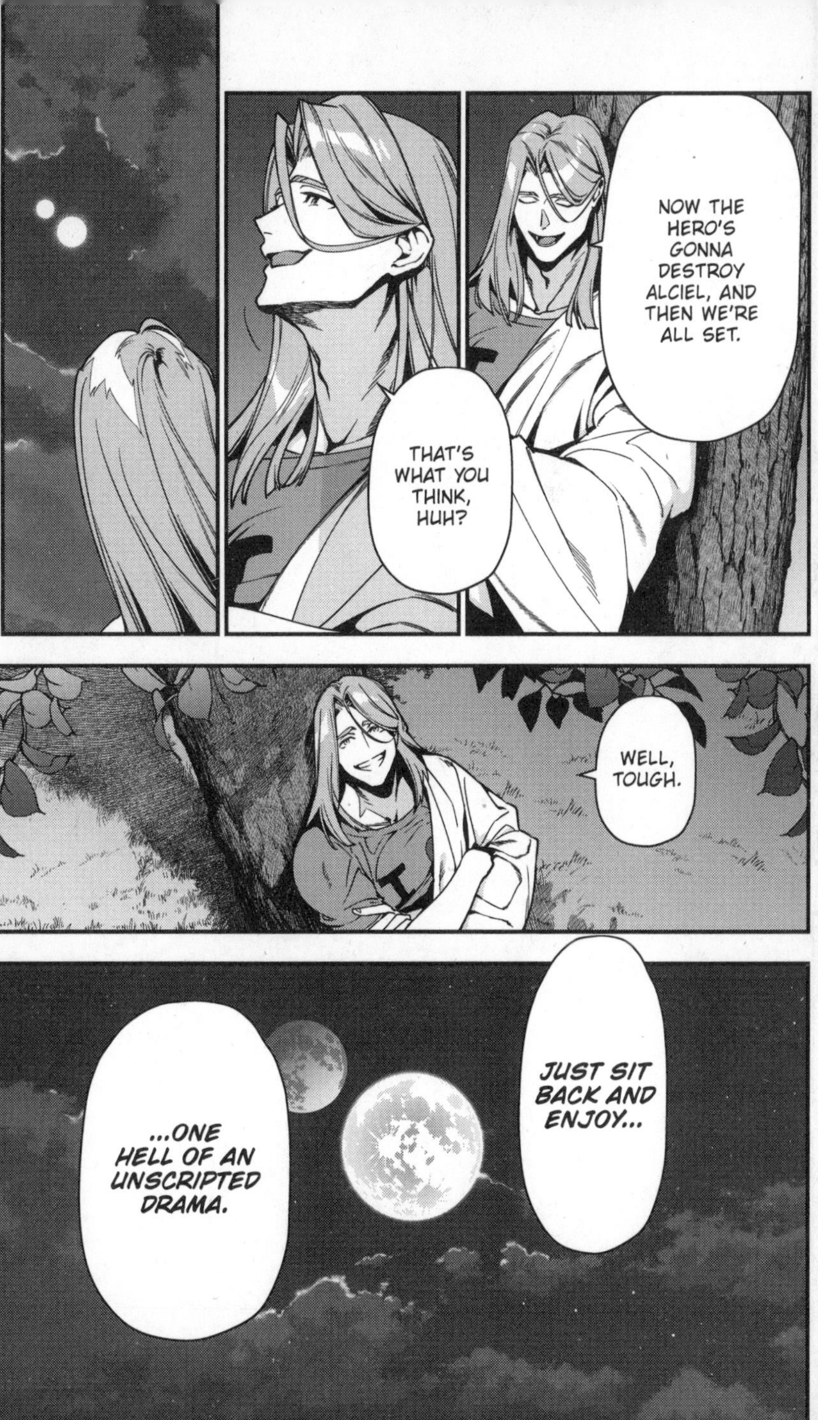
NOW THE HERO'S GONNA DESTROY ALCIEL, AND THEN WE'RE ALL SET.
THAT'S WHAT YOU THINK, HUH?
WELL, TOUGH.
JUST SIT BACK AND ENJOY...
...ONE HELL OF AN UNSCRIPTED DRAMA.

THE DEVIL IS A PART-TIMER!

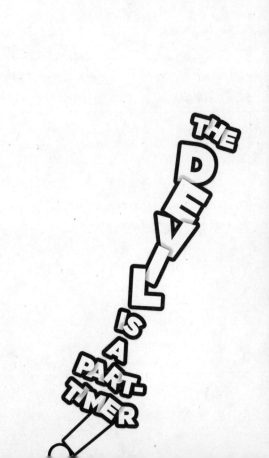

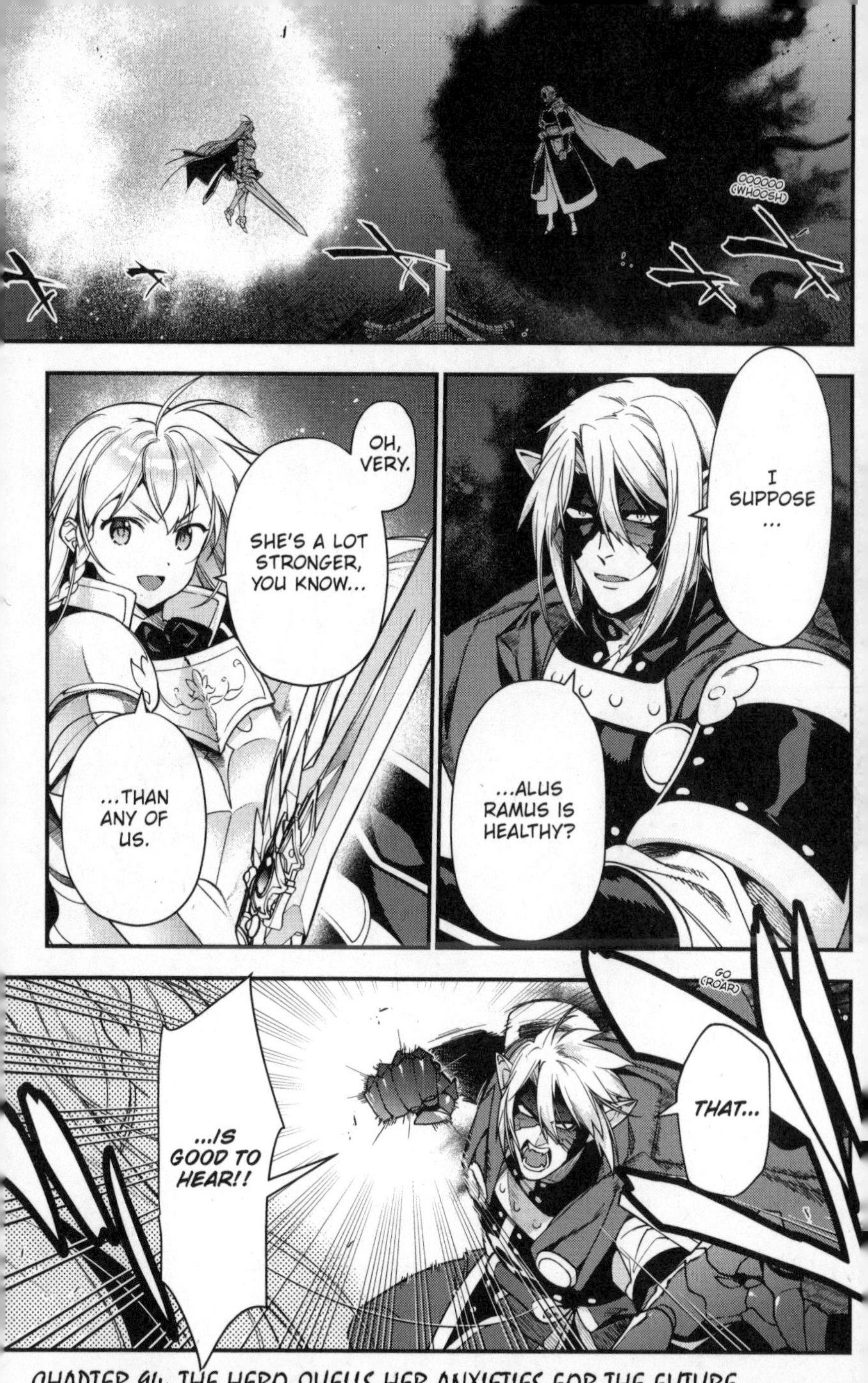
OOOOOO (WHOOSH)
I SUPPOSE...
...ALUS RAMUS IS HEALTHY?
OH, VERY.
SHE'S A LOT STRONGER, YOU KNOW...
...THAN ANY OF US.
GO (ROAR)
THAT...
...IS GOOD TO HEAR!!

CHAPTER 94: THE HERO QUELLS HER ANXIETIES FOR THE FUTURE

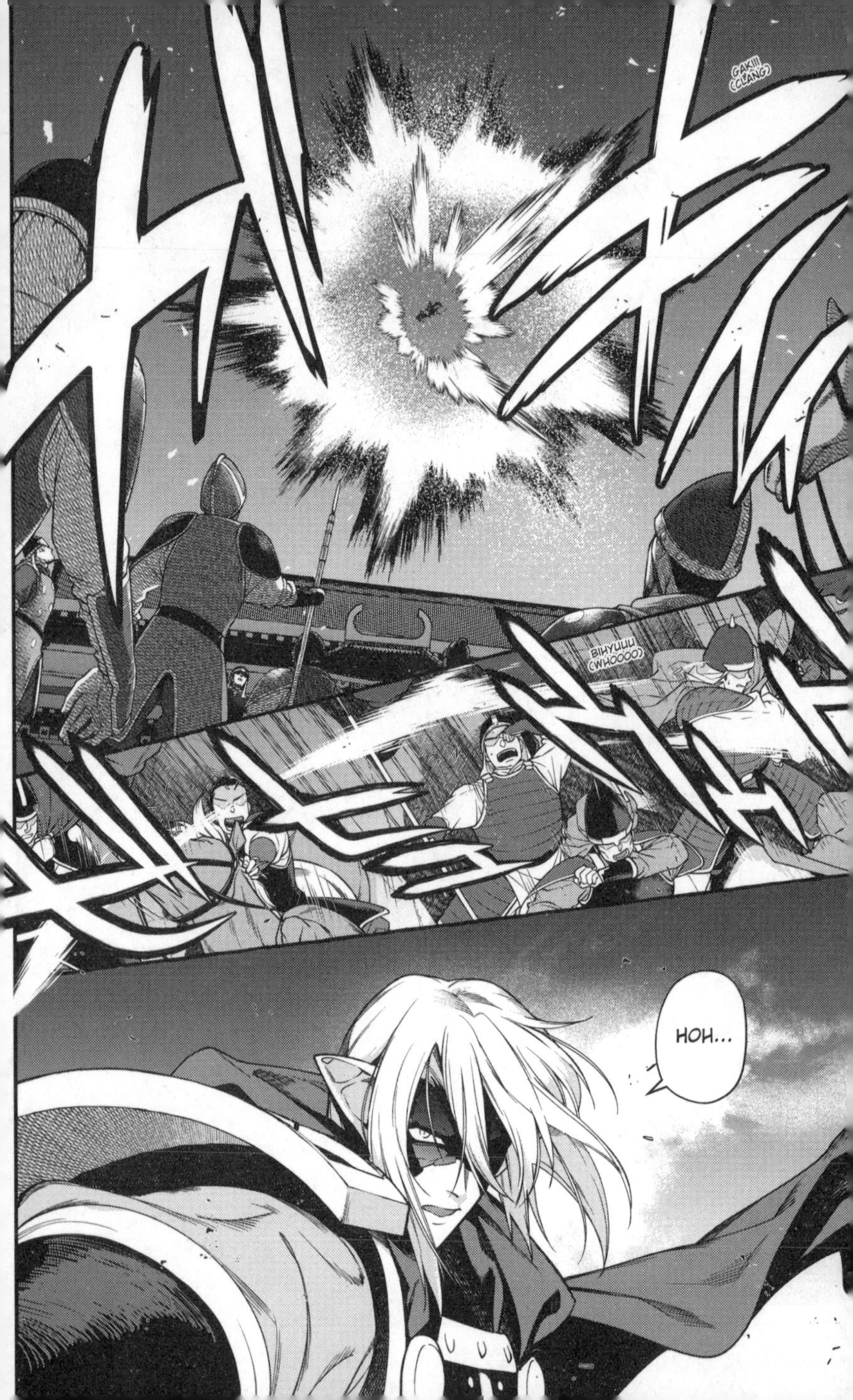
GAKIII
(CLANG)
BIHYUUU
(WHOOOO)
HOH...

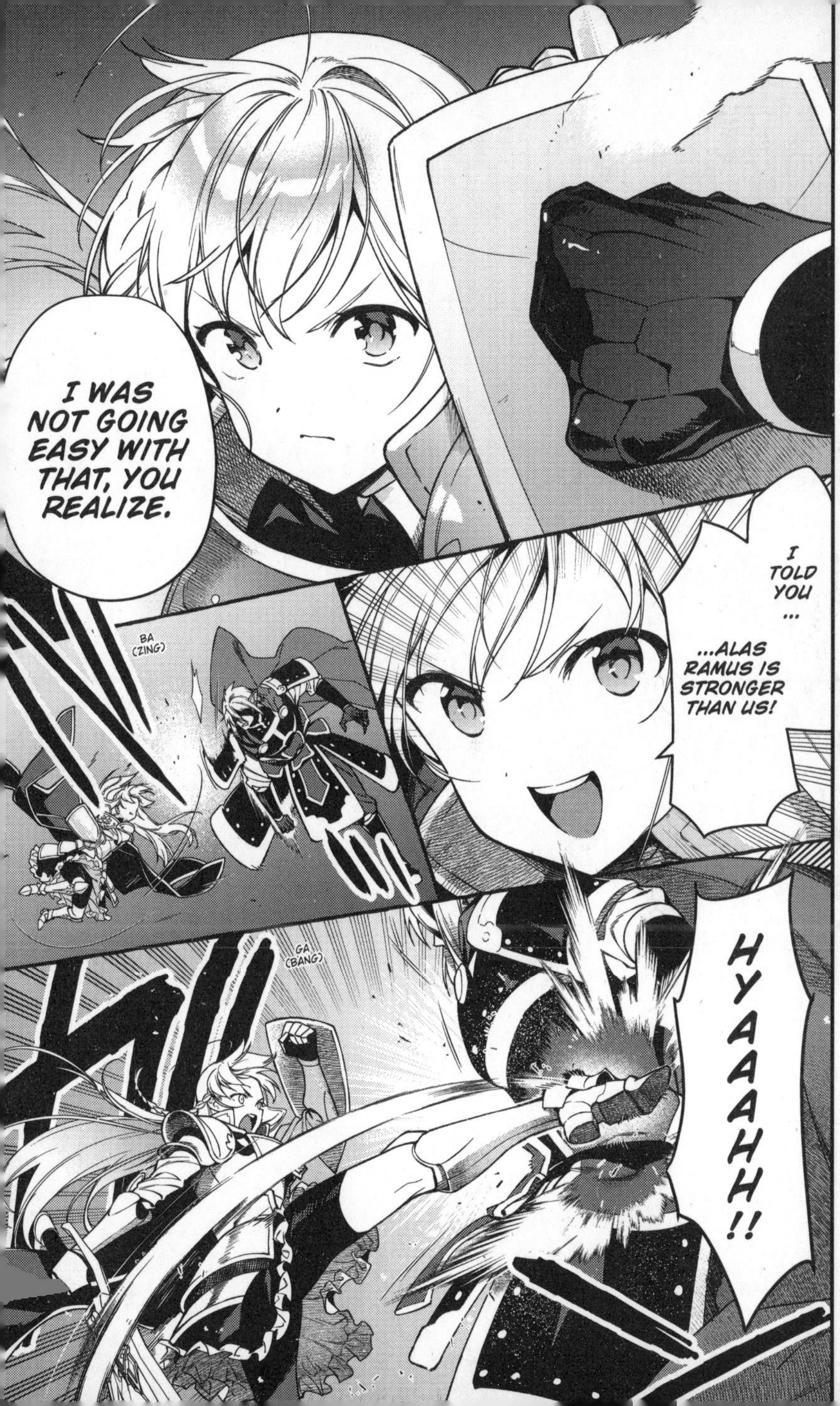
I WAS NOT GOING EASY WITH THAT, YOU REALIZE.
I TOLD YOU ...
...ALAS RAMUS IS STRONGER THAN US!
BA (ZING)
HYAAAAHH!!
GA (BANG)

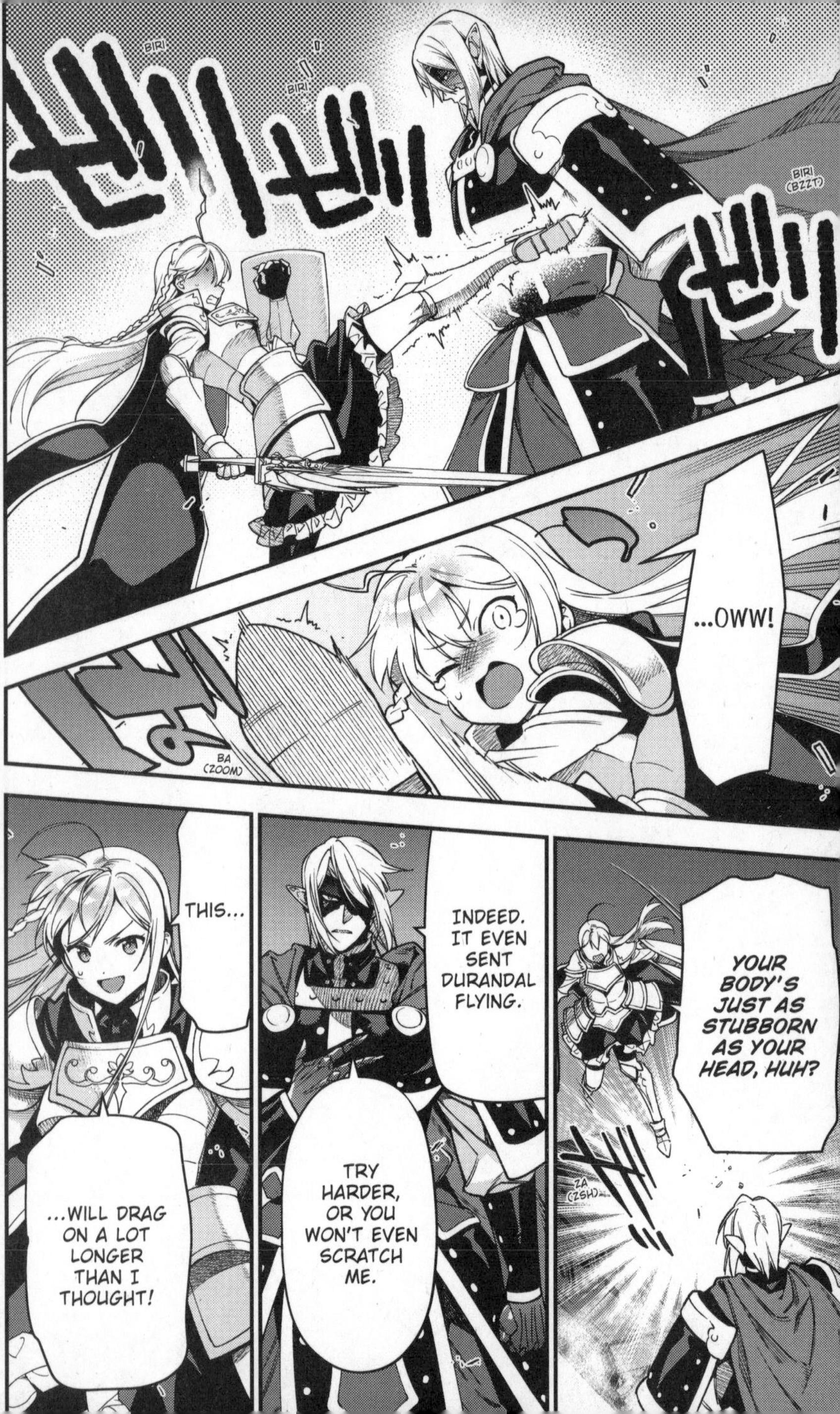
BIRI (BZZT)
BIRI
BIRI
...OWW!
BA (ZOOM)
YOUR BODY'S JUST AS STUBBORN AS YOUR HEAD, HUH?
ZA (ZSH)
INDEED. IT EVEN SENT DURANDAL FLYING.
TRY HARDER, OR YOU WON'T EVEN SCRATCH ME.
THIS...
...WILL DRAG ON A LOT LONGER THAN I THOUGHT!

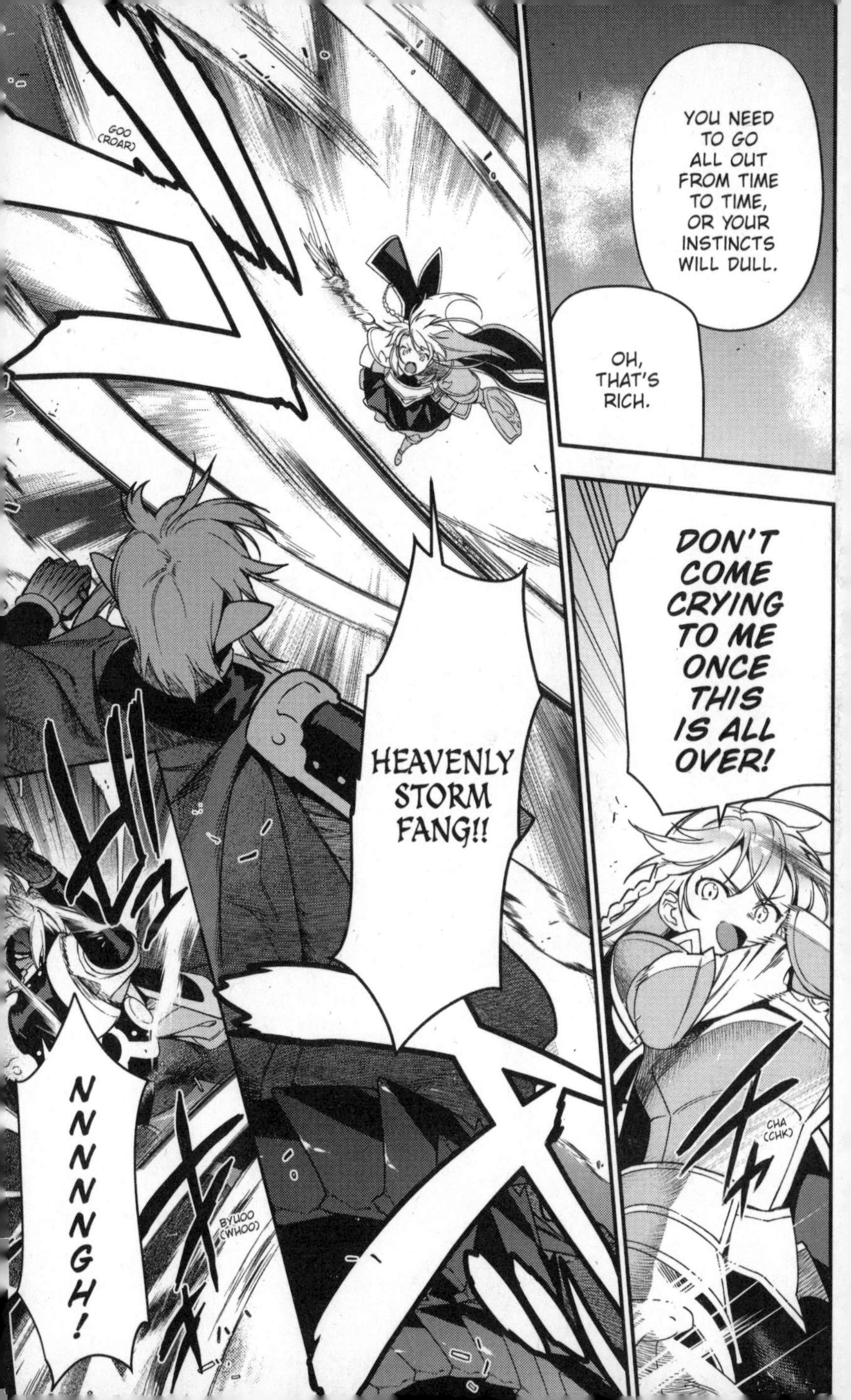
YOU NEED TO GO ALL OUT FROM TIME TO TIME, OR YOUR INSTINCTS WILL DULL.
OH, THAT'S RICH.
DON'T COME CRYING TO ME ONCE THIS IS ALL OVER!
CHA (CHK)
GOO (ROAR)
HEAVENLY STORM FANG!!
NNNNNGH!
BYUOO (WHOO)

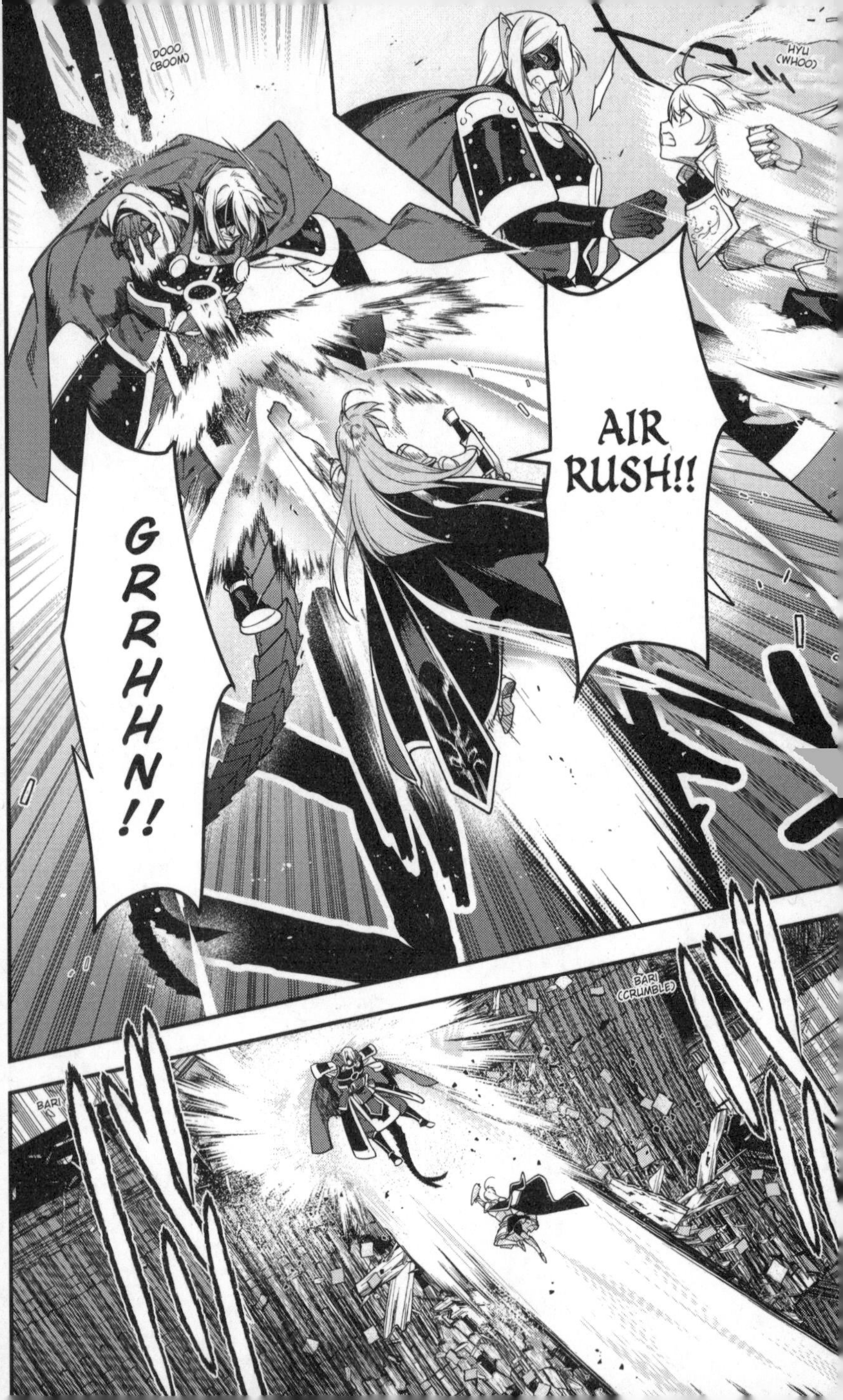
HYU (WHOO)
DOOO (BOOM)
AIR RUSH!!
GRRHHN!!
BARI (CRUMBLE)
BARI

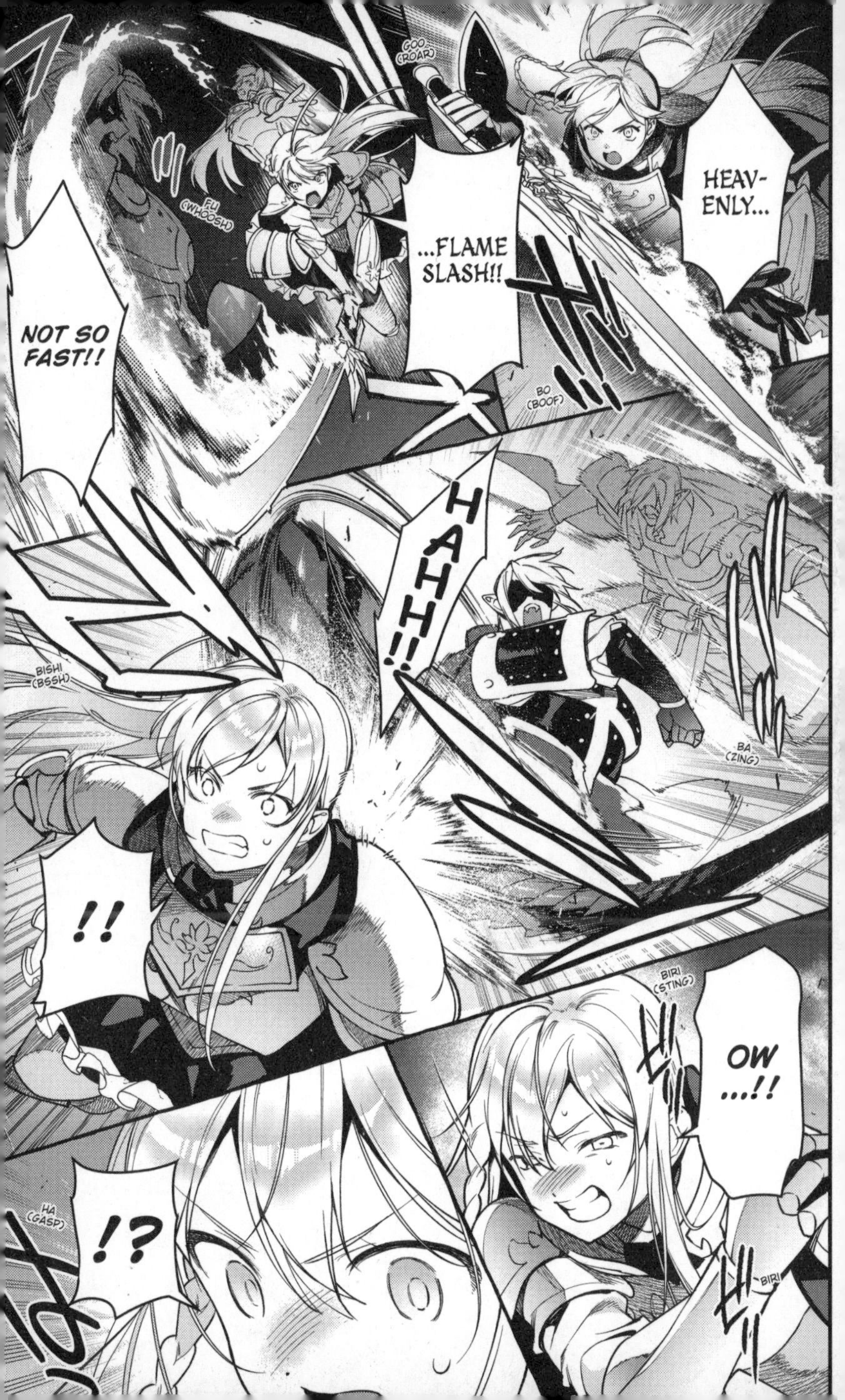
HEAV-ENLY...
GOO (ROAR)
...FLAME SLASH!!
FU (WHOOSH)
BO (BOOF)
NOT SO FAST!!
HAHHH!!!
BA (ZING)
BISHI (BSSH)
!!
BIRI (STING)
OW ...!!
BIRI
!?
HA (GASP)

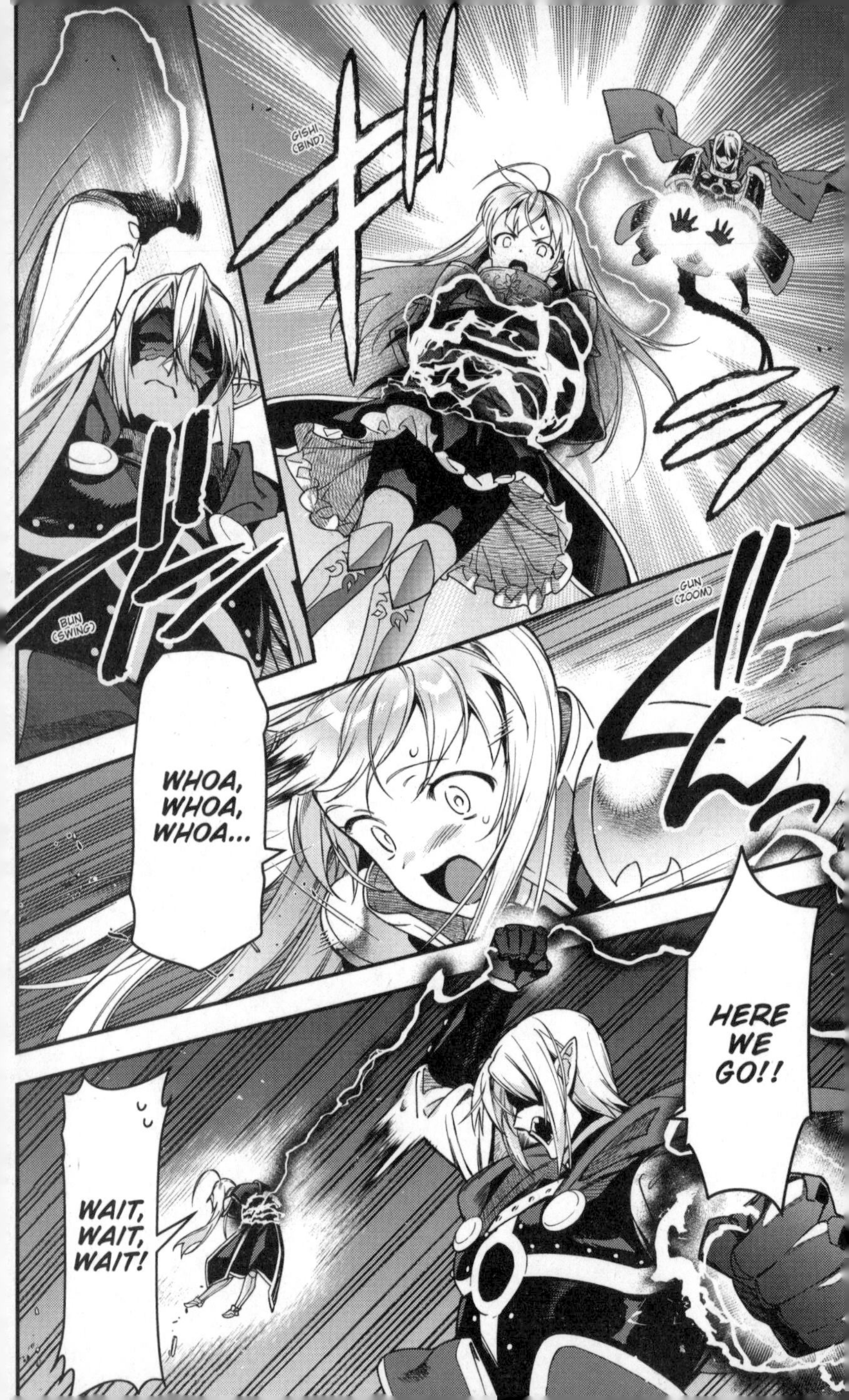
GISHI (BIND)
BUN (SWING)
GUN (ZOOM)
WHOA, WHOA, WHOA...
HERE WE GO!!
WAIT, WAIT, WAIT!

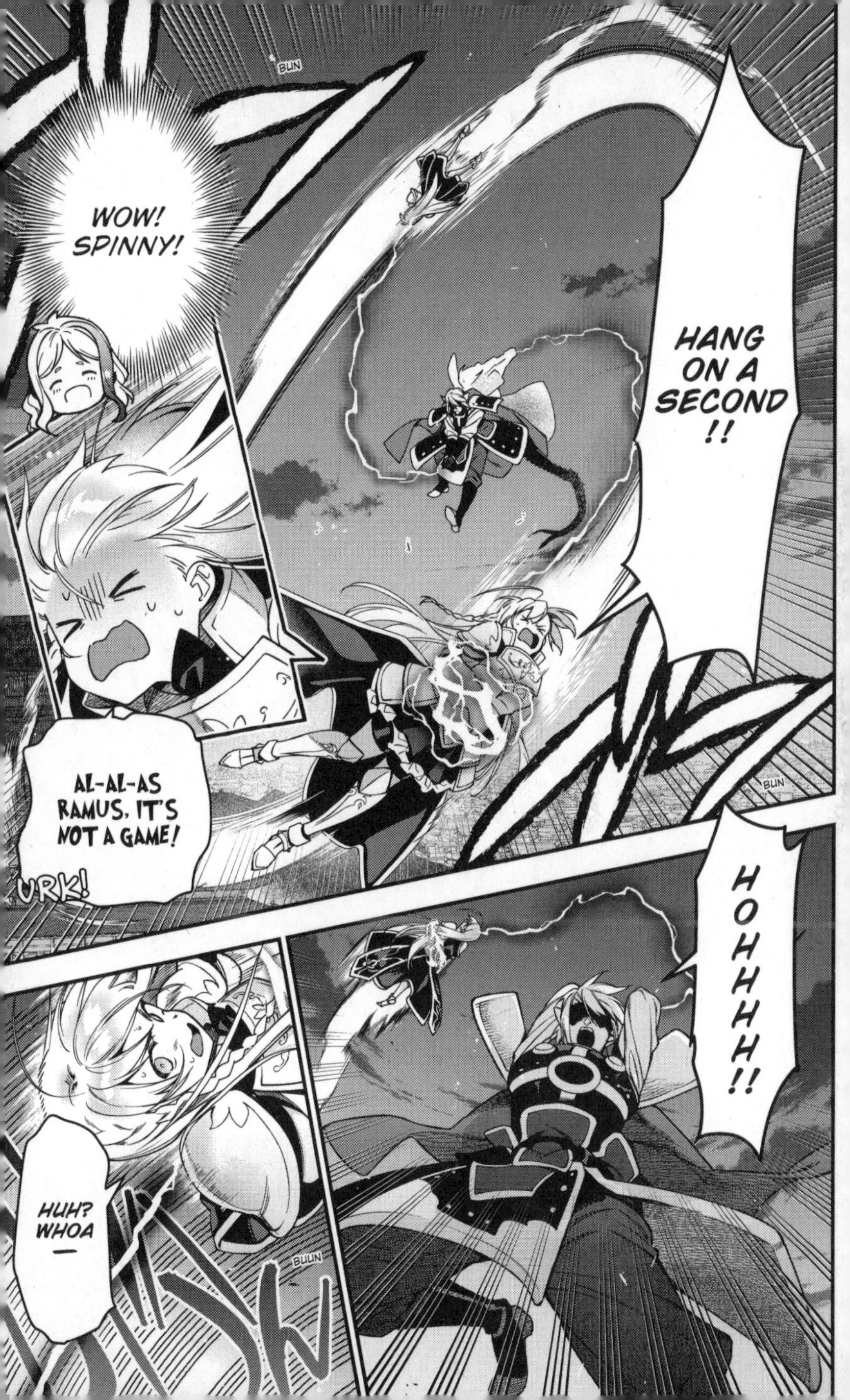
BUN
HANG ON A SECOND!!
WOW! SPINNY!
BUN
AL-AL-AS RAMUS, IT'S NOT A GAME!
URK!
HOHHHHH!!
HUH? WHOA—
BUN

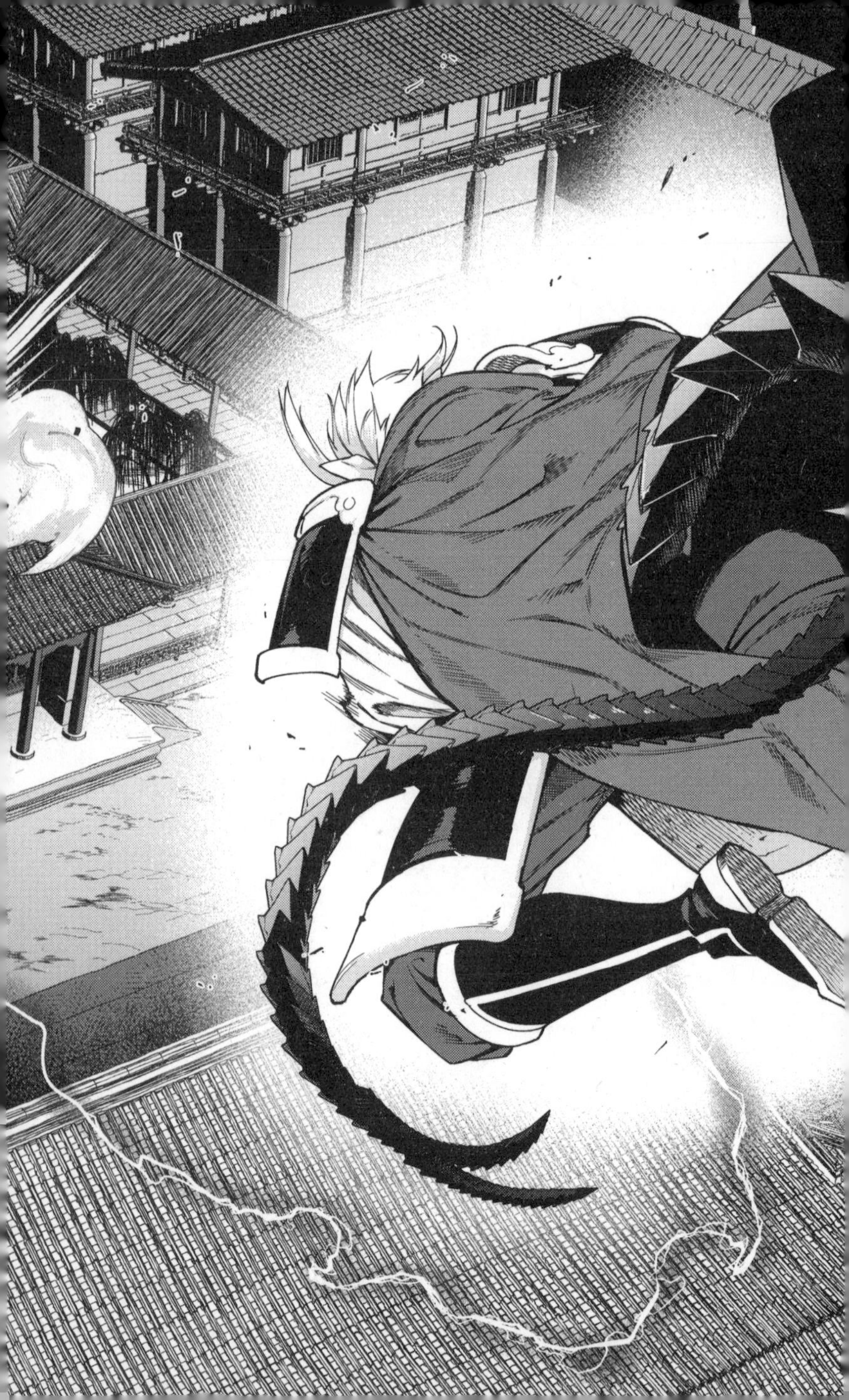

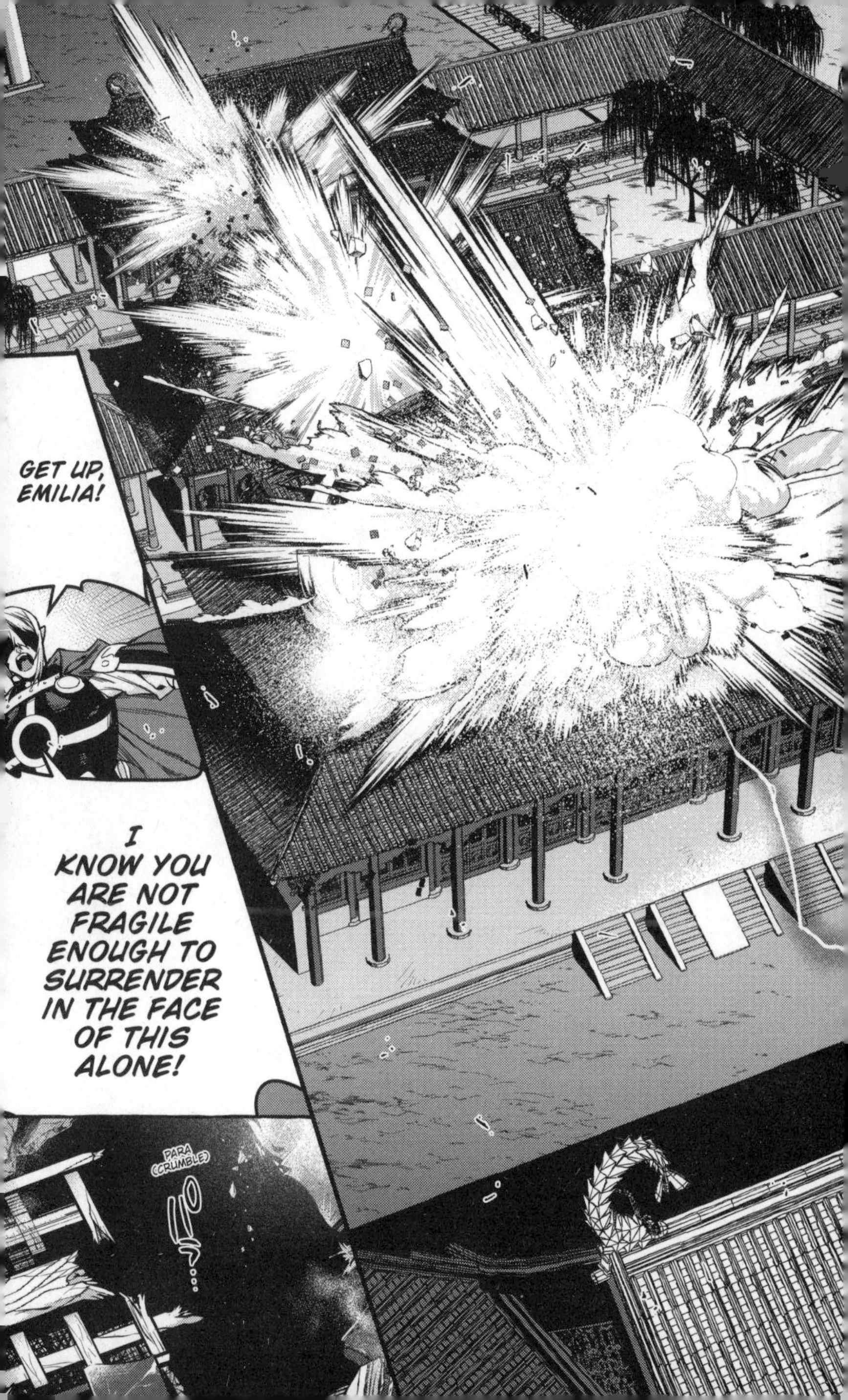
GET UP, EMILIA!
I KNOW YOU ARE NOT FRAGILE ENOUGH TO SURRENDER IN THE FACE OF THIS ALONE!
PARA (CRUMBLE)

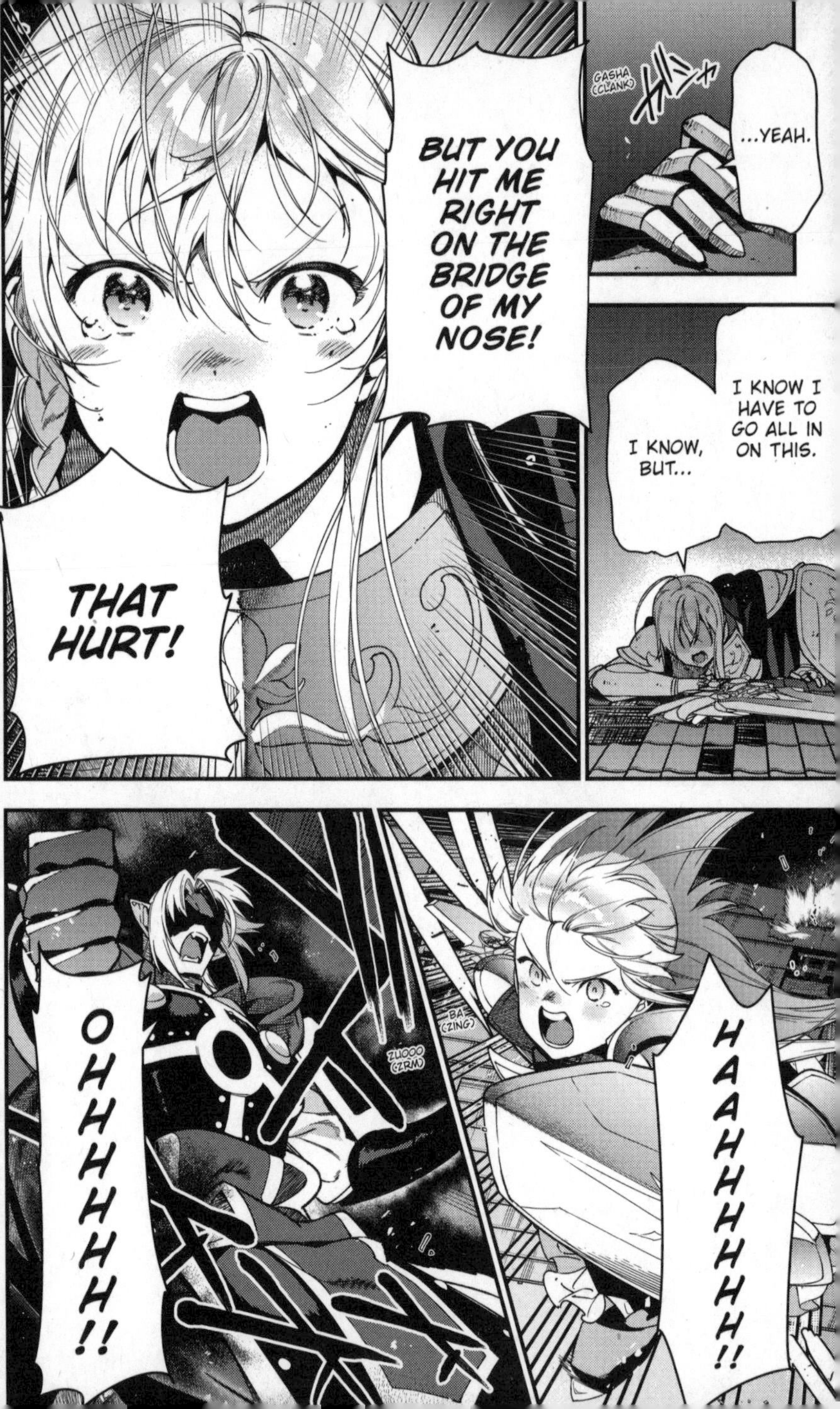
GASHA (CLANK)
...YEAH.
I KNOW I HAVE TO GO ALL IN ON THIS.
I KNOW, BUT...
BUT YOU HIT ME RIGHT ON THE BRIDGE OF MY NOSE!
THAT HURT!
HAAHHHHHHH!!
BA (ZING)
ZUOOO (ZRM)
OHHHHHHH!!

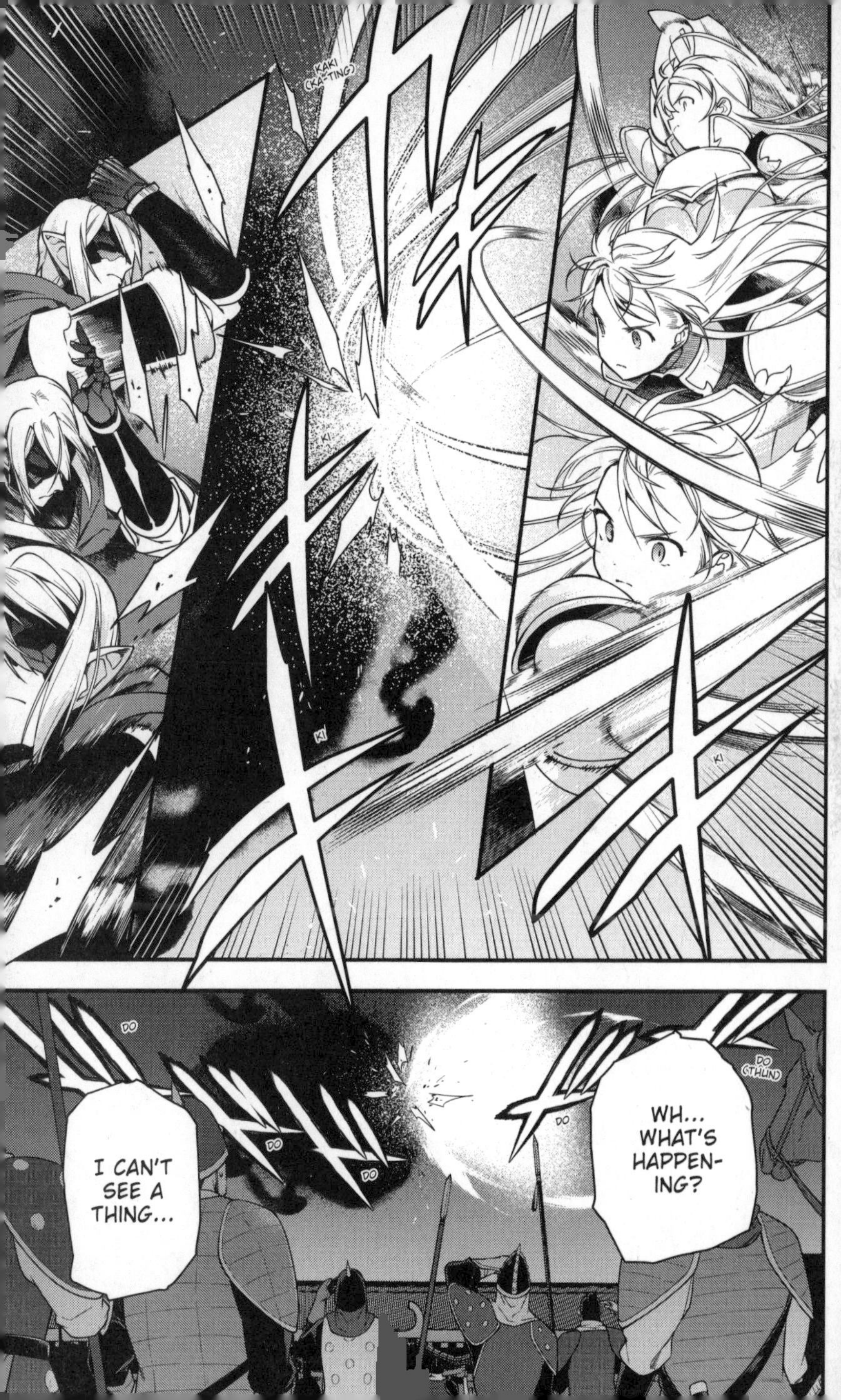
KAKI (KA-TING)
KI
KI
KI
DO (THUNK)
WH... WHAT'S HAPPEN-ING?
DO
DO
DO
DO
I CAN'T SEE A THING...

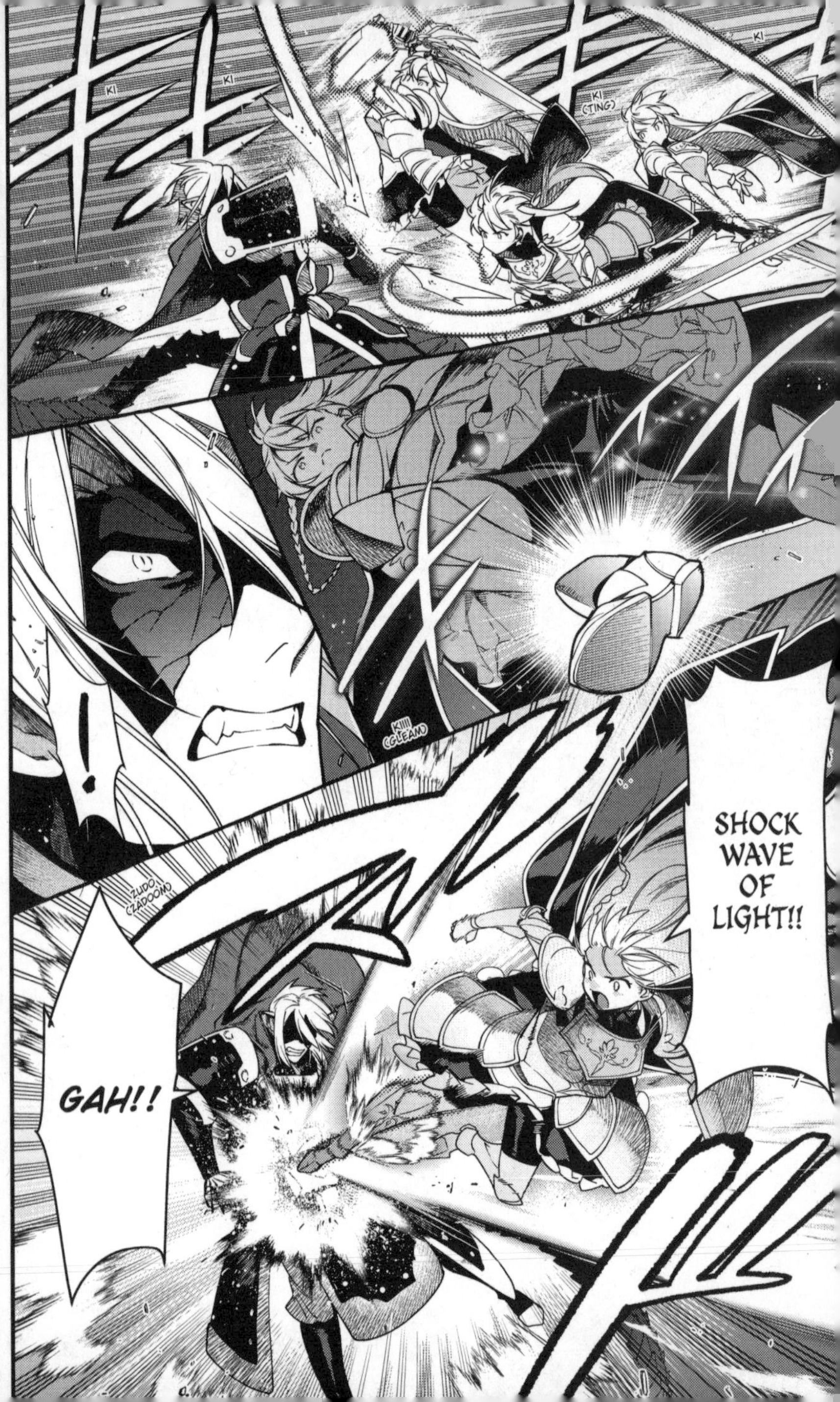
KI
KI (TING)
KI
KI
KIIII (GLEAM)
!
SHOCK WAVE OF LIGHT!!
ZUDO (ZADOOM)
GAH!!

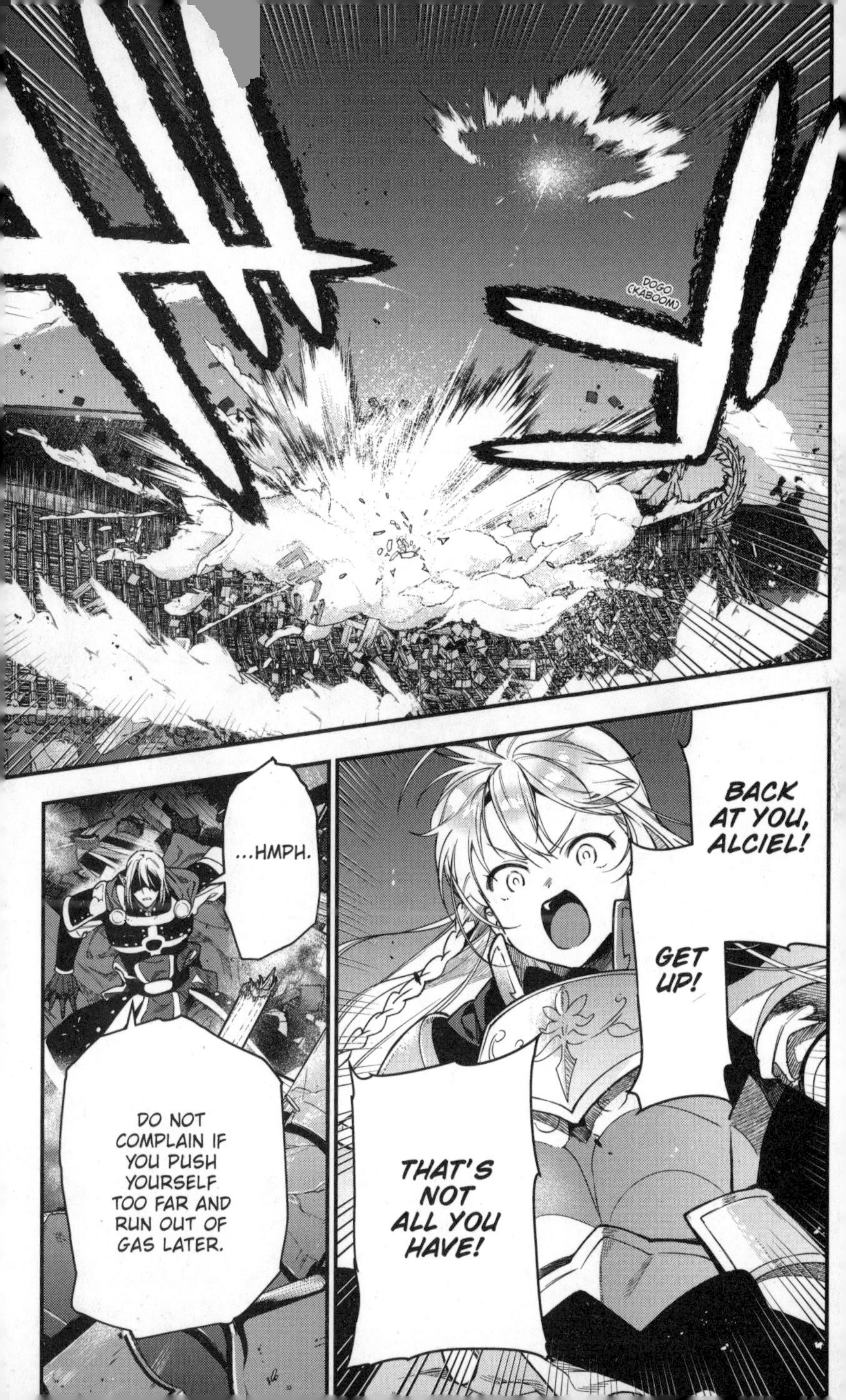
DOGO (KABOOM)
BACK AT YOU, ALCIEL!
GET UP!
THAT'S NOT ALL YOU HAVE!
...HMPH.
DO NOT COMPLAIN IF YOU PUSH YOURSELF TOO FAR AND RUN OUT OF GAS LATER.

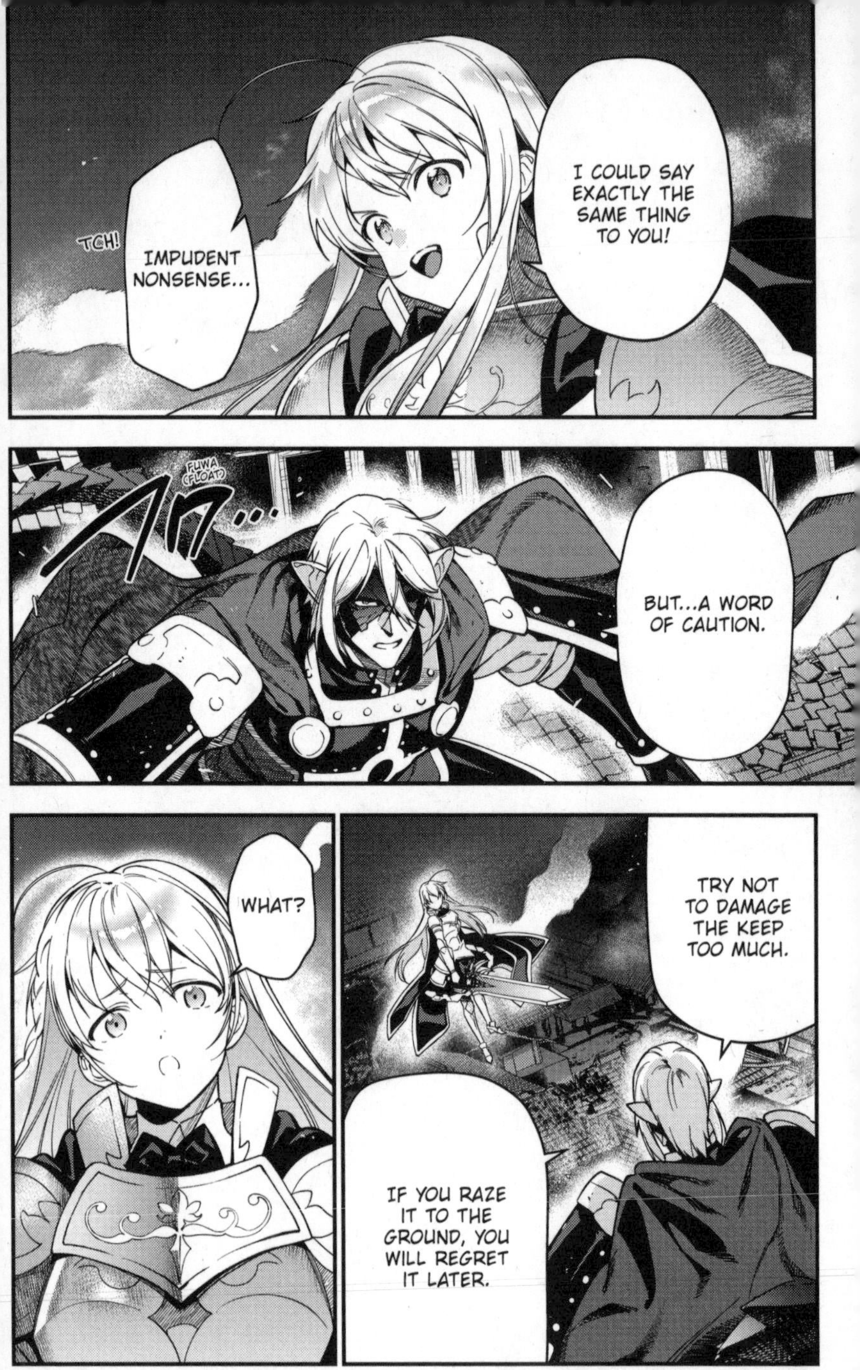
I COULD SAY EXACTLY THE SAME THING TO YOU!
TCH!
IMPUDENT NONSENSE...
BUT...A WORD OF CAUTION.
FUWA (FLOAT)
TRY NOT TO DAMAGE THE KEEP TOO MUCH.
IF YOU RAZE IT TO THE GROUND, YOU WILL REGRET IT LATER.
WHAT?

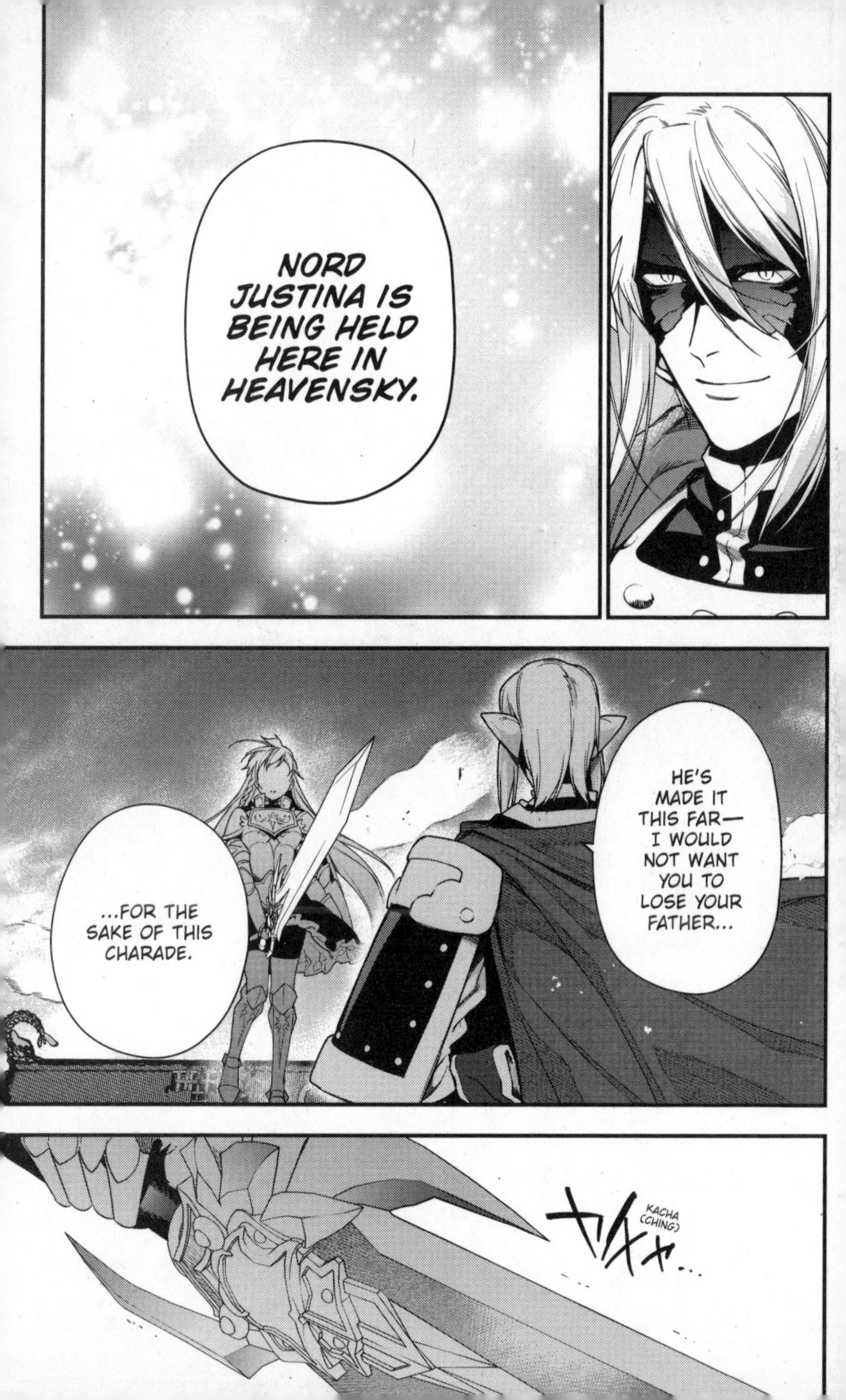
NORD JUSTINA IS BEING HELD HERE IN HEAVENSKY.
HE'S MADE IT THIS FAR— I WOULD NOT WANT YOU TO LOSE YOUR FATHER...
...FOR THE SAKE OF THIS CHARADE.
KACHA (CHING)

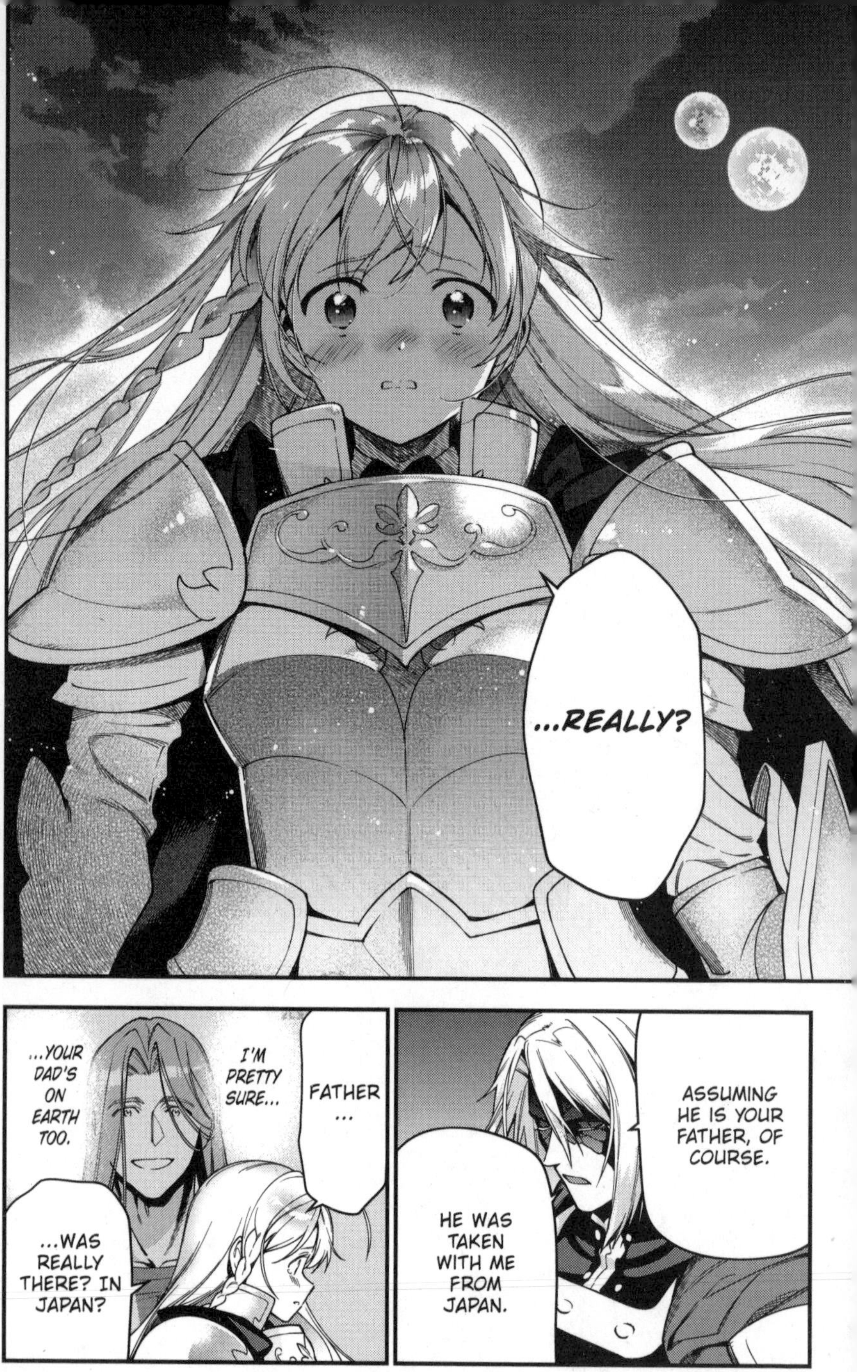
...REALLY?
ASSUMING HE IS YOUR FATHER, OF COURSE.
HE WAS TAKEN WITH ME FROM JAPAN.
FATHER ...
...WAS REALLY THERE? IN JAPAN?
I'M PRETTY SURE...
...YOUR DAD'S ON EARTH TOO.

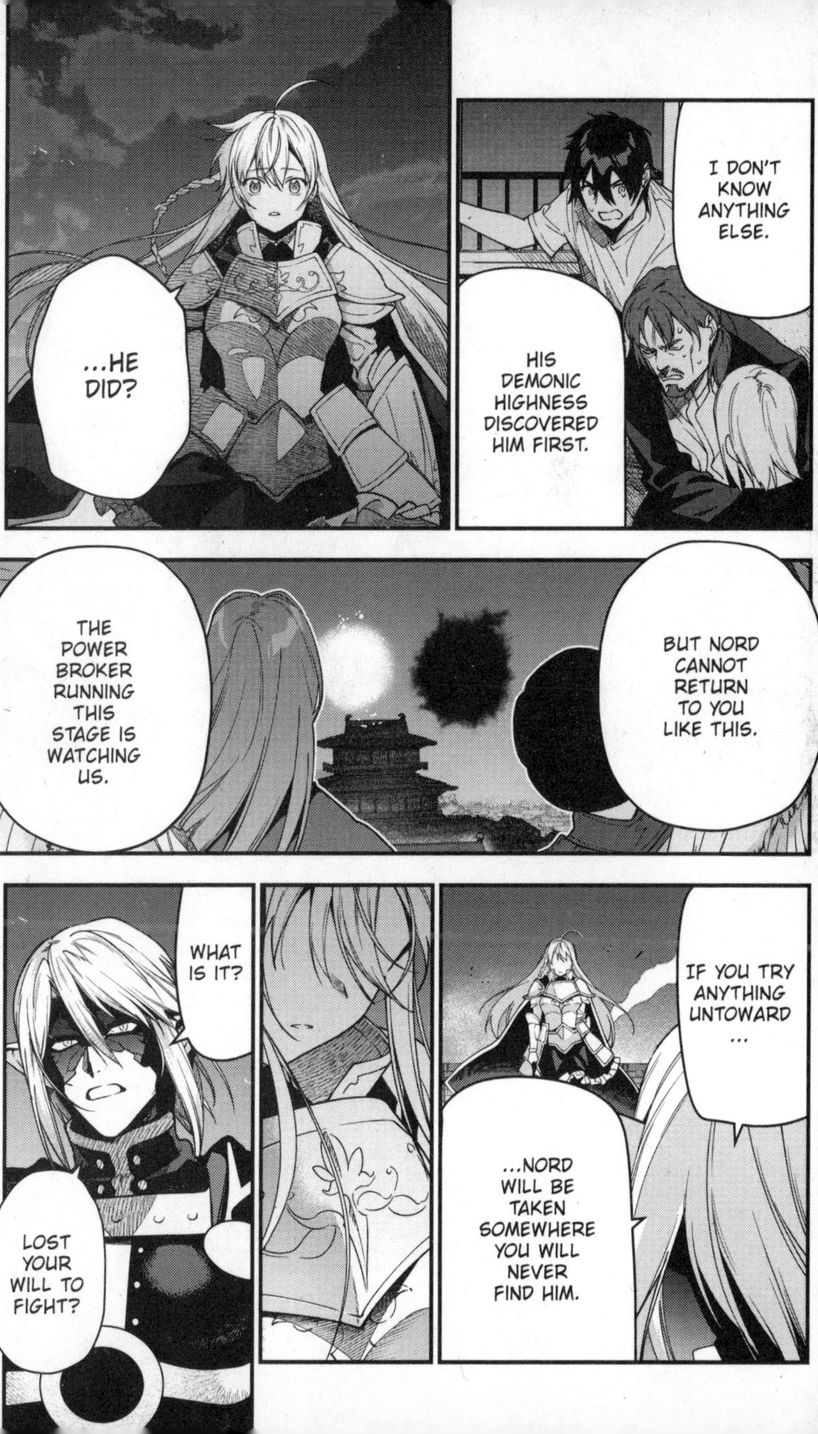

I DON'T KNOW ANYTHING ELSE.
HIS DEMONIC HIGHNESS DISCOVERED HIM FIRST.
...HE DID?
BUT NORD CANNOT RETURN TO YOU LIKE THIS.
THE POWER BROKER RUNNING THIS STAGE IS WATCHING US.
IF YOU TRY ANYTHING UNTOWARD ...
...NORD WILL BE TAKEN SOMEWHERE YOU WILL NEVER FIND HIM.
WHAT IS IT?
LOST YOUR WILL TO FIGHT?

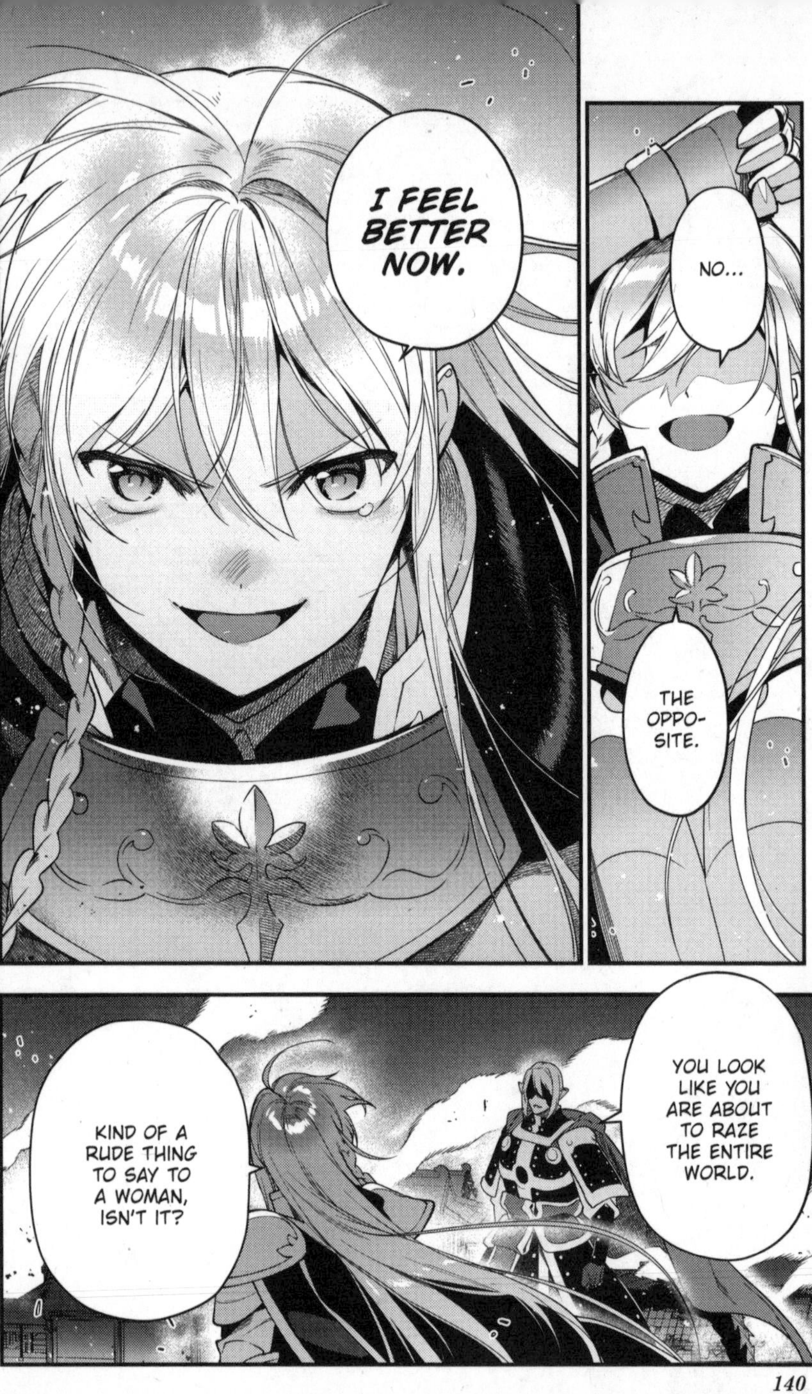
NO...
THE OPPOSITE.
I FEEL BETTER NOW.
YOU LOOK LIKE YOU ARE ABOUT TO RAZE THE ENTIRE WORLD.
KIND OF A RUDE THING TO SAY TO A WOMAN, ISN'T IT?

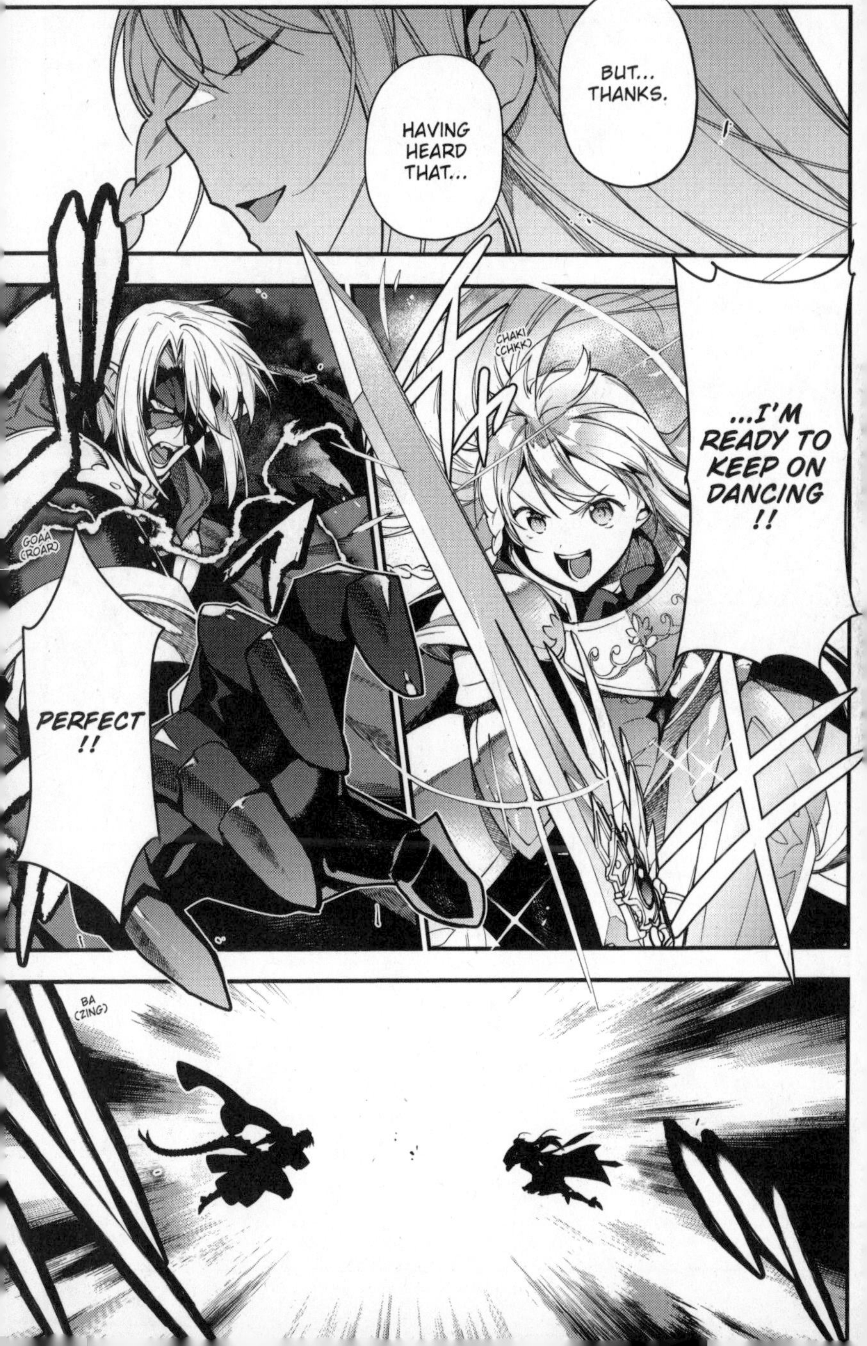
BUT... THANKS.
HAVING HEARD THAT...
...I'M READY TO KEEP ON DANCING!!
CHAKI (CHKK)
GOAA (ROAR)
PERFECT!!
BA (ZING)

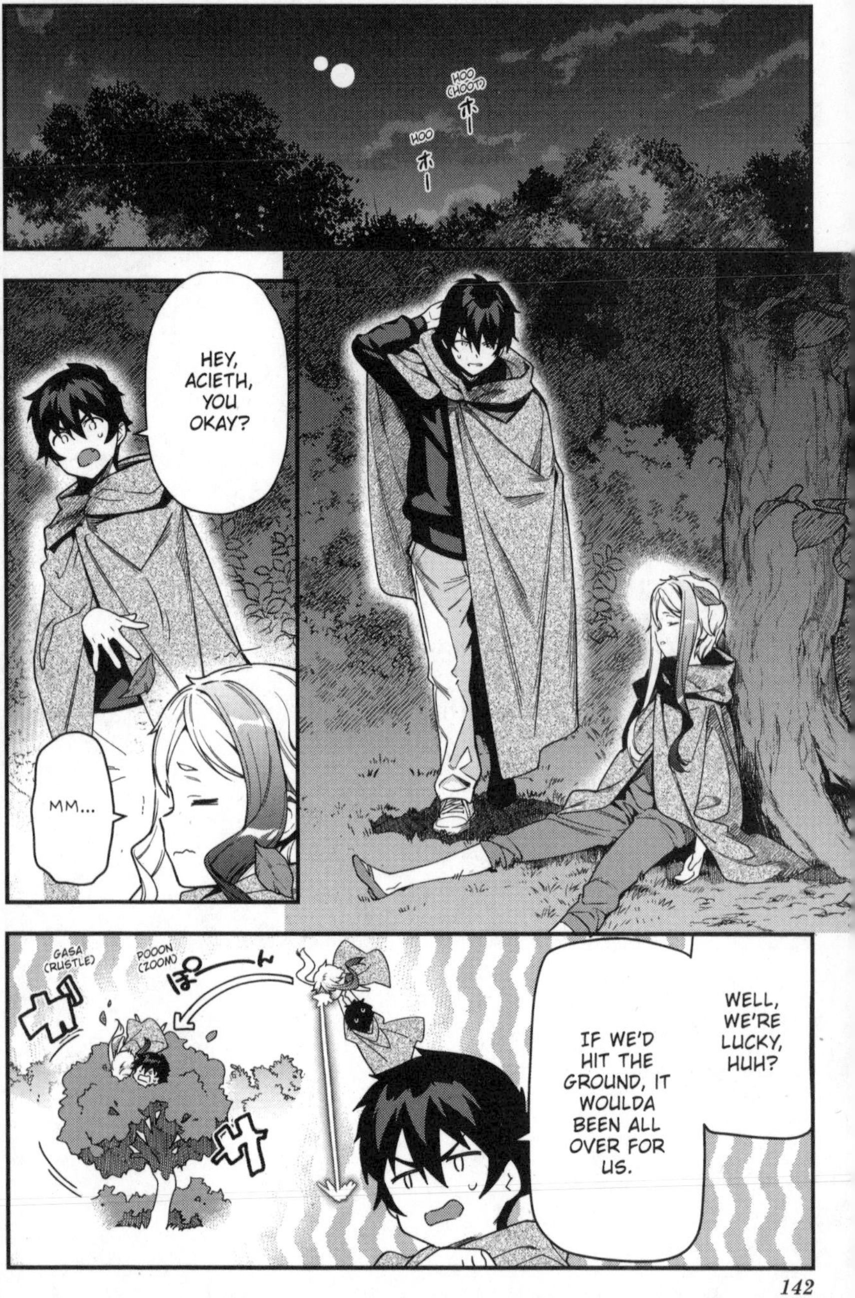
HOO (HOOT!)
ホー
HOO
ホー
HEY, ACIETH, YOU OKAY?
MM...
WELL, WE'RE LUCKY, HUH?
IF WE'D HIT THE GROUND, IT WOULDA BEEN ALL OVER FOR US.
POOON (ZOOM)
ぽーん
GASA (RUSTLE)

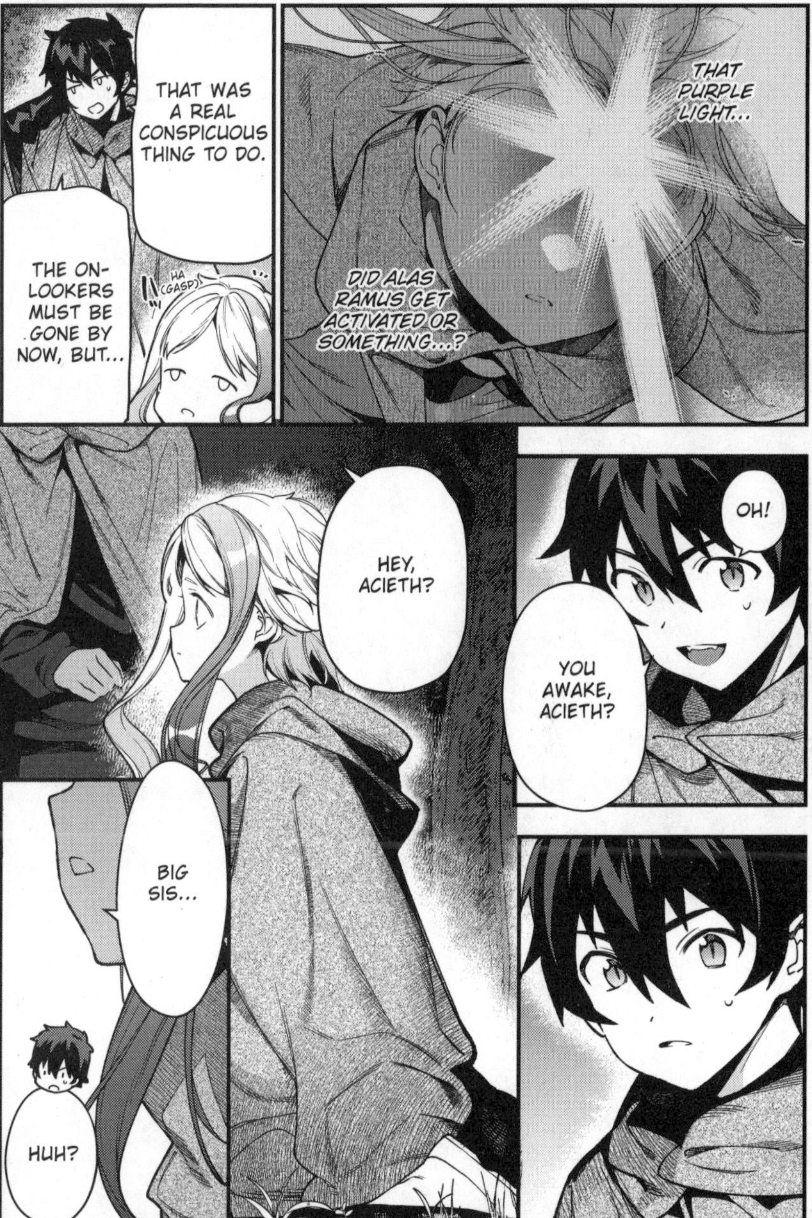
THAT PURPLE LIGHT...
DID ALAS RAMUS GET ACTIVATED OR SOMETHING...?
THAT WAS A REAL CONSPICUOUS THING TO DO.
THE ON-LOOKERS MUST BE GONE BY NOW, BUT...
HA (GASP)
OH!
YOU AWAKE, ACIETH?
HEY, ACIETH?
BIG SIS...
HUH?

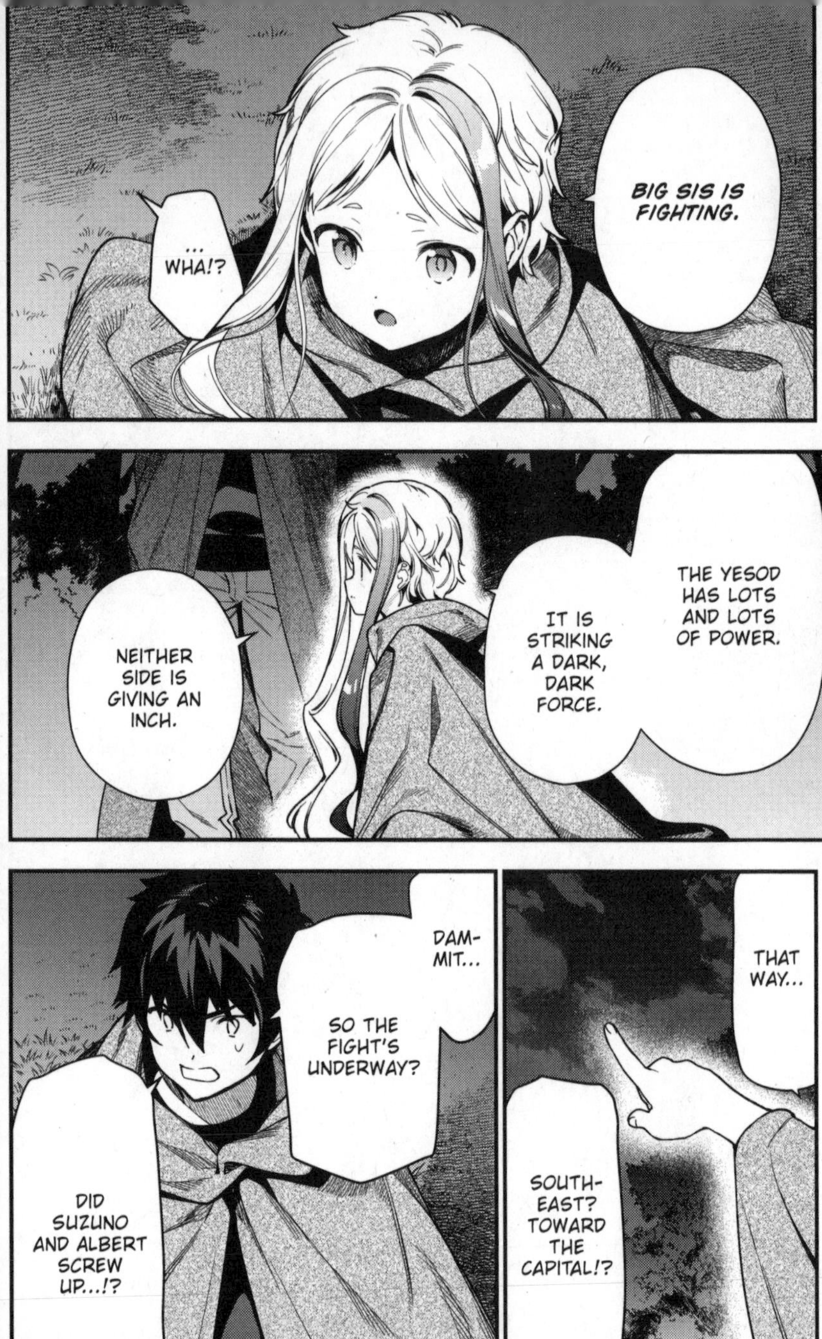
BIG SIS IS FIGHTING.
...WHA!?
THE YESOD HAS LOTS AND LOTS OF POWER.
IT IS STRIKING A DARK, DARK FORCE.
NEITHER SIDE IS GIVING AN INCH.
THAT WAY...
SOUTH-EAST? TOWARD THE CAPITAL!?
DAM-MIT...
SO THE FIGHT'S UNDERWAY?
DID SUZUNO AND ALBERT SCREW UP...!?

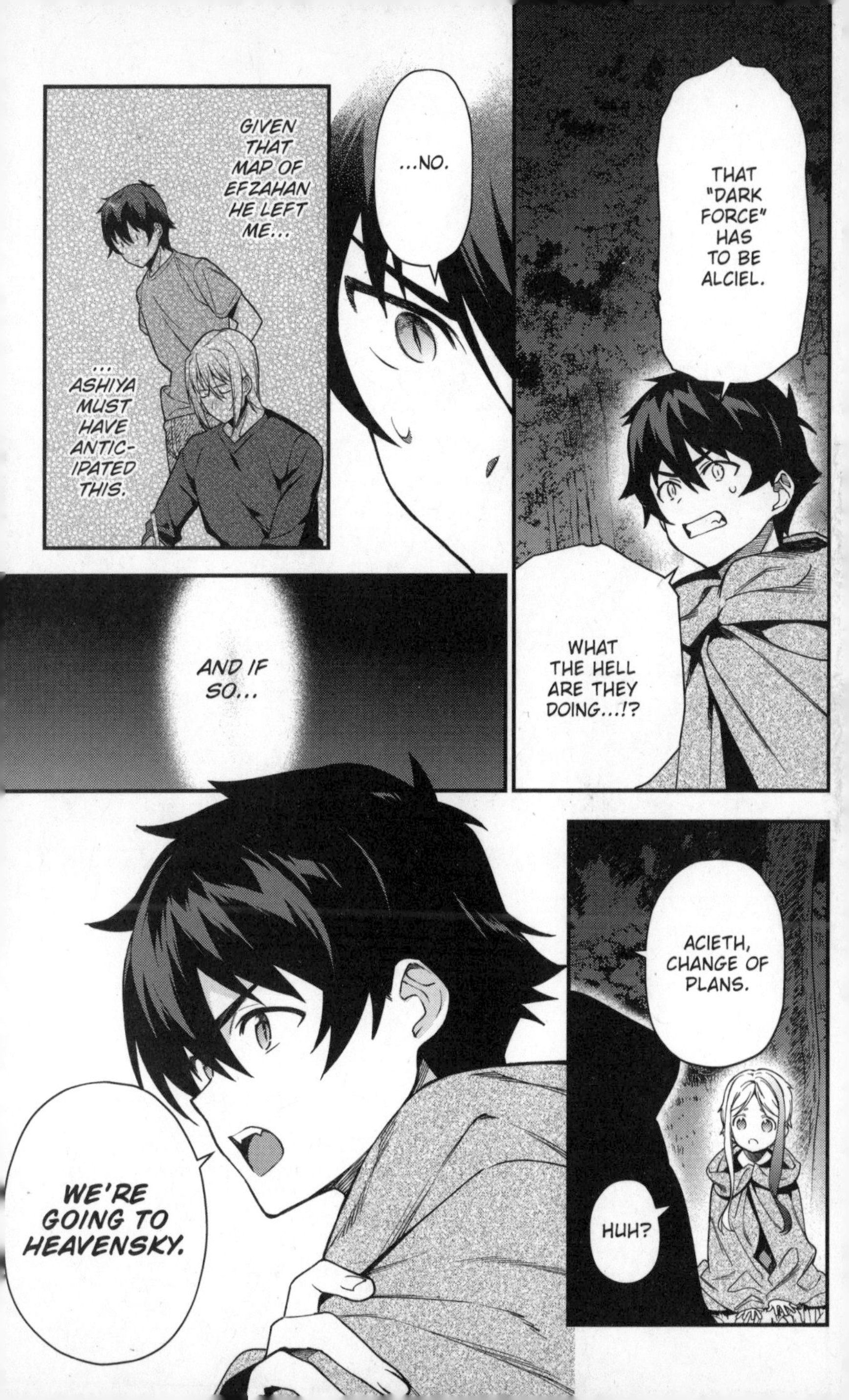
THAT "DARK FORCE" HAS TO BE ALCIEL.
WHAT THE HELL ARE THEY DOING...!?
...NO.
GIVEN THAT MAP OF EFZAHAN HE LEFT ME...
...ASHIYA MUST HAVE ANTIC-IPATED THIS.
AND IF SO...
ACIETH, CHANGE OF PLANS.
HUH?
WE'RE GOING TO HEAVENSKY.

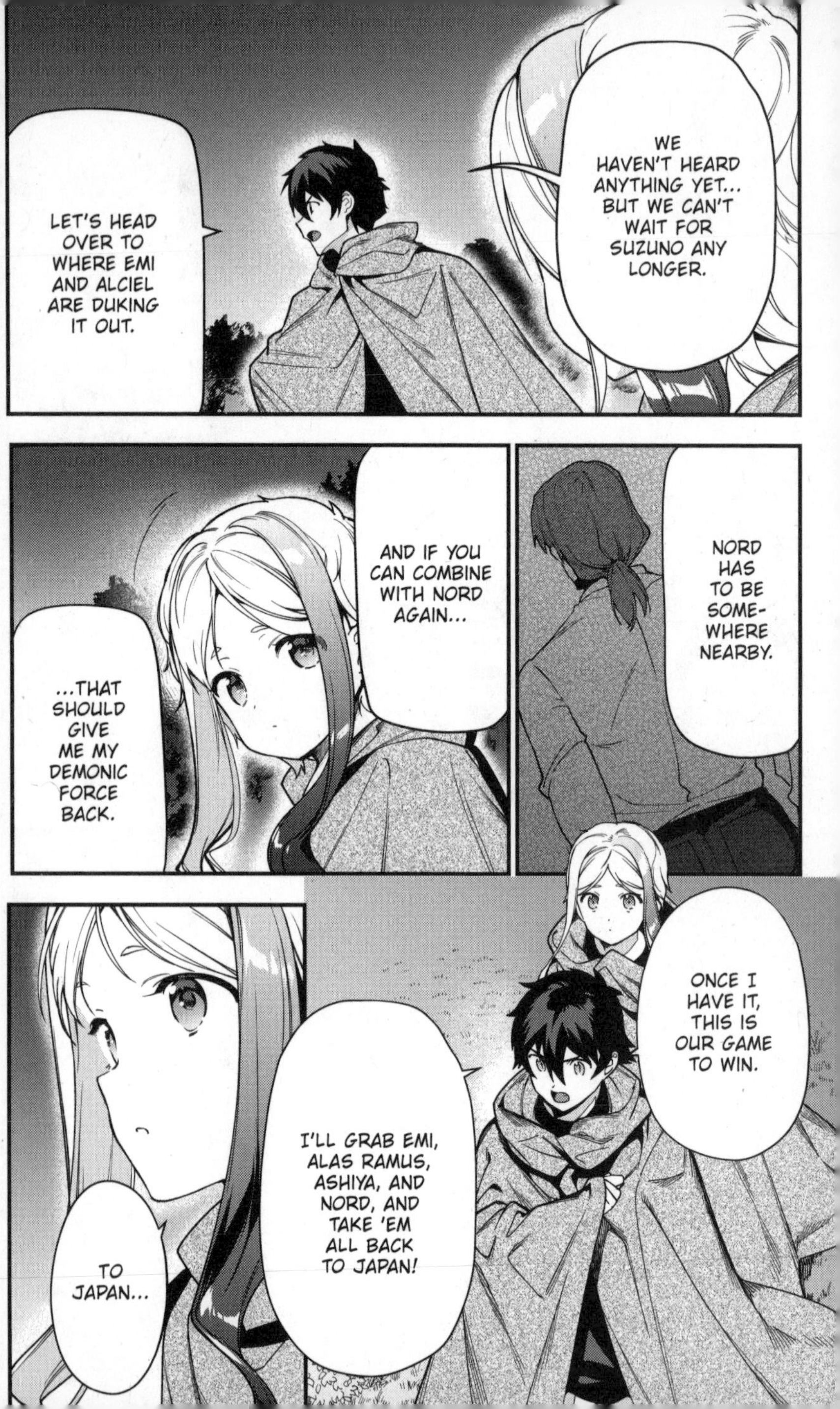
WE HAVEN'T HEARD ANYTHING YET... BUT WE CAN'T WAIT FOR SUZUNO ANY LONGER.
LET'S HEAD OVER TO WHERE EMI AND ALCIEL ARE DUKING IT OUT.
NORD HAS TO BE SOME-WHERE NEARBY.
AND IF YOU CAN COMBINE WITH NORD AGAIN...
...THAT SHOULD GIVE ME MY DEMONIC FORCE BACK.
ONCE I HAVE IT, THIS IS OUR GAME TO WIN.
I'LL GRAB EMI, ALAS RAMUS, ASHIYA, AND NORD, AND TAKE 'EM ALL BACK TO JAPAN!
TO JAPAN...

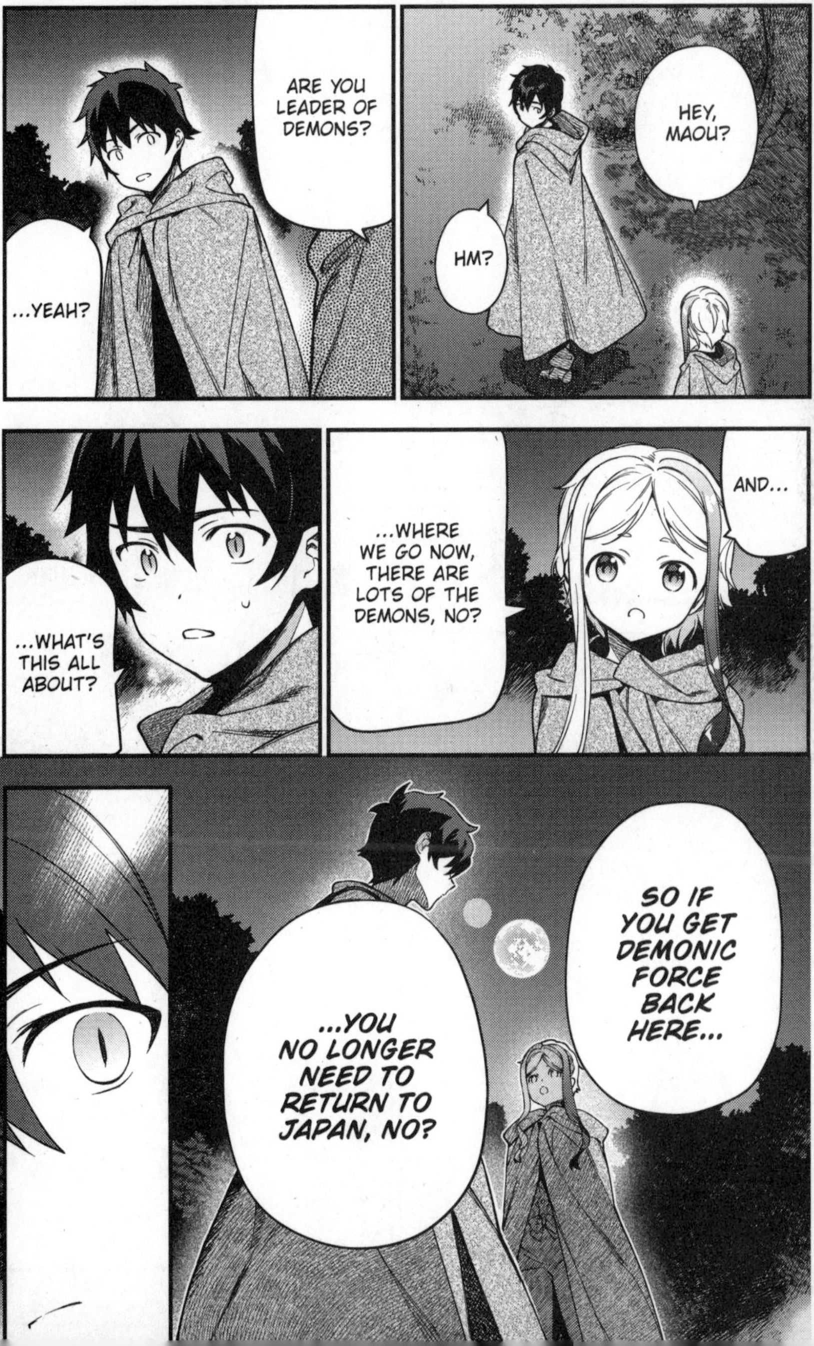
HEY, MAOU?
HM?
ARE YOU LEADER OF DEMONS?
...YEAH?
AND...
...WHERE WE GO NOW, THERE ARE LOTS OF THE DEMONS, NO?
...WHAT'S THIS ALL ABOUT?
SO IF YOU GET DEMONIC FORCE BACK HERE...
...YOU NO LONGER NEED TO RETURN TO JAPAN, NO?

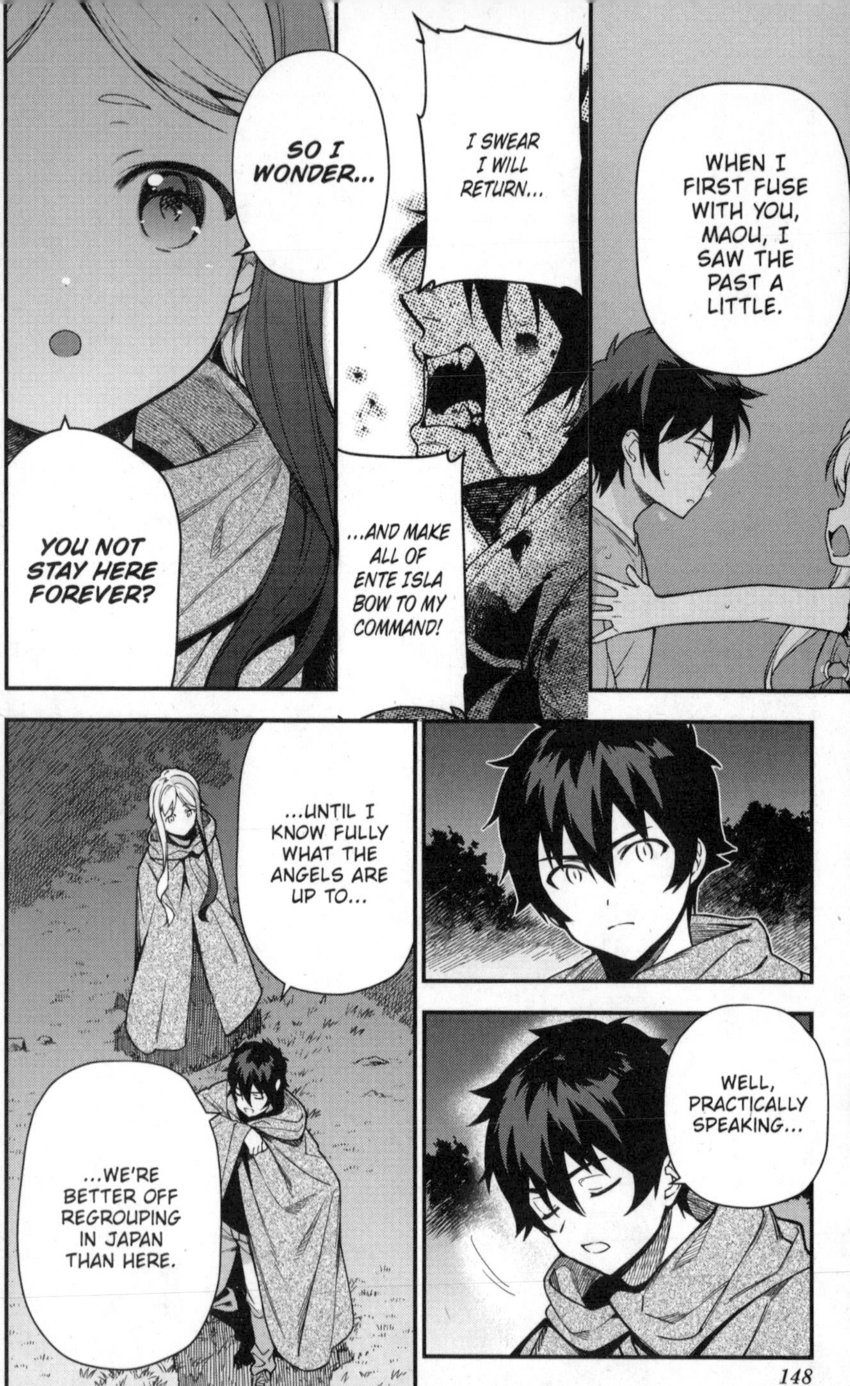
WHEN I FIRST FUSE WITH YOU, MAOU, I SAW THE PAST A LITTLE.
I SWEAR I WILL RETURN...
...AND MAKE ALL OF ENTE ISLA BOW TO MY COMMAND!
SO I WONDER...
YOU NOT STAY HERE FOREVER?
WELL, PRACTICALLY SPEAKING...
...UNTIL I KNOW FULLY WHAT THE ANGELS ARE UP TO...
...WE'RE BETTER OFF REGROUPING IN JAPAN THAN HERE.

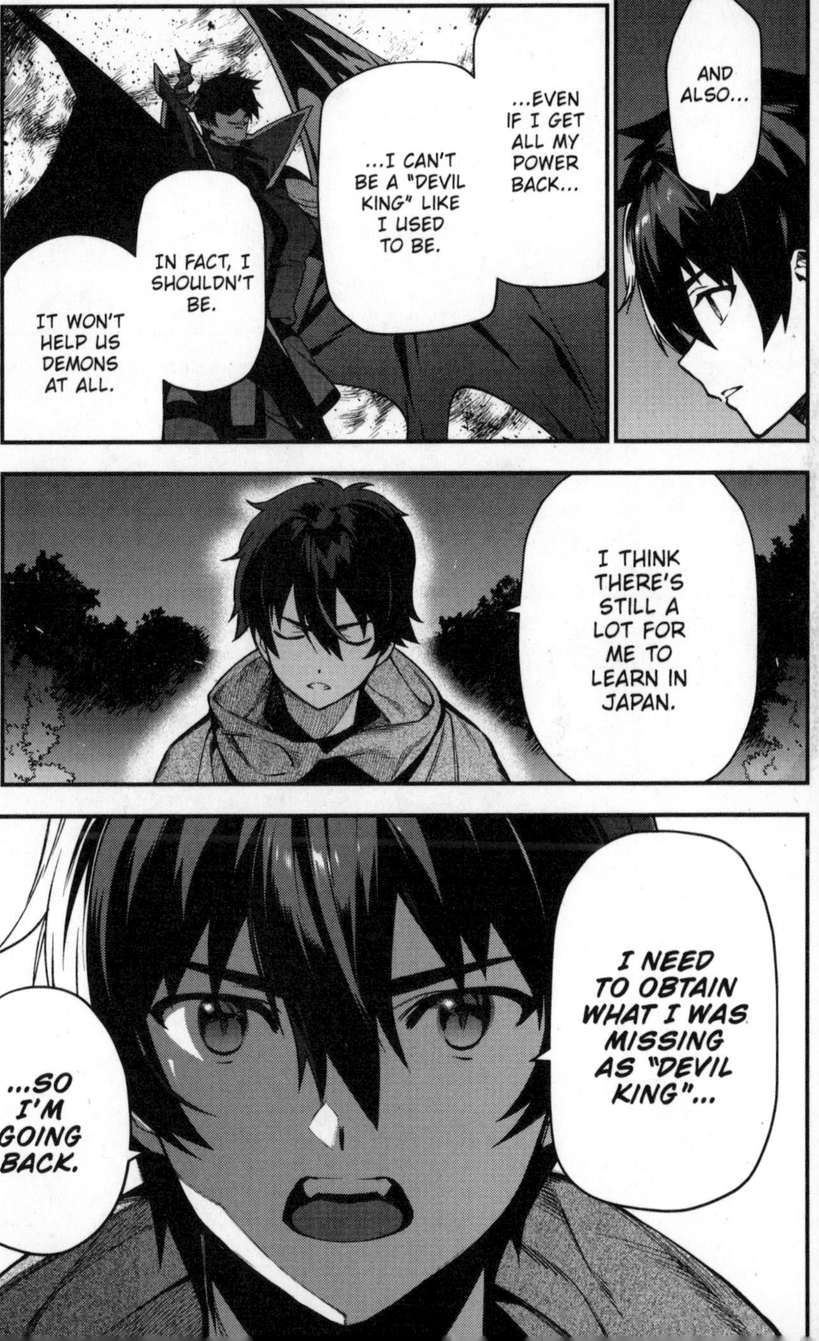
AND ALSO...
...EVEN IF I GET ALL MY POWER BACK...
...I CAN'T BE A "DEVIL KING" LIKE I USED TO BE.
IN FACT, I SHOULDN'T BE.
IT WON'T HELP US DEMONS AT ALL.
I THINK THERE'S STILL A LOT FOR ME TO LEARN IN JAPAN.
I NEED TO OBTAIN WHAT I WAS MISSING AS "DEVIL KING"...
...SO I'M GOING BACK.

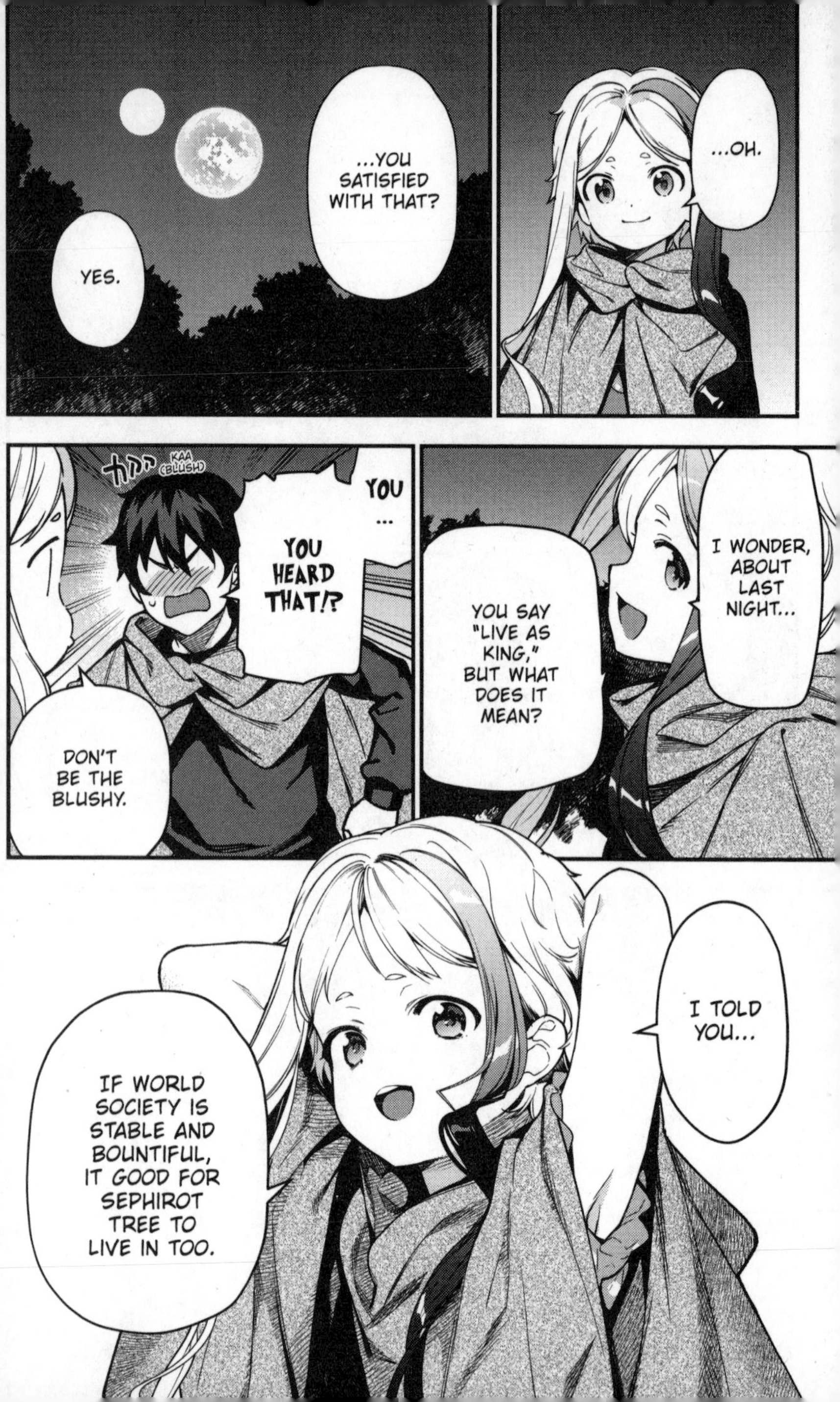
...OH.
...YOU SATISFIED WITH THAT?
YES.
I WONDER, ABOUT LAST NIGHT...
YOU SAY "LIVE AS KING," BUT WHAT DOES IT MEAN?
YOU ...
カァ KAA (BLUSH)
YOU HEARD THAT!?
DON'T BE THE BLUSHY.
I TOLD YOU...
IF WORLD SOCIETY IS STABLE AND BOUNTIFUL, IT GOOD FOR SEPHIROT TREE TO LIVE IN TOO.

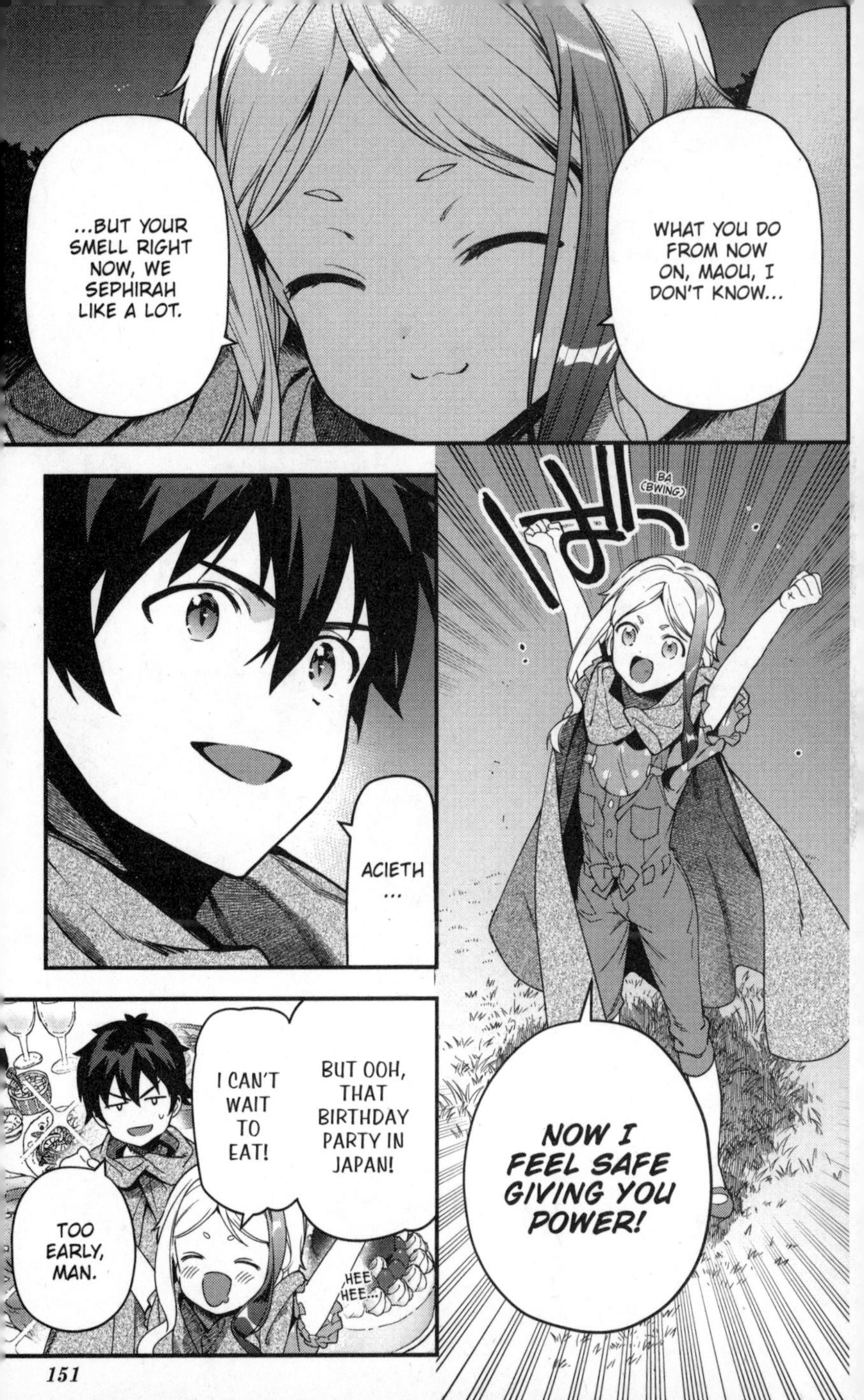
WHAT YOU DO FROM NOW ON, MAOU, I DON'T KNOW...
...BUT YOUR SMELL RIGHT NOW, WE SEPHIRAH LIKE A LOT.
BA (BWING)
NOW I FEEL SAFE GIVING YOU POWER!
ACIETH...
BUT OOH, THAT BIRTHDAY PARTY IN JAPAN!
I CAN'T WAIT TO EAT!
HEE HEE...
TOO EARLY, MAN.

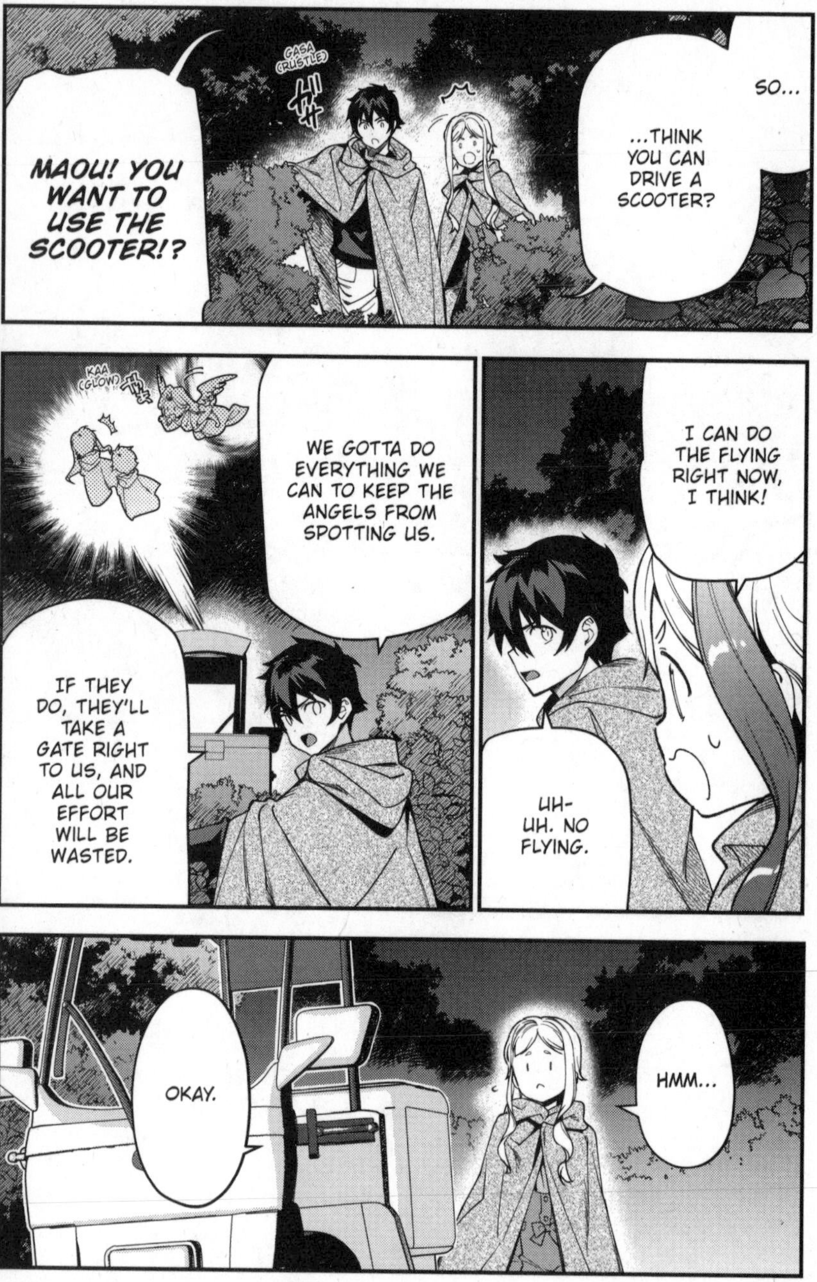
SO...
...THINK YOU CAN DRIVE A SCOOTER?
GASA (RUSTLE)
MAOU! YOU WANT TO USE THE SCOOTER!?
I CAN DO THE FLYING RIGHT NOW, I THINK!
UH-UH. NO FLYING.
WE GOTTA DO EVERYTHING WE CAN TO KEEP THE ANGELS FROM SPOTTING US.
KAA (GLOW)
IF THEY DO, THEY'LL TAKE A GATE RIGHT TO US, AND ALL OUR EFFORT WILL BE WASTED.
HMM...
OKAY.

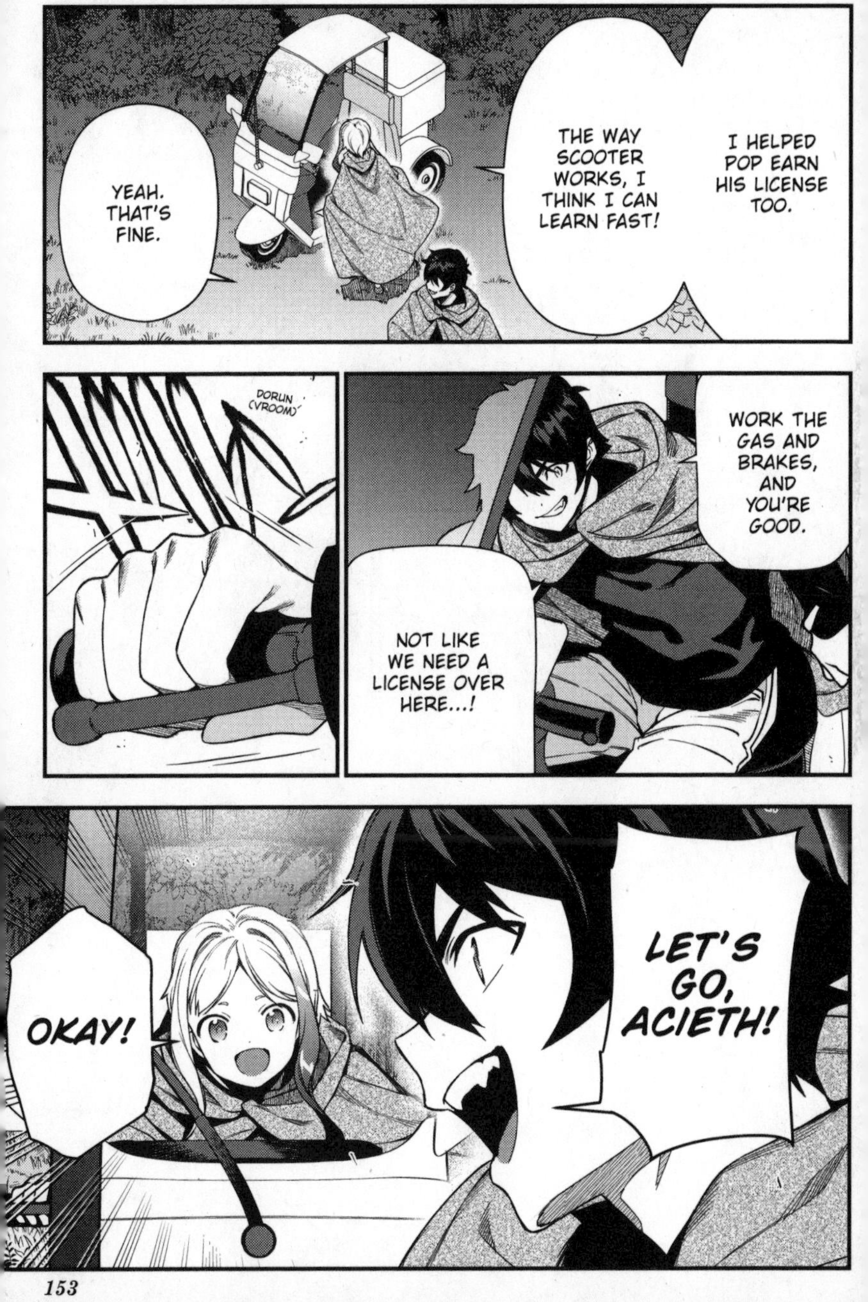
I HELPED POP EARN HIS LICENSE TOO.
THE WAY SCOOTER WORKS, I THINK I CAN LEARN FAST!
YEAH. THAT'S FINE.
WORK THE GAS AND BRAKES, AND YOU'RE GOOD.
NOT LIKE WE NEED A LICENSE OVER HERE...!
DORUN (VROOM)
LET'S GO, ACIETH!
OKAY!

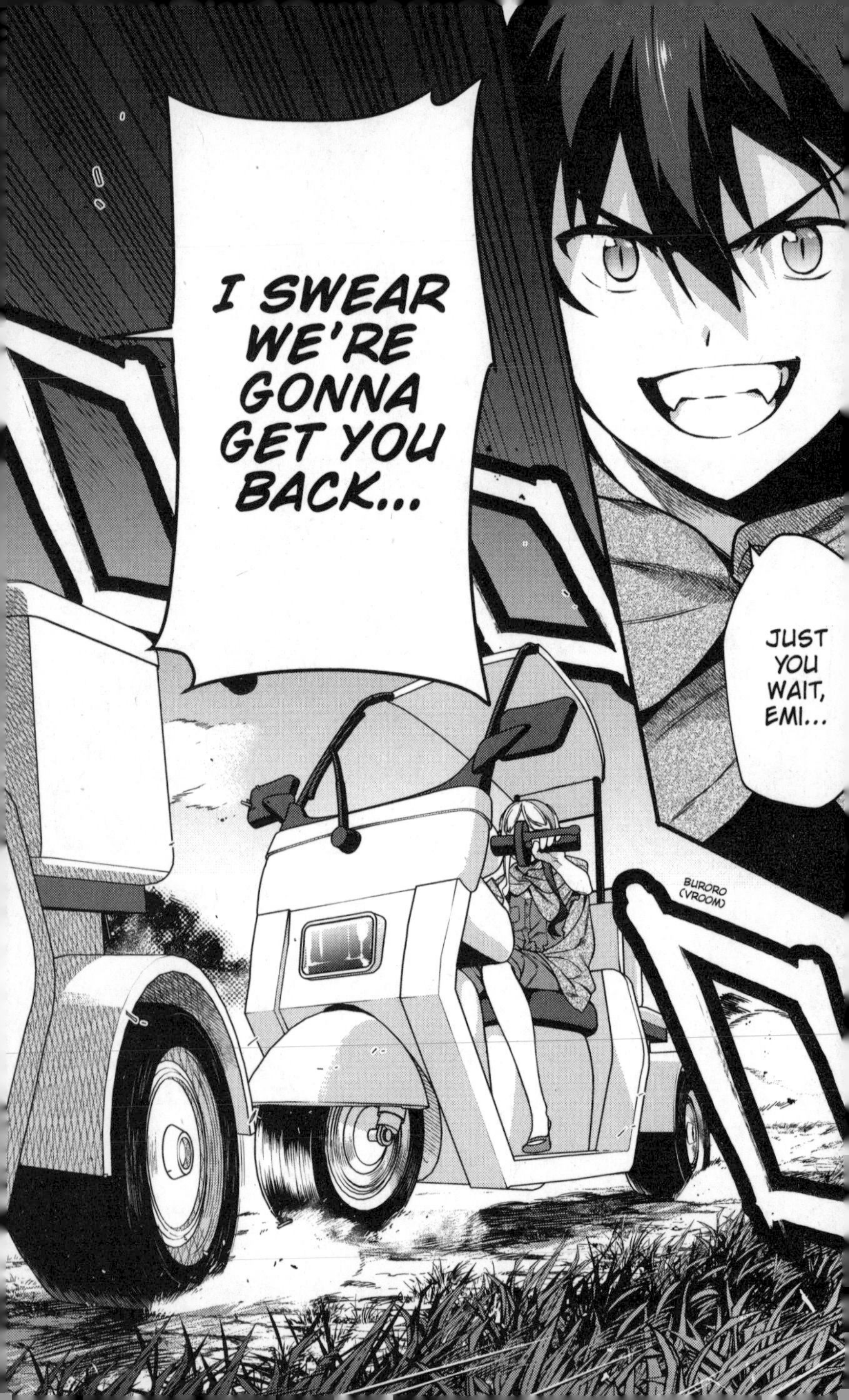
JUST YOU WAIT, EMI...
I SWEAR WE'RE GONNA GET YOU BACK...
BURORO (VROOM)

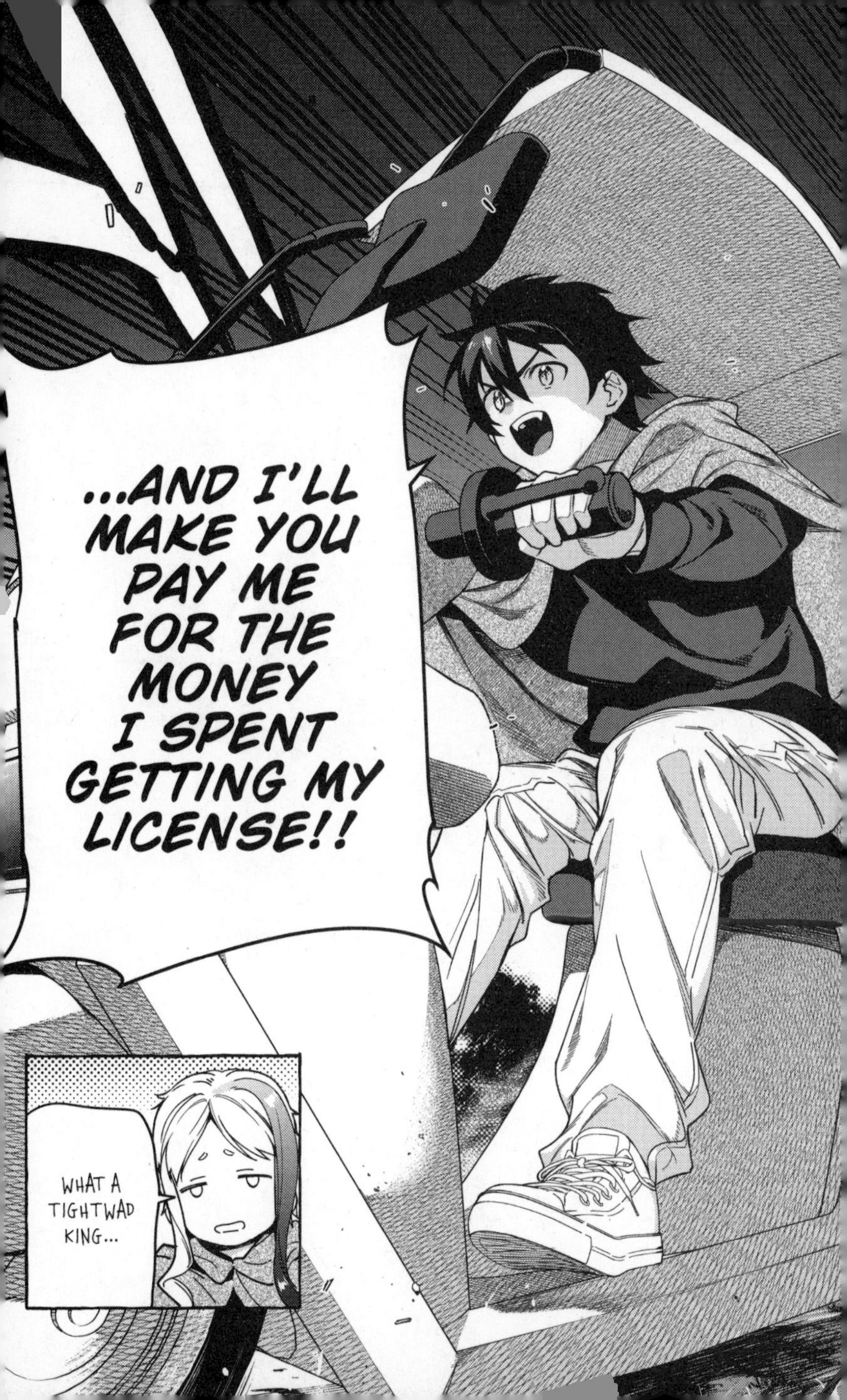
...AND I'LL MAKE YOU PAY ME FOR THE MONEY I SPENT GETTING MY LICENSE!!
WHAT A TIGHTWAD KING...

SERIES DESIGNS (ENTE ISLA ARC)

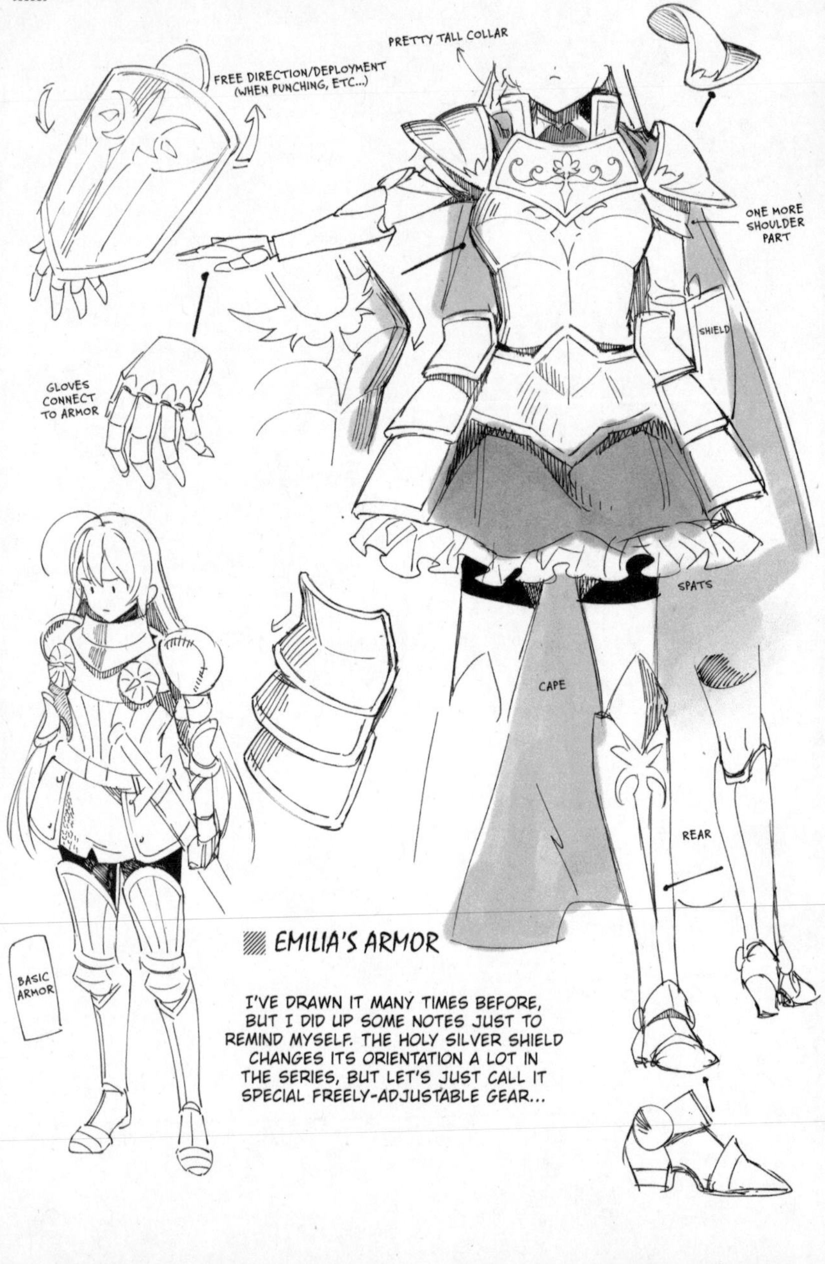
PRETTY TALL COLLAR
FREE DIRECTION/DEPLOYMENT
(WHEN PUNCHING, ETC...)
ONE MORE
SHOULDER
PART
SHIELD
GLOVES
CONNECT
TO ARMOR
SPATS
CAPE
REAR
BASIC
ARMOR

EMILIA'S ARMOR

I'VE DRAWN IT MANY TIMES BEFORE, BUT I DID UP SOME NOTES JUST TO REMIND MYSELF. THE HOLY SILVER SHIELD CHANGES ITS ORIENTATION A LOT IN THE SERIES, BUT LET'S JUST CALL IT SPECIAL FREELY-ADJUSTABLE GEAR...

HOLY SWORD (EVOLVED)

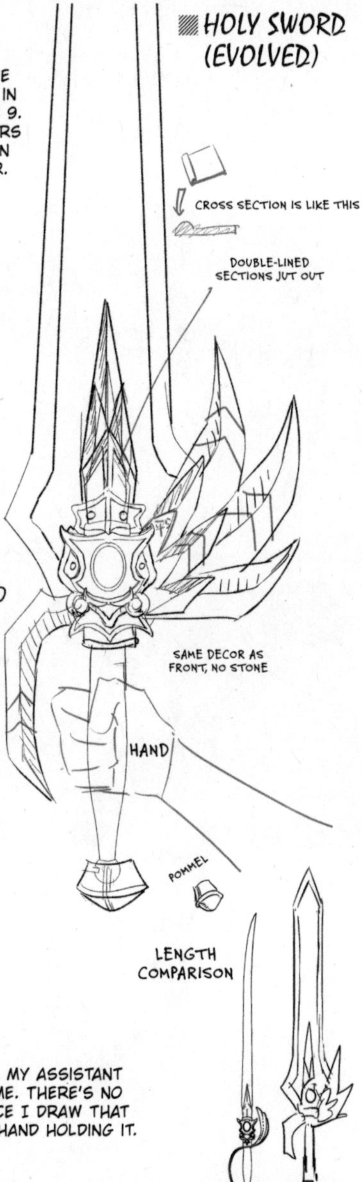

CROSS SECTION IS LIKE THIS
DOUBLE-LINED SECTIONS JUT OUT
SAME DECOR AS FRONT, NO STONE
HAND
POMMEL
LENGTH COMPARISON

PRISONER EMILIA OUTFIT

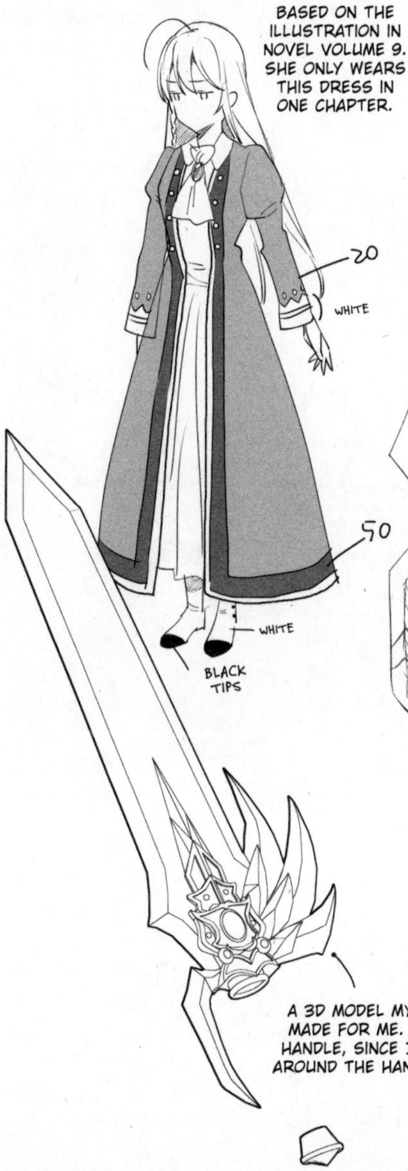

BASED ON THE ILLUSTRATION IN NOVEL VOLUME 9. SHE ONLY WEARS THIS DRESS IN ONE CHAPTER.
20
WHITE
50
WHITE
BLACK TIPS
A 3D MODEL MY ASSISTANT MADE FOR ME. THERE'S NO HANDLE, SINCE I DRAW THAT AROUND THE HAND HOLDING IT.

ALCIEL (DEMON VER.)

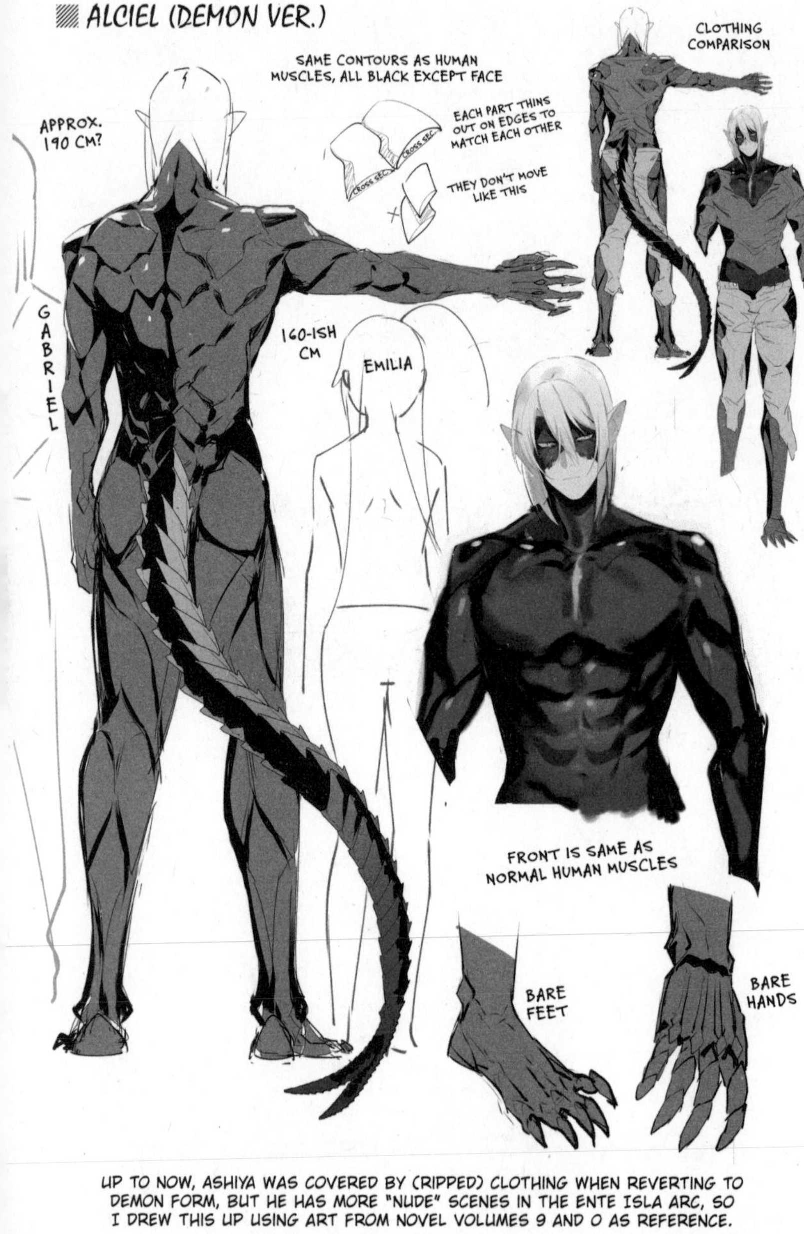
CLOTHING COMPARISON
SAME CONTOURS AS HUMAN MUSCLES, ALL BLACK EXCEPT FACE
APPROX. 190 CM?
EACH PART THINS OUT ON EDGES TO MATCH EACH OTHER
CROSS SEC.
CROSS SEC.
CROSS SEC.
THEY DON'T MOVE LIKE THIS
GABRIEL
160-ISH CM
EMILIA
FRONT IS SAME AS NORMAL HUMAN MUSCLES
BARE FEET
BARE HANDS

UP TO NOW, ASHIYA WAS COVERED BY (RIPPED) CLOTHING WHEN REVERTING TO DEMON FORM, BUT HE HAS MORE "NUDE" SCENES IN THE ENTE ISLA ARC, SO I DREW THIS UP USING ART FROM NOVEL VOLUMES 9 AND 0 AS REFERENCE.

ALCIEL ARMOR

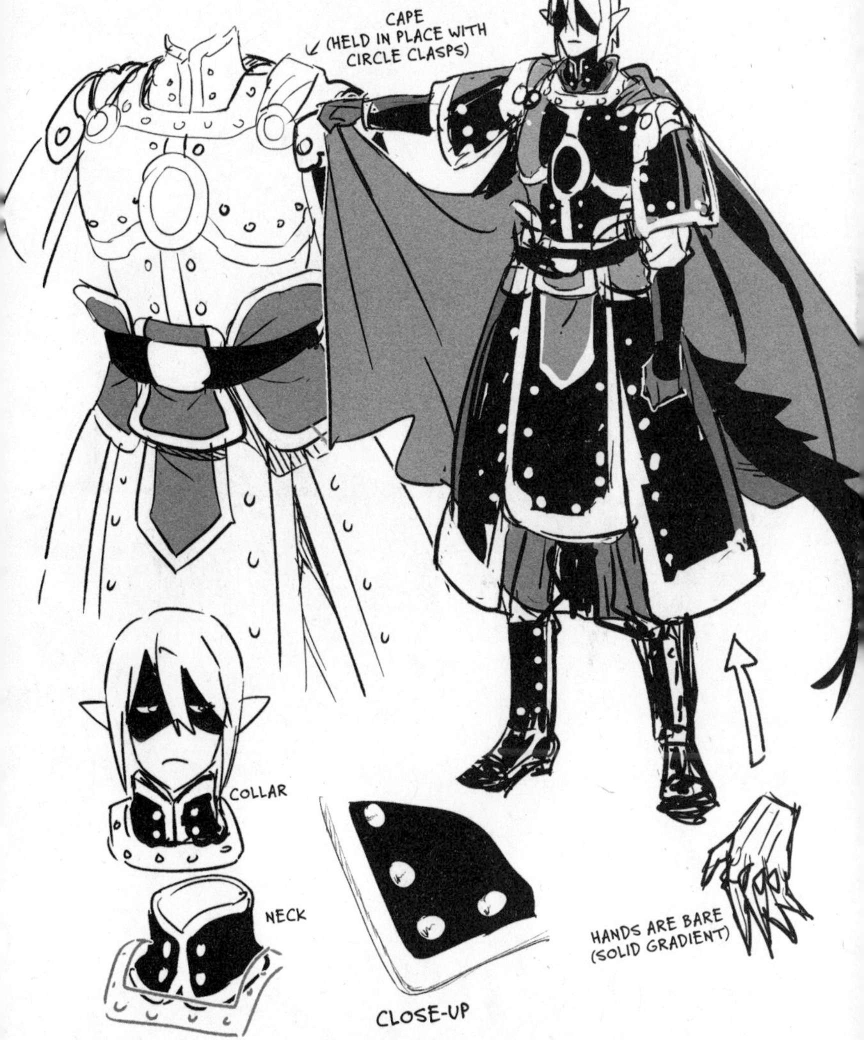
CAPE
(HELD IN PLACE WITH
CIRCLE CLASPS)
COLLAR
NECK
CLOSE-UP
HANDS ARE BARE
(SOLID GRADIENT)

THIS IS DEFINED TO BE FROM AN OLDER ERA THAN THE STANDARD EIGHT SCARVES GEAR. THE PRIORITY WAS TO GIVE A "STRONG ARMOR" IMPRESSION AT A SINGLE GLANCE.

The comic version has hit Volume 18!
We're now up to the battle between Emilia and Alciel,
one of the major climaxes of the lengthy Ente Isla arc.
It makes me incredibly happy to be able to draw it in so
much detail.

To Wagahara-sensei, Oniku-sensei, everyone involved
with *Devil*, and all the readers, I extend my grateful
thanks.

Next volume will mark the end of this arc!
From the artwork to the story, there was a lot of tricky
stuff that I didn't think I'd ever be drawing. It's been a
struggle to depict it all, but a real fun one for me. I want
to do everything in my power to make this exciting,
so here's hoping for your continued support!

Special thanks:
Akira Hisagi, Takashi Yamano,
and you!

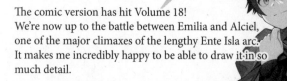

AKIO HIIRAGI

2021.
06

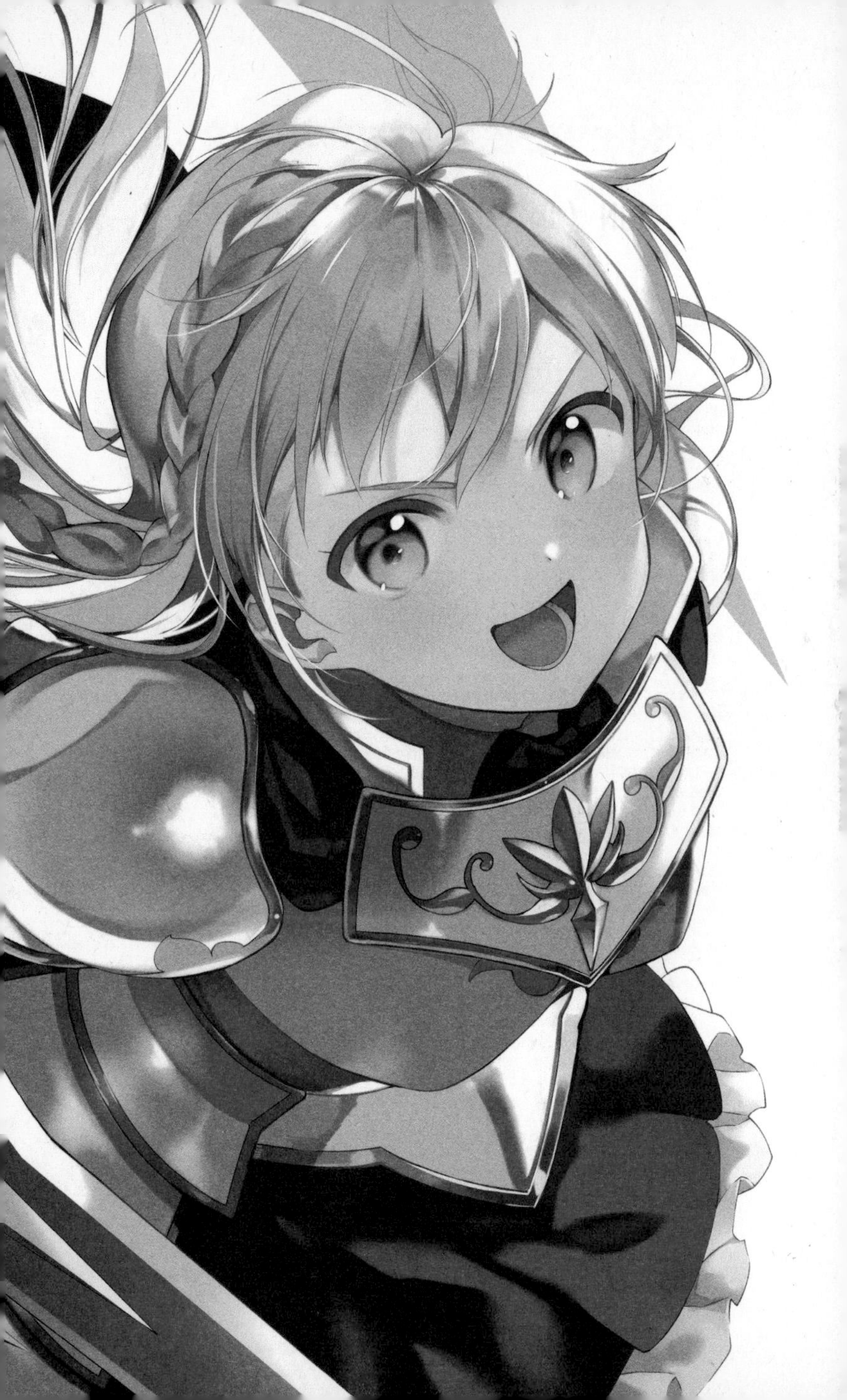

THE DEVIL IS A PART-TIMER! ⑱

JUN / 0 2022

ART: Akio Hiiragi
Original Story: Satoshi Wagahara
Character Design: 029 (Oniku)

Translation: Kevin Gifford

Lettering: Brandon Bovia

HATARAKU MAOUSAMA! Vol. 18
© Satoshi Wagahara / Akio Hiiragi 2021
First published in Japan in 2021 by KADOKAWA CORPORATION, Tokyo.
English translation rights arranged with KADOKAWA CORPORATION, Tokyo,
through Tuttle-Mori Agency, Inc., Tokyo.

English translation © 2022 by Yen Press, LLC

Yen Press
150 West 30th Street, 19th Floor
New York, NY 10001

Visit us at yenpress.com
facebook.com/yenpress
twitter.com/yenpress
yenpress.tumblr.com
instagram.com/yenpress

First Yen Press Edition: May 2022

Yen Press is an imprint of Yen Press, LLC.
The Yen Press name and logo are trademarks of Yen Press, LLC.

Library of Congress Control Number: 2014504637

ISBNs: 978-1-9753-4286-9 (paperback)
　　　 978-1-9753-4287-6 (ebook)

10 9 8 7 6 5 4 3 2 1

WOR

Printed in the United States of America